Arguments

3.75

W9-BYU-314

PARADISE
LOST

❦

JOHN
MILTON

M. born 1608
Thinks Arthurian epic 1638
patriot, pamphletteer
— 2 Marriages
1st wife back to father 1642

1652 Blindness almost total
1649 Charles execut!
1653 Cromwell in
ca 1658 - begins P.L.
1660 Restoration
1667 Paradise Lost pub.
3 yrs

WHEN
COFFEE?

justify god's ways
to man?

blindness
failed marriage
death of wife, son, second wife
failure of Puritan (repub.) ~~rebellion~~ revolt

Not of war but
" patience and
heroic martyrdom "

PARADISE LOST

JOHN MILTON

EDITED WITH AN INTRODUCTION BY
WILLIAM G. MADSEN
WASHINGTON UNIVERSITY

THE MODERN LIBRARY
New York

For Pat and Bill

Library of Congress Catalog Card Number: 69–11581

THE MODERN LIBRARY
is published by RANDOM HOUSE, INC.

Manufactured in the United States of America
Designed by Richard A. Roth

CONTENTS

INTRODUCTION

by WILLIAM G. MADSEN

Almost from the moment of its publication in 1667 *Paradise Lost* was regarded as a classic of the English language, great enough to take its place beside the epics of Homer, Virgil, and Tasso. It was dramatized by John Dryden, commented on in a series of *Spectator* papers by Addison, edited and emended by the great classical scholar Bentley, pillaged by Pope for his mock-heroic poem "The Rape of the Lock," and excised for middle-class consumption by John Wesley. For 200 years it was a dominant (sometimes, indeed, a tyrannical) influence on English poetry. For this very reason it was subjected, in the third, fourth, and fifth decades of the twentieth century, to as furious an onslaught of adverse criticism as any acknowledged masterpiece has ever received. Led by poets such as Ezra Pound and T. S. Eliot, who were trying to create an audience for a new poetic idiom, and by critics such as F. R. Leavis and A. J. A. Waldock, the attack proceeded on all fronts: stylistic, intellectual, religious, political, and personal. *Paradise Lost* was considered a bad poem: Its language was un-English, its rhythms rigid and mechanical, its imagery lacking in sensuous richness, its intellectual content simple-minded and trite to the point of fatuity, its narrative method crude and naïve, and its influence on English poetry disastrous. Milton himself, who once said that "he who would not be frustrate of his hope to write well here-after in laudable things, ought himself to be a true poem, that is, a composition and pattern of the best and honorablest things," was found to be no better than his poem.

The main lines of defense were at first somewhat over-hastily drawn. C. S. Lewis, whose Preface to *Paradise Lost* is still one of the best introductions to the poem, responds to F. R. Leavis' description of the style ("the inescapable monotony of the ritual") by saying that he agrees with Leavis about the properties of Milton's epic verse but that Leavis "sees and hates the very same that I see and love." *Paradise Lost,* Lewis says, is a secondary epic like Virgil's *Aeneid,* and the style of secondary epic is removed from and elevated above ordinary speech in diction and syntax; to introduce the colloquial speech of one of Donne's lyrics would be to commit a serious breach of decorum. More recent analysis of Milton's style, of which Christopher Ricks' *Milton's Grand Style* is perhaps the best example, detects additional qualities of simplicity of diction, complexity of thought, and verbal irony. The reader who wishes to acquire a feeling for the variety of styles that Milton commands may compare the rhetorical splendor of the debate in Hell in Book II with the simple beauty of the reconciliation between Adam and Eve near the end of Book X, and the complex perversions of logic and rhetoric in Satan's temptation speeches (IX, 532 ff.) with the breathless disingenuousness of Eve's report of her transgression (IX, 856 ff.).

Defenses of the intellectual content of *Paradise Lost* (in 1900 Sir Walter Raleigh called it a "monument to dead ideas") include Denis Saurat's characterization of Milton as an outflying precursor of nineteenth-century idealism, James Holly Hanford's plea that he was a secular humanist, and the view of critics such as C. S. Lewis and Douglas Bush that, whatever Milton's personal heresies might have been, *Paradise Lost* is essentially an orthodox poem in the central tradition of Christian humanism. The latter is no doubt the more nearly correct view, but the mere presence of other views suggests that the mythic and symbolic dimensions of *Paradise Lost* are large enough to accommodate non-Christian philosophies of the nature and destiny of man. As in any other great narrative fiction, the persons and events of *Paradise Lost* embody universally valid attitudes toward and patterns of experience.

Although most contemporary poets do not respond to Milton as a living presence in the way that Wordsworth and Keats, for example, did, it is nevertheless true that the reputation of *Paradise Lost* not only stands as high as it ever did among literary critics, including many poets, but also rests on a more secure foundation. The disciples of F. R. Leavis and A. J. A. Waldock, it is true, still regard the poem as a disaster; but the prevailing contemporary estimate is probably closer to Frank Kermode's in *The Romantic Image* (London, 1957): "The time cannot be far off when [*Paradise Lost*] will be read once more as the most perfect achievement of English poetry, perhaps the richest and most intricately beautiful poem in the world." Unlike many nineteenth-century paeans to the sonority of Milton's verse and the high seriousness of his thought, the current critical esteem in which *Paradise Lost* is held rests (ironically) upon those very methods of close analysis that the adverse critics of Milton were among the first to practice.

Verbal Texture

As an example of how well the poem stands up under close analysis, let us look at Milton's use of the word "fair." Because Milton presents Adam's fall as involving the choice of a lesser over a higher good and because "fair" can be applied both to physical beauty and to the more valuable kind of beauty that is moral and spiritual, the word is ideally suited to Milton's purposes. Its true meaning, which is to say its nonphysical meaning, is defined in Book IV where Eve tells Adam how she learned, presumably from him, that "beauty is excelled by manly grace/ And wisdom, which alone is truly fair" (IV, 490–491). But physical things are also fair in their way; and the word is used to describe the created universe both by Adam and by God, who says that he created the world "fair and good" (X, 618). Eve too is fair, like the physical creation of which she is both consummation and symbol; and the word is applied to her at least nine times in unambiguously favorable contexts.

But man, like Satan, "perverts best things/ To worst abuse, or to their meanest use" (IV, 203–204); and the perversion soon reveals itself in language. In the following passage, which contains the first appearance of "fair" in the poem, the process of degeneration occurs in the physical, moral, and linguistic realms:

> In Sion also not unsung, where stood
> Her temple on th' offensive mountain, built
> By that uxorious king, whose heart though large,
> Beguiled by fair idolatresses, fell
> To idols foul. . . .   (I, 442–446)

The descent fair-fell-foul, linguistically enacted in the regression from front to back vowels, is embodied in a visual symbol in the person of Sin, that monstrous issue of Satan's mind, who "seemed woman to the waist, and fair,/ But ended foul in many a scaly fold" (II, 650–651). "Fair" might almost be called Satan's favorite word. He speaks of Death as his "fair son" (II, 818) and of Paradise as "fair" (IV, 379); and he fully recognizes the dark potentialities of "fair Paradise" as he exclaims, with brilliant and diabolic irony, "O fair foundation laid whereon to build/ Their ruin! . . ." (IV, 521–522). In his soliloquy before the temptation he speaks of Eve as "divinely fair, fit love for gods" (IX, 489); and he proceeds to address her as "Fairest resemblance of thy Maker fair" (IX, 538). He uses the word eleven more times in this scene, applying it both to Eve and to the Tree of Knowledge; and he even dares to join with it God's epithet "good":

> Thenceforth to speculations high or deep
> I turned my thoughts, and with capacious mind
> Considered all things visible in heav'n,

> Or earth, or middle, all things fair and good;
> But all that fair and good in thy divine
> Semblance, and in thy beauty's heav'nly ray
> United I beheld; no fair to thine
> Equivalent or second . . .   (IX, 602–609)

Having learned from Adam that manly grace and wisdom alone are "truly fair," Eve should have recognized
Satan's perversion of values in his insistence on the literal, physical meaning of the word. But he succeeds in
convincing her that the literal fruit has spiritual properties. Lamenting her ignorance of good and evil she
says:

> Here grows the cure of all, this fruit divine,
> Fair to the eye, inviting to the taste,
> Of virtue to make wise: what hinders then
> To reach, and feed at once both body and mind?
>   (IX, 776–779)

Adam has no excuse, however, for he is well aware of
the danger of taking the word "fair" in too literal a
sense. In lecturing Eve on the psychology of temptation
(Adam's sentiments are irreproachable when he lectures
Eve) he says:

> But God left free the will, for what obeys
> Reason, is free, and reason he made right,
> But bid her well beware, and still erect,
> Lest by some fair appearing good surprised
> She dictate false, and misinform the will
>   (IX, 351–355)

Raphael tries to warn Adam that the "fair appearing
good" might be Eve herself:

> For what admir'st thou, what transports thee so,
> An outside? fair no doubt, and worthy well
> Thy cherishing, thy honoring, and thy love,
> Not thy subjection: weigh with her thyself;
> Then value . . .   (VIII, 567–571)

But manly grace and wisdom are forgotten when Eve
approaches with "A bough of fairest fruit that downy
smiled" (IX, 851). "O fairest of creation," Adam exclaims to himself, echoing the language of Satan:

> O fairest of creation, last and best
> Of all God's works, creature in whom excelled
> Whatever can to sight or thought be formed,
> Holy, divine, good, amiable, or sweet!
>
> (IX, 896–899)

Eve may be fairest to sight, but not to thought. Adam
eats of the "fair enticing fruit" (IX, 996); and the result
is a darkening of his intellectual vision, which manifests
itself immediately in a degradation of language:

> But come, so well refreshed, now let us play,
> As meet is, after such delicious fare;
> For never did thy beauty since the day
> I saw thee first and wedded thee, adorned
> With all perfections, so inflame my sense
> With ardor to enjoy thee, fairer now
> Than ever, bounty of this virtuous tree.
>
> (IX, 1027–1033)

"Fair Eve," the physical glory of God's "fair Paradise,"
has become a "fair idolatress." Adam, beguiled, has
fallen to "idols foul," and he now sees Eve as "fairer"
than she was when he thought of her as "fairest of creation." In the alembic of the mind—Adam's or Satan's
—the physical universe is transformed, and what began
as "fair and good" ends "foul in many a scaly fold"
(II, 651).

Milton's Career: Background to
Paradise Lost

Compared to most other great poets, Milton came to
the writing of his masterpiece rather late in his career
and after "long choosing," as he says in the prologue to

Book IX. For many years he had assiduously prepared himself by a program of private study, by conscious poetic experimentation, and (as it turned out) by active participation in public affairs to write a poem that would be "doctrinal and exemplary to a nation." In *The Reason of Church Government Urged Against Prelaty* (1642), the prose pamphlet from which the preceding quotation is taken, Milton speaks of his poetic ambitions. He was encouraged, he says, by his early teachers, who thought that his "style, by certain vital signs it had, was likely to live," by the poets and scholars he had met in Italy, and by an "inward prompting" to think that he "might perhaps leave something so written to aftertimes, as they should not willingly let it die." He goes on to say that instead of writing in Latin, he resolved "to fix all the industry and art I could unite to the adorning of my native tongue; not to make verbal curiosities the end, that were a toilsome vanity, but to be an interpreter and relater of the best and sagest things among mine own citizens throughout this island in the mother dialect." He then discusses the various genres and models available to him, mentioning first the epic:

> Time serves not now, and perhaps I might seem too profuse to give any certain account of what the mind at home in the spacious circuits of her musing hath liberty to propose to herself, though of highest hope and hardest attempting; whether that epic form whereof the two poems of Homer and those other two of Virgil and Tasso are a diffuse, and the book of Job a brief model: or whether the rules of Aristotle herein are strictly to be kept, or nature to be followed, which in them that know art and use judgment, is no transgression but an enriching of art: and lastly, what king or knight before the conquest might be chosen in whom to lay the pattern of a Christian hero. And as Tasso gave to a prince of Italy his choice whether he would command him

to write of Godfrey's expedition against the Infidels, or Belisarius against the Goths, or Charlemain against the Lombards; if to the instinct of nature and the emboldening of art aught may be trusted, and that there be nothing adverse in our climate or the fate of this age, it haply would be no rashness, from an equal diligence and inclination, to present the like offer in our own ancient stories.

One hero from England's ancient stories is of course Arthur; and in 1638 in a Latin poem addressed to John Baptista Manso, the distinguished patron of Tasso whom he had met in Italy, Milton speaks of his intention to write an Arthurian epic:

> O, if my lot might but bestow such a friend upon me, a friend who understands how to honor the devotees of Phoebus—if ever I shall summon back our native kings into our songs, and Arthur, waging his wars beneath the earth, or if ever I shall proclaim the magnanimous heroes of the table which their mutual fidelity made invincible, and (if only the spirit be with me) shall shatter the Saxon phalanxes under the British Mars!

In 1640 Milton again refers to his Arthuriad, this time in a Latin elegy mourning the death of his friend Charles Diodati:

> I, for my part, am resolved to tell the story of the Trojan ships in the Rutupian sea and of the ancient kingdom of Inogene, the daughter of Pandrasus, and of the chiefs, Brennus and Arviragus, and of old Belinus, and of the Armorican settlers who came at last under British law. Then I shall tell of Igraine pregnant with Arthur by fatal deception, the counterfeiting of Gorlois' features and arms by Merlin's treachery.

About this time Milton drew up a long list of possible subjects for poems and plays drawn from the Bible and from British history, a list that fortunately survives in a manuscript now in Trinity College, Cambridge, but the name of Arthur nowhere appears. While it may be that Milton drew up another list of possible epic subjects that has not survived, it is perhaps significant that King Alfred is mentioned as an epic hero:

> A Heroicall Poem may be founded somwhere in Alfreds reigne, especially at his issuing out of Edelingsey on the Danes; whose actions are wel like those of Ulysses.

We hear no more of the projected Arthuriad, and reasons are not far to seek. For one thing, Milton had already begun his researches into British history that were to result in his *History of Britain* (pub. 1670); and in that work he expresses grave doubts about Arthur as a historical person. An even more important consideration is that the absolutist claims of the Stuart monarchs were closely tied up with the mystique of the Arthurian legend. Milton's developing republicanism no doubt led him to a more sympathetic view of the Anglo-Saxon tradition, to which the supporters of the Parliamentary cause traced the customary liberties of the English people.

The subject of what was to become *Paradise Lost* is found in this same Trinity Manuscript in the form of two lists of characters and two outlines for tragedies, the first of which is entitled *Paradise Lost* and the second *Adam Unparadiz'd.* Milton apparently got further than a mere outline, for his nephew Edward Phillips tells us in his *Life of Milton* that lines 32–41 of Satan's soliloquy in Book IV were shown to him and some others "several years before the poem was begun . . . as designed for the very beginning of the said tragedy." Because neither of the outlines begins with Satan speaking, it would seem, if Phillips is to be trusted, that Milton discarded his earlier plans for still another one. How far he progressed with this version we do not know, but scholars have detected passages in the poem that may be vestiges of the drama.

The epic poem that Milton finally wrote is very different from what it would have been had he written it in his thirties instead of in his fifties. As a younger man Milton was an orthodox Anglican and a Royalist. By 1637, when he wrote "Lycidas," he was sufficiently disillusioned with the Anglican hierarchy to include in that poem an attack on "our corrupted Clergy then in their height," but he was not yet ready for direct involvement in the Puritan attacks on the policies of Archbishop Laud. From the spring of 1638 to the summer of 1639 he journeyed in Italy; and when he returned to England, he undertook the teaching of his two nephews, Edward and John Phillips. This occupation afforded him opportunity to continue his program of private study. The calling of the Long Parliament in the fall of 1640, however, brought the great public issues very much to Milton's attention; and in 1641 and 1642 he wrote five antiepiscopal pamphlets, the longest and most interesting of which is *The Reason of Church Government,* a defense of the Presbyterian form of church government. Although Milton soon came to think the Presbyterians as tyrannical as the Anglicans— "New Presbyter is but Old Priest writ Large"—this tract is of enduring interest both because of its personal digression (see quotation above) and because of its clear statement of many of Milton's most fundamental religious principles, the chief of which is that Christianity is a purely spiritual religion and that the formal and ceremonial observances that the Anglican apologists traced back to the Old Testament had been completely abrogated by the coming of Christ. This opposition between the "inward power and purity of the gospel" and the "outward carnality of the law," between the preaching of the Word and "idolatrous and Gentilish rites and ceremonies," between "faith" and "sight and visibility" is central to Milton's religious thought and informs his last three poems, *Paradise Lost, Paradise Regained,* and *Samson Agonistes.*

In *The Reasons of Church Government* Milton is still an avowed Royalist, but we know from entries in his Commonplace Book that he was already interested in the republican form of government. By late 1648 he was an avowed anti-Royalist and a champion of the Independent, anti-Presbyterian party in Parliament. His *Tenure of Kings and Magistrates,* a defense of "regicide," was published on February 13, 1649, two weeks after the execution of Charles I. Here is Milton's account of how he came to write it:

> But when, at length, some Presbyterian ministers, who had formerly been the most bitter enemies to Charles, became jealous of the growth of the Independents, and of their ascendancy in the Parliament, most tumultuously clamored against the sentence, and did all in their power to prevent the execution, though they were not angry so much on account of the act itself as because it was not the act of their party; and when they dared to affirm, that the doctrine of the Protestants, and of all the reformed churches, was abhorrent to such an atrocious proceeding against kings; I thought that it became me to oppose such a glaring falsehood; and accordingly, without any immediate or personal application to Charles, I showed, in an abstract consideration of the question, what might lawfully be done against tyrants.

Now totally committed to the revolutionary cause, Milton was appointed on March 15, 1649 to the post of Secretary for Foreign Tongues to the Council of State; his duties were to translate and sometimes actually to compose the Commonwealth's correspondence with foreign states. In addition, the Council of State expected to use Milton's considerable rhetorical abilities in the

defense of the Commonwealth, and they were not dis-
appointed, for within seven months Milton published
Eikonoklastes ("Image Breaker"), an attack on the
Eikon Basilike ("King's Image"), which purported to be
the private meditations of Charles I in his last years.
This book, which had actually been written by Charles'
chaplain, Bishop John Gauden, had aroused an alarm-
ing degree of public sympathy for Charles; and Milton
was ruthless in his attack on the book as well as on the
memory of Charles.

Early in 1650 Milton was asked to write another book,
this one in response to a continental attack entitled
Defensio Regia pro Carolo I, written for Charles II by
a French scholar, Claude Saumaise, or Salmasius. *John
Milton's Defence of the English People Against Claude
Saumaise's Defence of the King,* written in Latin for an
international audience, was published in February 1651
and won for Milton universal notoriety if not acclaim.
In 1654, in response to an attack on the *First Defence,*
he published a *Second Defence of the English People,*
an impassioned work in which he realized to some degree his ambition to proclaim (if not to "sing") "the
deeds and triumphs of just and pious nations doing
valiantly through faith against the enemies of Christ."

Six years later, with the restoration of Charles II, it
was all over. In 1641 Milton had been confident that
God would not lead his chosen English people out of
the Egypt of Catholicism only to let them perish in the
wilderness of Anglicanism; he had even thought that
the Second Coming was imminent. In 1660 he feared
that the English were "choosing them a captain back for
Egypt" in the person of Charles II. *The Ready and Easy
Way to Establish a Free Commonwealth,* written just
before the Restoration, ends with the following words:

> But I trust I shall have spoken persuasion to abun-
> dance of sensible and ingenuous men; to some,
> perhaps, whom God may raise of these stones to

become children of reviving liberty; and may re-claim, though they seem now choosing them a cap-tain back for Egypt, to bethink themselves a little, and consider whither they are rushing; to exhort this torrent also of the people, not to be so im-petuous, but to keep their due channel; and at length recovering and uniting their better resolu-tions, now that they see already how open and un-bounded the insolence and rage is of our common enemies, to stay these ruinous proceedings, justly and timely fearing to what a precipice of destruc-tion the deluge of this epidemic madness would hurry us, through the general defection of a mis-guided and abused multitude.

A few years later he could say that "one's country is wherever it is well with one." The course of public events had forced Milton to apply to politics those prin-ciples of inwardness and spirituality that lay at the heart of his understanding of Christianity. He could no longer write a great national epic.

During these years of public activity Milton's faith was severely tested by a series of personal tragedies, which began in 1642 with his unfortunate marriage. "About *Whitsuntide* [1642] it was, or a little after," writes his nephew Edward Phillips, "that he took a Journey into the Country; no body about him certainly knowing the Reason, or that it was any more than a Journey of Recreation: after a Month's stay, home he returns a Married-man, that went out a Batchelor." His wife was Mary Powell, the pleasure-loving and "un-Miltonic" daughter of a Royalist living near Oxford. The marriage appeared to end almost as soon as it had begun: Within a few months Mary went home to visit her parents, and she did not return for three years. (Milton took advantage of this unexpected release from domestic care to publish four scholarly and dispassion-ate defenses of divorce as well as the little tractate *Of*

Education and his prose masterpiece, *Areopagitica*.) The return of Mary (probably in the late summer of 1645) is charmingly described by Phillips:

> [Friends on both sides desiring a reunion and Milton having made one of his frequent visits to the home of a relative] the Wife was ready in another Room, and on a sudden he was surprised to see one whom he thought to have never seen more, making Submission and begging Pardon on her Knees before him; he might probably at first make some shew of aversion and rejection; but partly his own generous nature, more inclinable to Reconciliation than to perseverance in Anger and Revenge; and partly the strong intercession of Friends on both sides, soon brought him to an Act of Oblivion, and a firm League of Peace for the future.

Those who believe that Milton was a confirmed misogynist and who insist on regarding Adam's savage denunciation of Eve after the Fall as Milton's final word on the subject of woman might do well to set this passage from Phillips' *Life* beside the beautiful and moving reconciliation scene between Adam and Eve in Book X, lines 909–965. It is possible that the proud Milton, like Adam, learned from a woman something about the humiliation that exalts. What slender evidence we have suggests that Milton's life with Mary (and, incidentally, with his mother-in-law) was not very happy; but we would like to think that he enjoyed a few years of wedded love before the public and personal defeats of the 1650s.

Milton's eyesight had never been strong, and in 1651 it began to fail rapidly. Total blindness overtook him by March 1652, about two months before the death of his wife Mary and three months before the death of his son, John. It must have been for him a veritable dark night of the soul, and we are not surprised to learn that in August of 1653 he translated the first eight Psalms.

Lord in thine anger do not reprehend me,
  Nor in thy hot displeasure me correct;
Pity me, Lord, for I am much deject,
  Am very weak and faint; heal and amend me,
For all my bones, that even with anguish ache,
  Are troubled, yea my soul is troubled sore;
And thou, O Lord, how long? turn Lord, restore
  My soul, O save me for thy goodness' sake,
For in death no remembrance is of thee;
  Who in the grave can celebrate thy praise?
Wearied I am with sighing out my days,
  Nightly my couch I make a kind of sea;
My bed I water with my tears; mine eye
  Through grief consumes, is waxen old and dark
I' th' midst of all mine enemies that mark.

                                    (*Psalm 6*)

In the *Second Defence* (1654) Milton, having been re-
proached for his blindness by the anonymous author of
*The Royal Blood Crying to Heaven for Vengeance on
the English Parricides,* could say that "To be blind is
not miserable; not to be able to bear blindness, that is
miserable." He recalls the blind prophets and poets of
antiquity and says that his blindness "deprives things
merely of their color and surface, but takes not from
the mind's contemplation whatever is real and perma-
nent in them." "The divine law, the divine favor, has
made us not merely secure, but as it were sacred, from
the injuries of men, nor would seem to have brought
this darkness upon us so much by inducing a dimness
of the eyes as by the overshadowing of heavenly wings,
and not unfrequently is wont to illumine it again, when
produced, by an inward and far surpassing light." Every
page of *Paradise Lost* bears witness to the inward light
with which Milton was recompensed, and the magnificent prologue to Book III is Milton's prayer both of
petition and of thanksgiving.

  In the twenty years or so between the writing of
"Lycidas" at age twenty-nine and the beginning of sus-

tained work on *Paradise Lost* at age forty-nine or fifty,
Milton apparently wrote no more than 250 lines of
original English verse. At the age of fifty he had indeed
achieved the European fame for which he had longed,
but as a patriot not as a poet. Perhaps he was content
to have lost his poetic fame, as well as his eyesight, in
liberty's defense, his noble task "Of which all Europe
talks from side to side" (Sonnet XXII). But the death of
Oliver Cromwell in 1658, three months before Milton
completed his fiftieth year, must have induced in him
the same despair that his friend Andrew Marvell recorded in his poem on the death of Cromwell. The Second Coming of Christ no longer seemed imminent, as it
had in 1641; and by 1660 the English people, whom
God had been preparing in the early 1640s for a new
revelation, had become a "misguided and abused multitude." If Milton paused to take stock of himself on
December 9, 1658, as he had so often done on earlier
occasions, he could have reflected bitterly that *Jerusalem
Delivered* was completed when Tasso was in his thir-
tieth year, that Virgil was in his forties when he wrote
the *Aeneid,* that all of Shakespeare's plays were written
by the time he was forty-nine, and that Dante was only
a few years past fifty when he finished the *Divine Comedy.* Only Cervantes (whom Milton never alludes to)
and Sophocles would have afforded him examples of
great literary artists all of whose major work was done
after they were fifty. And yet the world was all before
him.

No one today, it may be supposed, laments the
twenty-year descent into darkness that enabled Milton
to rise so triumphantly into the realms of light. *Paradise Lost,* like the *Divine Comedy,* could only have
been written by a man who had entered the gates of
Hell and waited there in patient resignation, like the
saints of the Old Testament, until his Saviour should
come to release him from bondage. Milton learned in
those twenty years many things about himself, about
the relations between man and woman, about freedom

and tyranny, about human nature in general; but the chief thing he learned was the virtue of patience. None of Milton's last poems could have been written by the young revolutionary of the early 1640s, who thought that the English Puritans had God in their pocket. The failure of the Commonwealth and the Restoration of the hated monarchy and episcopacy taught Milton that "Justice divine/ Mends not her slowest pace for prayers or cries" (X, 858–859). It was with a purified inner vision and a strong new voice that the blind poet at long last turned to "fresh woods, and pastures new."

Approaching *Paradise Lost*

The reader who is approaching *Paradise Lost* for the first time may feel himself at a disadvantage, especially if he has been told that Milton's language is more Latinate than English and that his poems are full of obscure allusions to the classics and to the Bible. It would be dishonest to pretend that Milton does not make strenuous demands on his readers, but the demands are no more strenuous than those of, say, Yeats and Eliot. Milton could certainly expect his seventeenth-century readers to be more familiar with the Bible than are most modern readers, and probably he could expect more familiarity with classical literature and mythology. But such ignorance as ours is not invincible, and the student who is willing to follow the leads given in the notes—or in such a book as Davis P. Harding's *The Club of Hercules*—will find himself well rewarded. The more we know, the richer our reading becomes.

As for the Latinate quality of the language of *Paradise Lost,* it has been greatly exaggerated. It is true that if one counts only the number of different words, the vocabulary is about 57 percent classical in origin and 37 percent English and Teutonic. If, however, one counts the total number of words, English and Teutonic words outweigh all others by 77 percent to 23 percent. In his syntax Milton tries to free English from the

tyranny of word order and confer on it the flexibility
that is enjoyed by an inflected language such as Latin,
in which the function of a word is determined by its
form rather than by its position in the sentence. What
Milton sacrifices thereby in the immediacy of normal
spoken English, he more than makes up for in weighty,
succinct, and memorable utterance.

Another apparent obstacle to the rational enjoyment
of *Paradise Lost* is the poem's supposed "world view."
We have heard much in recent years about the delight
we must take in the ideas of order, degree, hierarchy,
right reason, and whatnot if we expect to appreciate
Paradise Lost. No doubt we must; but that depends on
how these terms are defined. The prelapsarian world
of *Paradise Lost* is indeed a hierarchical one, but the
Fall introduces disorder not only into the universe but
also into the mind of man, whose ability to discern the
essential orderliness of things is seriously impaired.
There is a passage in which Raphael compares the
dance of the angels to the movements of the heavenly
bodies that perfectly images the complexity of Milton's
idea of order:

> That day, as other solemn days, they spent
> In song and dance about the sacred hill,
> Mystical dance, which yonder starry sphere
> Of planets and of fixed in all her wheels
> Resembles nearest, mazes intricate,
> Eccentric, intervolved, yet regular
> Then most, when most irregular they seem.
>
> *(V, 618–624)*

Milton's mature works suggest that for him the images
of religious and social order in seventeenth-century
England were mainly false images, idols: the ecclesiastical hierarchy, the royalty, the nobility, the censorship
laws, the laws against divorce. Milton believed in an
ultimate providential order, not because he saw evidence of it all around him, but in spite of the fact that
after the Restoration he thought himself "fall'n on evil

days : . ./ In darkness, and with dangers compassed
'ound," threatened by the "barbarous dissonance/ Of
Bacchus and his revellers . . ." (Book VII, Prologue).
Milton was no spokesman for the Establishment; that
role is Satan's.

A good example of how Milton handles the theme of
essential order as opposed to superficial order may be
seen in his use of the names traditionally assigned to
the angelic hierarchies. In orthodox Christian theology
the nine orders of angels were ranked as follows: Seraphim, Cherubim, Thrones, Dominations, Virtues, Powers, Principalities, Archangels, and Angels. In *Paradise
Lost* some angels are superior to others (just as in the
Second Defence Cromwell, for example, was superior
to other men), and all angels are superior *by nature* to
men. So Satan, disguised as a good angel, bows low to
Uriel "As to superior spirits is wont in Heav'n,/ Where
honor due and reverence none neglects" (III, 737–738),
and Adam bows low to Raphael "with submiss approach
and reverence meek,/ As to a superior nature . . ."
(V, 359–360). At the same time, however, Milton uses
the names of the angelic ranks almost interchangeably,
calling Raphael now a Virtue, now a Seraph, and now
an Archangel, as if to imply that these outward mani-
festations of degree and hierarchy only imperfectly re-
flect the inner reality. The devils, on the other hand,
set great store by names and titles:

> "Thrones and imperial Powers, offspring of
>   Heav'n,
> Ethereal Virtues; or these titles now
> Must we renounce, and changing style be called
> Princes of Hell?" . . .   *(II, 310–313)*

Another aspect of the poem's world view that the
modern reader must familiarize himself with is the pre-
Copernican cosmology, which Milton uses largely for
its symbolic value. In this system the earth is surrounded
by ten concentric spheres: the moon, Mercury, Venus,
the sun, Mars, Jupiter, Saturn, the fixed stars, the

primum mobile, which moves the other spheres, and an outer crystalline sphere, mentioned in Book III, line 482. Enveloping the tenth sphere is a crystalline ocean (VII, 271), and beyond that is chaos. "Above" the universe is God's Heaven, and "below" it is Hell. That Milton adopted this scheme largely for its imagistic and symbolic value is clear from the dialogue on astronomy between Raphael and Adam in Book VIII, where Raphael, without ever committing himself to one system or the other, allows that the earth may very well revolve around the sun. Milton's interest in such questions is moral rather than scientific. The lesson that Adam draws from Raphael's discussion about the rival theories is

> That not to know at large of things remote
> From use, obscure and subtle, but to know
> That which before us lies in daily life,
> Is the prime wisdom; what is more, is fume,
> Or emptiness, or fond impertinence,
> And renders us in things that most concern
> Unpractised, unprepared, and still to seek.
>
> *(VIII, 191–197)*

The theology of *Paradise Lost* has occasioned special kinds of difficulty: some readers simply cannot take it seriously; others take it very seriously indeed but cannot agree on what it is. To deal with the latter problem first, much of the theological furor over the alleged heterodoxy of *Paradise Lost* stems from the (in my opinion) mistaken assumption that Milton's theological treatise, *De Doctrina Christiana*, should be used as a gloss on the poem. This Latin prose work, for which Milton had collected materials over a long period and which he apparently completed during the years he worked on *Paradise Lost*, lay for many years unnoticed in the Public Record Office, where it was discovered in 1823. It was published in 1825 with an English translation by Bishop Charles Sumner. What it reveals is that Milton's mature religious thought was much more dar-

ing than even his worst enemies had suspected. That
he believed in divorce was of course common knowledge; but for 150 years orthodox Christian readers of
Paradise Lost and *Paradise Regained* had not realized
that he rejected the orthodox doctrines that God is
three Persons in one Nature, that matter was created
by God out of nothing (*ex nihilo*), and that the Soul is
by nature immortal. In the *Christian Doctrine* Milton
affirms that the Son is a divine person but not equal in
nature with the Father, that the Holy Spirit is not a
person at all, that matter was created *ex Deo* (out of
God) not *ex nihilo,* and that the soul dies with the body,
to be resurrected with it on the Last Day. Although it
is true that none of these heresies is contradicted in
Paradise Lost, it is also true that none of them is ex-
plicitly and unequivocally affirmed. The point that
needs to be made is that Milton's theology, both in the
treatise and in the poem, is centered in the language of
the Bible. In the treatise he interprets this language; in
the poem he lets it speak for itself, and every reader is
free to interpret it in his own way. In choosing this
strategy Milton's sense of decorum did not fail him: It
is surely not the task of a Christian epic poet to disturb
settled beliefs.

To the reader who cannot take the theology seriously
one can only say that he need not, although Milton
would surely have wished him to. The story of the Fall,
viewed simply as a fiction, has been variously interpreted, and the superhuman characters of God, Christ,
and the angels, whom Milton regarded as real persons,
may be regarded as fictional images of truth, love, order,
evil, or whatever. Many of the events in the poem Milton himself must surely have regarded as fictional, and
we have already seen that he did not intend his description of the physical universe to be taken literally.

Whether we approach *Paradise Lost* as Christian
readers or not, however, we must recognize the central
function of Christ in the symbolic and thematic struc-
tures of the poem: He is the symbolizing center of its

image patterns, and he is the supreme exemplar for the moral and spiritual life of man. He is alluded to at the very beginning of Book I as the "one greater Man" who will "Restore us, and regain the blissful seat," and at the end of Book XII it is hearing Michael's sermon about the humiliating, redemptive death of Christ that enables Adam to achieve his most profound spiritual insight:

> Henceforth I learn, that to obey is best,
> And love with fear the only God, to walk
> As in his presence, ever to observe
> His providence, and on him sole depend,
> Merciful over all his works, with good
> Still overcoming evil, and by small
> Accomplishing great things, by things deemed weak
> Subverting worldly strong, and worldly wise
> By simply meek; that suffering for truth's sake
> Is fortitude to highest victory,
> And to the faithful death the gate of life;
> Taught this by his example whom I now
> Acknowledge my Redeemer ever blest.
>
> (*XII, 561–573*)

As the "Image of [God] in all things" (VI, 736) Christ appears at the very center of the poem in his dual role of Judge and Creator: At the end of Book VI he judges the rebel angels, and at the beginning of Book VII he rides out into chaos to create the universe. From this central point his image irradiates the entire poem. In Book V the Father metaphorically "begets" (that is, exalts) the Son; and in Book VIII Adam literally begets Eve and exalts her above all creation, with the result that it is her voice he listens to rather than Christ's (X, 145–146). In Book IV the Garden is a fleshly foreshadowing of the spiritual "Paradise within" (XII, 587), which is the image of Christ in man; and in Book IX occurs the event that destroys that Garden and makes the metaphoric transformation possible, with the literalist Satan enacting the role of a false Christ through

.is "foul descent" and bestial incarnation (IX, 163–
67) and his promise of godhead by eating the literal
ruit. In Book III Christ is revealed as man's Intercessor and re-Creator; and in Book X he comes to the
Garden to judge him. Finally, his absence in the fallen
world of the devils in Books I and II is the most terrify-
ng example of his justice; and his presence in the fallen
world of man in Books XI and XII is the most glorious
example of his mercy.

This Edition

Paradise Lost was first published in 1667 as "A Poem
Written in Ten Books." In 1674, the year of Milton's
leath, a second edition appeared as *Paradise Lost. A
Poem in Twelve Books.* For this second edition Milton
split the original Book VII into the present Books VII
and VIII, and the original Book X into the present
Books XI and XII, adding a few transitional lines at
the beginning of each new book. Why he did this and
whether the twelve-book division more clearly reveals
the essential structure of the poem is matter for debate.
The cases for the ten-book and the twelve-book divisions
have been presented by John T. Shawcross and Arthur
E. Barker, respectively, in the articles listed in the
bibliography.

For the present edition, the editor has modernized
the 1674 edition in spelling, capitalization, and use of
italics, but the original punctuation, which is rhetorical
rather than grammatical, has been tampered with as
little as possible. Occasionally a reading from the 1667
edition has been adopted, as have several universally
accepted emendations. A few spellings that seem pecul-
iarly Miltonic, such as "highth" for "height," have been
retained. Where these are likely to give trouble to the
modern reader, they have been footnoted. Metrically significant marks of elision have been preserved and regu-
larized. Thus "Heav'n" is one syllable; "th' infernal" is
three. With a view to avoiding unnecessary obscurities

and an unattractive-looking page, marks of elision are eliminated whenever possible. Past participles are spelled out ("throned" instead of "thron'd"); when the "ed" is to be pronounced (contrary to modern usage), it receives an accent mark: "thronéd" is two syllables. "Power," which is always pronounced as one syllable, is spelled out, as are verbals formed on the analogy of "wandering" and "listening," which are almost invariably two syllables. It should be pointed out that *Paradise Lost* has a great many lines containing metrical elisions that are not indicated in the original editions. For example, in the line "Wand'ring shall in a glorious temple enshrine" (XII, 334), "glorious" is two syllables, and "temple enshrine" is three. The reader who makes a practice of reading *Paradise Lost* out loud will soon learn how to cope with such lines. The following rules for capitalization have been followed: names and titles of the Father (Almighty, Creator, Author, and so forth), of the Son (Redeemer, Word, Intercessor), of the angelic hierarchies (Cherubim, Seraphim), and of Satan (Fiend, Serpent); personifications (Sin, Death, Chaos, Night); Heaven (when the word refers to the abode of God); Hell; and of course all proper names.

I wish to acknowledge my great debt to the many studies of Milton listed in the bibliography and to the editions of *Paradise Lost* that I have consulted, especially those of A. W. Verity, Merritt Y. Hughes, and Douglas Bush. Grateful acknowledgment is also made to The Odyssey Press for permission to quote from Milton's Latin poetry in the English version of Merritt Y. Hughes and to the Dell Publishing Company for permission to use, in slightly altered form, several paragraphs from my introduction to the Laurel Poetry Series edition of Milton. The 1674 title page of *Paradise Lost* is reproduced by "Courtesy of the Huntington Library and Art Gallery."

1608	Dec. 9. John Milton born in Bread Street, Cheapside, London.
1617?	Began attending St. Paul's School.
1625	Feb. 12. Matriculated at Christ's College, Cambridge.
1632	July 3. Took the M. A. degree.
1632–1638	Resided at Hammersmith, Middlesex, and Horton, Buckinghamshire.
1634	Sept. *Comus* performed at Ludlow Castle.
1638	May? to 1639, July? Italian journey.
1640	Began teaching in London.
	Nov. The Long Parliament convened.
1641	May. *Of Reformation in England* published.
	July. *Animadversions upon the Remonstrant's Defence against Smectymnuus* published.
1642	Feb. *The Reason of Church Government Urged Against Prelaty* published.
	May? Married Mary Powell. *An Apology Against a Modest Confutation* published.
	July? Mary Powell Milton returned to her father's home.
	Aug. The Civil War began.
1643	Aug. *The Doctrine and Discipline of Divorce* published.
1644	June. *Of Education* published.
	Aug. *The Judgment of Martin Bucer Concerning Divorce* published.
	Nov. *Areopagitica* published.
1645	March. *Tetrachordon* and *Colasterion* published.

	Summer? Mary returned to live with Milton in London.
	Oct. 6. *Poems of Mr. John Milton* entered in the *Stationers Register*. It was published by January 2, 1646.
1646	July. Daughter Ann born.
1648	Oct. Daughter Mary born.
1649	Jan. King Charles executed.
	Feb. *The Tenure of Kings and Magistrates* published.
	March. Milton appointed Secretary for Foreign Tongues to the Council of State.
	Oct. *Eikonoklastes* published.
1651	Feb. *Defensio Pro Populo Anglicano* (*A Defence of the English People*) published.
	March. Son John born.
1652	Feb.? His blindness became almost total.
	May 2. Daughter Deborah born.
	May 5. Mary Powell Milton died.
	June 16. Son John died.
1653	Dec. Cromwell became Lord Protector.
1654	May. *Defensio Secunda* (*A Second Defence of the English People*) published.
1655	Aug. *Defensio Pro Se* (*A Defence of Himself*) published.
1656	Nov. Married Katherine Woodcock.
1658	March. Katherine Woodcock Milton died.
	Sept. Cromwell died.
1659	Feb.? *A Treatise of Civil Power in Ecclesiastical Causes* published.
1660	March. *The Ready and Easy Way to Establish a Free Commonwealth* published.
	May. Parliament voted for the restoration of Charles II.
1663	Feb. Married Elizabeth Minshull.
1667	Aug.? *Paradise Lost. A Poem Written in Ten Books* published.
1670	*The History of Britain* published.

BIBLIOGRAPHY

The following abbreviations have been used:

ELH	ELH: A Journal of English Literary History.
JEGP	Journal of English and Germanic Philology
JAAC	Journal of Aesthetics and Art Criticism
MLN	Modern Language Notes
MLQ	Modern Language Quarterly
MP	Modern Philology
PMLA	PMLA: Publications of the Modern Language Association
PQ	Philological Quarterly
SP	Studies in Philology
UTQ	University of Toronto Quarterly

LIFE AND WORKS

The fullest *Life of Milton* is David Masson's (London, 1859–1894. 7 vols. Vol. I, rev. ed., 1881). A more recent biography is James Holly Hanford, *John Milton: Englishman* (New York: Crown, 1949). The fourth edition of Hanford's *A Milton Handbook* (New York: Appleton-Century-Crofts, 1946) is still useful. Of special interest are *Early Lives of Milton,* Helen Darbishire (ed.) (London: Constable, 1932), and *Milton on Himself,* John S. Diekhoff (ed.) New York: Oxford University Press, 1939), a collection of autobiographical passages. Books combining biography and criticism are those of Walter Raleigh (London: E. Arnold, 1900), E. M. W. Tillyard (London: Chatto & Windus, 1930),

Kenneth Muir (London: Longmans Green, 1955), and Douglas Bush (New York: Macmillan, 1964).

The standard edition of Milton's collected works is the Columbia edition in 18 volumes (New York, 1931–1938). A convenient one-volume edition of the Columbia text of all the poetry and most of the prose is *The Student's Milton*, F. A. Patterson (ed.) (New York: Appleton-Century-Crofts, 1933). Excellent annotated editions of the poetry are those of A. W. Verity (Cambridge, Cambridge University Press, 1921), Merritt Y. Hughes (New York: The Odyssey Press, 1957), and Douglas Bush (Boston: Houghton Mifflin, 1965). Four volumes of a projected eight-volume edition of the *Prose Works* have been published by the Yale University Press (New Haven, Conn., 1953–).

There are bibliographical guides by David Stevens covering the period from 1800 to 1929 (Chicago: Chicago University Press, 1930) and Calvin Huckabay covering the period from 1929 to 1957 (Pittsburgh: Duquesne University Press, 1960). Intended for students is the *Goldentree Bibliography*, James Holly Hanford (ed.) (New York: Appleton-Century-Crofts, 1966). Annual bibliographies of Milton studies appear in the May issue of *Studies in Philology* and the June (formerly May) issue of *PMLA*.

COLLECTIONS OF ESSAYS AND ARTICLES

Barker, Arthur E. (ed.). *Milton: Modern Essays in Criticism*. New York: Oxford University Press, 1965.

Kermode, Frank (ed.). *The Living Milton*. London: Routledge & Kegan Paul, 1960.

Martz, Louis L. (ed.). *Milton: A Collection of Critical Essays*. Englewood Cliffs, N.J.: Prentice-Hall, 1966.

Thorpe, James (ed.). *Milton Criticism: Selections from Four Centuries*. New York: Rinehart, 1950.

BOOK-BY-BOOK COMMENTARIES ON
Paradise Lost

Broadbent, J. B. *Some Graver Subject.* London: Chatto & Windus, 1960.

Burden, Dennis H. *The Logical Epic.* Cambridge, Mass.: Harvard University Press, 1967.

Diekhoff, John S. *Milton's 'Paradise Lost.'* New York: Columbia University Press, 1946.

Fish, Stanley Eugene. *Surprised by Sin.* London: Macmillan; New York: St. Martin's Press, 1967.

Peter, John. *A Critique of* Paradise Lost. New York: Columbia University Press, 1960.

Summers, Joseph H. *The Muse's Method.* Cambridge, Mass.: Harvard University Press, 1962.

Wright, B. A. *Milton's 'Paradise Lost.'* London: Methuen, 1962.

OTHER BOOKS AND ARTICLES ON
Paradise Lost

Adamson, J. H. "The War in Heaven: Milton's Version of the Merkabah," *JEGP*, 57 (October 1958), 690–703.

Allen, Don Cameron. *The Harmonious Vision.* Baltimore: The Johns Hopkins University Press, 1954.

Barker, Arthur E. "Structural Pattern in *Paradise Lost*." *PQ*, 28 (January 1949), 17–30.

Barker, Arthur E. "Structural and Doctrinal Pattern in Milton's Later Poems," in Millar MacLure and F. W. Watt (eds.), *Essays in English Literature.* Toronto: University of Toronto Press, 1964.

Bell, Millicent. "The Fallacy of the Fall in *Paradise Lost*," *PMLA*, 68 (1953), 863–883. See also *PMLA*, 70 (September 1955), 1185–1203.

Berger, Harry. "*Paradise Lost* Evolving: Books I–IV. Toward a New View of the Poem as the Speaker's Experience," *The Centennial Review*, 11 (Fall 1967), 483–531.

Bowra, C. M. *From Virgil to Milton*. London: Macmillan, 1945.

Brooks, Cleanth. "Eve's Awakening," in *Essays in Honor of Walter Clyde Curry*. Nashville: Vanderbilt University Press, 1954.

————. "Milton and Critical Re-estimates," *PMLA*, 66 (December 1951), 1045–1054.

Bush, Douglas. Paradise Lost *in Our Time*. Ithaca, N.Y.: Cornell University Press, 1945.

Cirillo, Albert R. "Noon-Midnight and the Temporal Structure of *Paradise Lost*," *ELH*, 29 (December 1962), 372–395.

Coffin, Charles M. "Creation and the Self in *Paradise Lost*," *ELH*, 29 (March 1962), 1–18.

Colie, Rosalie L. "Time and Eternity: Paradox and Structure in *Paradise Lost*," *Journal of the Warburg and Courtauld Institutes*, 23 (January 1960), 127–138.

Cope, Jackson I. *The Metaphoric Structure of* Paradise Lost. Baltimore: The Johns Hopkins University Press, 1962.

Daiches, David. *Milton*. London: Hutchinson's Universal Library, 1957.

Durr, Robert A. "Dramatic Pattern in *Paradise Lost*," *JAAC*, 15 (June 1955), 520–526.

Eliot, T. S. *On Poetry and Poets*. London: Faber & Faber, 1957.

Empson, William. *Milton's God*. London: Chatto & Windus, 1961.

Ferry, Anne Davidson. *Milton's Epic Voice: The Narrator in* Paradise Lost. Cambridge, Mass.: Harvard University Press, 1963.

Frye, Northrop. *The Return of Eden*. Toronto: University of Toronto Press, 1965.

Gardner, Helen. *A Reading of* Paradise Lost. Oxford: The Clarendon Press, 1965.

Gilbert, Allan H. "The Theological Basis of Satan's Rebellion and the Function of Abdiel in *Paradise Lost*," *MP*, 40 (August 1942), 19–42.

————. *On the Composition of* Paradise Lost. Chapel Hill: University of North Carolina Press, 1947.

Hanford, James Holly. *John Milton: Poet and Humanist.* Cleveland: 1966.

Harding, Davis P. *The Club of Hercules: Studies in the Classical Background of 'Paradise Lost.'* Urbana: University of Illinois Press, 1962.

Hughes, Merritt Y. *Ten Perspectives on Milton.* New Haven, Conn.: Yale University Press, 1965.

Kelley, Maurice. *This Great Argument: A Study of Milton's* De doctrina christiana *As a Gloss Upon* Paradise Lost. Princeton, N.J.: Princeton University Press, 1941.

Knight, Douglas M. "The Dramatic Center of *Paradise Lost,*" *South Atlantic Quarterly,* 63 (Winter 1964), 44–59.

Leavis, F. R. *The Common Pursuit.* London: Chatto & Windus, 1952.

————. *Revaluation.* London: Chatto & Windus, 1936.

Lewalski, Barbara Kiefer. "Structure and the Symbolism of Vision in Michael's Prophecy, *Paradise Lost,* Books XI–XII," *PQ,* 42 (January 1963), 25–35.

Lewis, C. S. *A Preface to* Paradise Lost. London: Oxford University Press, 1942.

Lovejoy, A. O. "Milton and the Paradox of the Fortunate Fall," *Essays in the History of Ideas.* Baltimore: The Johns Hopkins University Press, 1948.

MacCaffrey, Isabel Gamble. Paradise Lost *as "Myth."* Cambridge, Mass.: Harvard University Press, 1959.

MacCallum, H. R. "Milton and Sacred History: Books XI and XII of *Paradise Lost,*" in Millar MacLure and F. W. Watt (eds.), *Essays in English Literature.* Toronto: University of Toronto Press, 1964.

MacKenzie, Phyllis. "Milton's Visual Imagination: an Answer to T. S. Eliot," *UTQ,* 16 (July 1946), 17–29.

Madsen, William G. "The Fortunate Fall in *Paradise Lost.*" *MLN,* 74 (February 1959), 103–105.

———— *From Shadowy Types to Truth: Studies in*

Milton's Symbolism. New Haven, Conn.: Yale University Press, 1968.

Martz, Louis L. *The Paradise Within*. New Haven, Conn.: Yale University Press, 1964.

Miller, Milton. "*Paradise Lost*: The Double Standard." *UTQ*, 20 (April 1951), 183–199.

Morris, John N. "*Paradise Lost* Now," *American Scholar*, 33 (Winter 1963–1964), 65–83.

Murray, Patrick. *Milton: The Modern Phase. A Study of Twentieth-century Criticism*. London: Longmans Green, 1967.

Prince, F. T. *The Italian Element in Milton's Verse*. Oxford: The Clarendon Press, 1954.

———. "On the Last Two Books of *Paradise Lost*," *Essays and Studies*, 11 (1958), 38–52.

Radzinowicz, Mary Ann Nevins. "Eve and Dalila: Renovation and the Hardening of the Heart," in J. A. Mazzeo (ed.), *Reason and the Imagination*. New York: Columbia University Press, 1962.

Rajan, B. *Paradise Lost and the Seventeenth-Century Reader*. London: Chatto & Windus, 1947.

Revard, Stella. "The Dramatic Function of the Son in *Paradise Lost*: A Commentary on Milton's 'Trinitarianism,' " *JEGP*, 66 (January 1967), 45–58.

Ricks, Christopher. *Milton's Grand Style*. Oxford: The Clarendon Press, 1963.

Saurat, Denis. *Milton: Man and Thinker*. London: Jonathan Cape, 1925.

Schultz, Howard. "Satan's Serenade," *PQ*, 27 (January 1948), 17–26.

Shawcross, John T. "The Balanced Structure of *Paradise Lost*," *SP*, 62 (October 1965), 696–718.

Steadman, John M. *Milton and the Renaissance Hero*. Oxford: The Clarendon Press, 1967.

Stein, Arnold. *Answerable Style*. Minneapolis: University of Minnesota Press, 1953.

Stoll, E. E. *From Shakespeare to Joyce*. Garden City, N.Y.: Doubleday, 1944.

————. *Poets and Playwrights*. Minneapolis: University of Minnesota Press, 1930.

Svendsen, Kester. *Milton and Science*. Cambridge, Mass.: Harvard University Press, 1956.

Thompson, E. N. S. "For *Paradise Lost,* XI–XII," *PQ,* 22 (October 1943), 376–382.

Tillyard, E. M. W. *Studies in Milton*. London: Chatto & Windus, 1951.

Toliver, Harold E. "Complicity of Voice in *Paradise Lost,*" *MLQ,* 25 (June 1964), 153–170.

Waldock, A. J. A. Paradise Lost *and Its Critics*. Cambridge: Cambridge University Press, 1947.

Watkins, W. B. C. *An Anatomy of Milton's Verse*. Baton Rouge: Louisiana State University Press, 1955.

Whaler, James. "The Miltonic Simile," *PMLA,* 46 (December 1931), 1034–1074.

Wilkes, G. A. *The Thesis of Paradise Lost*. Melbourne: Melbourne University Press, 1961.

Woodhouse, A. S. P. "Pattern in *Paradise Lost,*" *UTQ,* 22 (January 1953), 109–127.

Wrenn, C. L. "The Language of Milton," *Studies in English Language and Literature Presented to Professor Karl Brunner* (Wiener Studien zur englischen Philologie, LXV, 1957).

Paradiſe Loſt.

A
POEM
IN
TWELVE BOOKS.

The Author
JOHN MILTON.

𝔗𝔥𝔢 𝔖𝔢𝔠𝔬𝔫𝔡 𝔈𝔡𝔦𝔱𝔦𝔬𝔫
Reviſed and Augmented by the
ſame Author.

LONDON,
Printed by *S. Simmons* next door to the
Golden Lion in *Alderſgate-ſtreet*, 1674.

ON PARADISE LOST

When I beheld the poet blind, yet bold,
In slender book his vast design unfold,
Messiah crowned, God's reconciled decree,
Rebelling angels, the forbidden tree,
Heav'n, Hell, earth, chaos, all; the argument
Held me a while misdoubting his intent,
That he would ruin (for I saw him strong)
The sacred truths to fable and old song
(So Samson groped the temple's posts in spite)
The world o'erwhelming to revenge his sight.

Yet as I read, soon growing less severe,
I liked his project, the success did fear;
O'er which lame faith leads understanding blind;
Lest he perplexed the things he would explain,
And what was easy he should render vain.

Or if a work so infinite he spanned,
Jealous I was that some less skilful hand
(Such as disquiet always what is well,
And by ill imitating would excell)
Might hence presume the whole creation's day
To change in scenes, and show it in a play.

Pardon me, mighty poet, nor despise
My causeless, yet not impious, surmise.
But I am now convinced, and none will dare
Within thy labors to pretend a share.
Thou hast not missed one thought that could be fit,
And all that was improper dost omit:
So that no room is here for writers left,
But to detect their ignorance or theft.

That majesty which through thy work doth reign
Draws the devout, deterring the profane.
And things divine thou treatst of in such state
As them preserves, and thee, inviolate.
At once delight and horror on us seize,
Thou sing'st with so much gravity and ease;
And above human flight dost soar aloft
With plume so strong, so equal, and so soft,
The bird named from that Paradise you sing
So never flags, but always keeps on wing.

Where could'st thou words of such a compass find?
Whence furnish such a vast expense of mind?
Just Heav'n thee like Tiresias to requite
Rewards with prophecy thy loss of sight.

Well might'st thou scorn thy readers to allure
With tinkling rhyme, of thy own sense secure;
While the Town-Bayes writes all the while and spells,
And like a pack-horse tires without his bells:
Their fancies like our bushy-points appear,
The poets tag them, we for fashion wear.
I too transported by the mode offend,
And while I meant to praise thee must commend.
Thy verse created like thy theme sublime,
In number, weight, and measure, needs not rhyme.

A[NDREW] M[ARVELL]

THE VERSE

The measure is English heroic verse without rhyme,
as that of Homer in Greek, and of Virgil in Latin;
rhyme being no necessary adjunct or true ornament of
poem or good verse, in longer works especially, but the
invention of a barbarous age, to set off wretched matter
and lame meter; graced indeed since by the use of some
famous modern poets, carried away by custom, but
much to their own vexation, hindrance, and constraint
to express many things otherwise, and for the most part

worse than else they would have expressed them. Not without cause therefore some both Italian and Spanish poets of prime note have rejected rhyme both in longer and shorter works, as have also long since our best English tragedies, as a thing of itself, to all judicious ears, trivial and of no true musical delight: which consists only in apt numbers, fit quantity of syllables, and the sense variously drawn out from one verse into another, not in the jingling sound of like endings, a fault avoided by the learned ancients both in poetry and all good oratory. This neglect then of rhyme so little is to be taken for a defect, though it may seem so perhaps to vulgar readers, that it rather is to be esteemed an example set, the first in English, of ancient liberty recovered to heroic poem from the troublesome and modern bondage of rhyming.

PARADISE LOST ❧ ❧ ❧

❧ ❧ ❧ ❧ ❧ ❧

BOOK I ❧ ❧

THE ARGUMENT

The first book proposes, first in brief, the whole subject, man's disobedience, and the loss thereupon of Paradise wherein he was placed: then touches the prime cause of his fall, the serpent, or rather Satan in the serpent; who revolting from God, and drawing to his side many legions of angels, was by the command of God driven out of Heaven with all his crew into the great deep. Which action passed over, the poem hastes into the midst of things, presenting Satan with his angels now fallen into Hell, described here, not in the center (for heaven and earth may be supposed as yet not made, certainly not yet accursed) but in a place of utter darkness, fitliest called Chaos: here Satan with his angels lying on the burning lake, thunder-struck and astonished, after a certain space recovers, as from confusion, calls up him who next in order and dignity lay by him; they confer of their miserable fall. Satan awakens all

his legions, who lay till then in the same manner confounded; they rise, their numbers, array of battle, their
chief leaders named, according to the idols known after-
wards in Canaan and the countries adjoining. To these
Satan directs his speech, comforts them with hope yet of
regaining Heaven, but tells them lastly of a new world
and new kind of creature to be created, according to an
ancient prophecy or report in Heaven; for that angels
were long before this visible creation, was the opinion
of many ancient Fathers. To find out the truth of this
prophecy, and what to determine thereon he refers to a
full council. What his associates thence attempt. Pandemonium the palace of Satan rises, suddenly built out
of the deep: the infernal peers there sit in council.

Of man's first disobedience, and the fruit
Of that forbidden tree, whose mortal taste
Brought death into the world, and all our woe,
With loss of Eden, till one greater Man
Restore us, and regain the blissful seat,
Sing heav'nly Muse, that on the secret top

1–5. The hero of *PL* is not an individual man like Odysseus or
Aeneas but Everyman, whose spiritual history encompasses the first
disobedience of Adam and the restoration "as from a second root"
(III, 288) in *one greater Man*, Christ, the second Adam. Cf. III,
274–341.

6–17. By invoking the Muse here and at the beginning of Books
III, VII, and IX, M. follows classical precedent and at the same
time asserts the superiority both of his source of inspiration, which
is God, and of his subject matter, which he refers to as "this great
argument" in line 24 and as "higher argument" in IX, 42. The
glancing allusions to classical epic in line 15 (*th' aonian mount*
is Mount Helicon) and to Renaissance epic in line 16, which is an
ironic reference to the opening of Ariosto's *Orlando Furioso*, are
expanded in IX, 13–47, where M. boldly asserts that in its subject
matter his poem is "not less but more heroic" than other epic
poems. By referring to his Muse variously as "Spirit," "Celestial
Light" (III, 51), "Urania" (VII, 1), and "Celestial Patroness" (IX,
21), and by stating that he calls on "the meaning, not the name"
(VII, 5), M. leaves open the question, which has vexed modern
scholars, whether he has in mind the Father or the Son.

Of Oreb, or of Sinai, didst inspire
That shepherd, who first taught the chosen seed,
In the beginning how the heav'ns and earth
Rose out of Chaos: or if Sion hill   10
Delight thee more, and Siloa's brook that flowed
Fast by the oracle of God; I thence
Invoke thy aid to my adventrous song,
That with no middle flight intends to soar
Above th' Aonian mount, while it pursues
Things unattempted yet in prose or rhyme.
And chiefly Thou O Spirit, that dost prefer
Before all temples th' upright heart and pure,
Instruct me, for Thou know'st; Thou from the first
Wast present, and with mighty wings outspread   20
Dove-like satst brooding on the vast abyss
And mad'st it pregnant: what in me is dark
Illumine, what is low raise and support;
That to the highth of this great argument
I may assert eternal Providence,
And justify the ways of God to men.
    Say first, for Heav'n hides nothing from thy view
Nor the deep tract of Hell, say first what cause
Moved our grand parents in that happy state,
Favored of Heav'n so highly, to fall off   30
From their Creator, and transgress his will
For one restraint, lords of the world besides?

---

8. *that shepherd:* Moses, to whom God appeared in a burning
bush on Mount Oreb (Horeb in Exodus 3:1) and to whom he gave
the Law on Mount Sinai (Exodus 19–31). Sinai is the lower part of
the mountain range Horeb.

10–12. Mount Zion, the site of David's palace, and Mount
Moriah, the site of Solomon's Temple (*the oracle of God*), are divided by the Tyropoeon valley and form the western and eastern
sides respectively of Jerusalem. *Siloa* (or Shiloah) is a subterranean
brook that issues in a pool at the southern extremity of the Tyropoeon valley and thence flows into the Brook Kidron. Cf. the allusion to "Sion and the flow'ry brooks beneath" in III, 30. The pool
Siloam is where the blind man received his sight by washing away
the clay with which Jesus had anointed his eyes (John 9:7).

24. *argument:* subject.

Who first seduced them to that foul revolt?
Th' infernal Serpent; he it was, whose guile
Stirred up with envy and revenge, deceived
The mother of mankind, what time his pride
Had cast him out from Heav'n, with all his host
Of rebel angels, by whose aid aspiring
To set himself in glory above his peers,
He trusted to have equaled the Most High,   40
If he opposed; and with ambitious aim
Against the throne and monarchy of God
Raised impious war in Heav'n and battle proud
With vain attempt. Him the Almighty Power
Hurled headlong flaming from th' ethereal sky
With hideous ruin and combustion down
To bottomless perdition, there to dwell
In adamantine chains and penal fire,
Who durst defy th' Omnipotent to arms.
Nine times the space that measures day and night   50
To mortal men, he with his horrid crew
Lay vanquished, rolling in the fiery gulf
Confounded though immortal: but his doom
Reserved him to more wrath; for now the thought
Both of lost happiness and lasting pain
Torments him; round he throws his baleful eyes
That witnessed huge affliction and dismay
Mixed with obdúrate pride and steadfast hate:
At once as far as angels ken he views
The dismal situation waste and wild,   60
A dungeon horrible, on all sides round
As one great furnace flamed, yet from those flames
No light, but rather darkness visible
Served only to discover sights of woe,
Regions of sorrow, doleful shades, where peace
And rest can never dwell, hope never comes

---

46. *ruin:* falling.
57. *witnessed:* gave witness to, revealed.
66. Cf. Dante's *Inferno*, III, 9, "All hope abandon, ye who enter here."

That comes to all; but torture without end
Still urges, and a fiery deluge, fed
With ever-burning sulphur unconsumed:
Such place eternal Justice had prepared   70
For those rebellious, here their prison ordained
In utter darkness, and their portion set
As far removed from God and light of Heav'n
As from the center thrice to th' utmost pole.
O how unlike the place from whence they fell!
There the companions of his fall, o'erwhelmed
With floods and whirlwinds of tempestuous fire,
He soon discerns, and weltering by his side
One next himself in power, and next in crime,
Long after known in Palestine, and named   80
Beëlzebub. To whom th' Arch-Enemy,
And thence in Heav'n called Satan, with bold words
Breaking the horrid silence thus began.
    "If thou beest he; but O how fall'n! how changed
From him, who in the happy realms of light
Clothed with transcendent brightness didst outshine
Myriads though bright: if he whom mutual league,
United thoughts and counsels, equal hope
And hazard in the glorious enterprise,
Joined with me once, now misery hath joined   90   *Read*
In equal ruin: into what pit thou seest
From what highth fall'n, so much the stronger proved   *cf*
He with his thunder: and till then who knew   *Zeus*
The force of those dire arms? yet not for those,   *Jove*
Nor what the potent victor in his rage   *Thor*

---

68. *urges:* afflicts.

72. *utter:* outer.

74. The indication of spatial distance need not be taken literally.

81. *Beëlzebub* means "lord of the flies." He is referred to as "the prince of the devils" in Matthew 12:24.

82. *Satan* means "adversary."

84–85. Cf. Isaiah 14:12, "How art thou fallen from Heaven, O Lucifer, son of the morning!" and *Aeneid,* II, 274–275, "quantum mutatus ab illo Hectore" (how changed from that Hector).

Read

Can else inflict, do I repent or change,
Though changed in outward luster; that fixed mind
And high disdain, from sense of injured merit,
That with the mightiest raised me to contend,
And to the fierce contention brought along   1
Innumerable force of spirits armed
That durst dislike his reign, and me preferring,
His utmost power with adverse power opposed
In dubious battle on the plains of Heav'n,
And shook his throne. What though the field be lost?
All is not lost; the unconquerable will,
And study of revenge, immortal hate,
And courage never to submit or yield:
And what is else not to be overcome?
That glory never shall his wrath or might   1.
Extort from me. To bow and sue for grace
With suppliant knee, and deify his power,
Who from the terror of this arm so late
Doubted his empire, that were low indeed,
That were an ignominy and shame beneath
This downfall; since by fate the strength of gods
And this empyreal substance cannot fail,
Since through experience of this great event
In arms not worse, in foresight much advanced,
We may with more successful hope resolve   12
To wage by force or guile eternal war
Irreconcilable, to our grand foe,

97–105. Satan's propagandistic allusions to the war in Heaven
should be compared with the more authoritative account o
Raphael in Books V and VI. There we learn, for example, tha
God was far from using his *utmost power*.

107. *study:* pursuit.

109. "And in what else does not being overcome consist (be
sides retaining one's courage, hate, etc.)?"

115. *ignominy:* pronounced "ignomy."

116. *fate:* The first of many diabolic references to a power sup
posedly superior to God. In VII, 173, the reader learns that wha
God wills is fate. *gods:* The word is frequently applied to the
angels both by the narrator and by God himself (III, 341).

120. *successful hope:* hope of success.

Who now triumphs, and in th' excess of joy
Sole reigning holds the tyranny of Heav'n."
    So spake th' apostate angel, though in pain,
Vaunting aloud, but racked with deep despair:
And him thus answered soon his bold compeer.
    "O Prince, O chief of many thronéd Powers,
That led th' embattled Seraphim to war
Under thy conduct, and in dreadful deeds   130
Fearless, endangered Heav'n's perpetual King;
And put to proof his high supremacy,
Whether upheld by strength, or chance, or fate,
Too well I see and rue the dire event,
That with sad overthrow and foul defeat
Hath lost us Heav'n, and all this mighty host
In horrible destruction laid thus low,
As far as gods and heav'nly essences
Can perish: for the mind and spirit remains
Invincible, and vigor soon returns,   140
Though all our glory extinct, and happy state
Here swallowed up in endless misery.
But what if he our conqueror, (whom I now
Of force believe almighty, since no less
Than such could have o'erpowered such force as ours)
Have left us this our spirit and strength entire
Strongly to suffer and support our pains,
That we may so suffice his vengeful ire,
Or do him mightier service as his thralls
By right of war, whate'er his business be   150
Here in the heart of Hell to work in fire,
Or do his errands in the gloomy deep;
What can it then avail though yet we feel
Strength undiminished, or eternal being
To undergo eternal punishment?"
Whereto with speedy words th' Arch-Fiend replied.
    "Fall'n Cherub, to be weak is miserable
Doing or suffering: but of this be sure,
To do aught good never will be our task,

---

148. *suffice:* satisfy.

But ever to do ill our sole delight,   160
As being the contrary to his high will
Whom we resist. If then his providence
Out of our evil seek to bring forth good,
Our labor must be to pervert that end,
And out of good still to find means of evil;
Which ofttimes may succeed, so as perhaps
Shall grieve him, if I fail not, and disturb
His inmost counsels from their destined aim.
But see the angry victor hath recalled
His ministers of vengeance and pursuit   170
Back to the gates of Heav'n: the sulphurous hail
Shot after us in storm, o'erblown hath laid
The fiery surge, that from the precipice
Of Heav'n received us falling, and the thunder,
Winged with red lightning and impetuous rage,
Perhaps hath spent his shafts, and ceases now
To bellow through the vast and boundless deep.
Let us not slip th' occasion, whether scorn,
Or satiate fury yield it from our foe.
Seest thou yon dreary plain, forlorn and wild,   180
The seat of desolation, void of light,
Save what the glimmering of these livid flames
Casts pale and dreadful? Thither let us tend
From off the tossing of these fiery waves,
There rest, if any rest can harbor there,
And reassembling our afflicted powers,
Consult how we may henceforth most offend
Our enemy, our own loss how repair,
How overcome this dire calamity,
What reinforcement we may gain from hope,   190
If not what resolution from despair."
     Thus Satan talking to his nearest mate
With head uplift above the wave, and eyes
That sparkling blazed, his other parts besides

---

167. *if I fail not:* if I am not mistaken.
186. *afflicted:* stricken.
187. *offend:* strike at, harm.

Prone on the flood, extended long and large
Lay floating many a rood, in bulk as huge
As whom the fables name of monstrous size,
Titanian, or Earth-born, that warred on Jove,
Briareos or Typhon, whom the den
By ancient Tarsus held, or that sea-beast   200
Leviathan, which God of all his works
Created hugest that swim th' ocean stream:
Him haply slumbering on the Norway foam
The pilot of some small night-foundered skiff,
Deeming some island, oft, as seamen tell,
With fixéd anchor in his scaly rind
Moors by his side under the lee, while night
Invests the sea, and wishéd morn delays:
So stretched out huge in length the Arch-Fiend lay
Chained on the burning lake, nor ever thence   210
Had ris'n or heaved his head, but that the will
And high permission of all-ruling Heav'n
Left him at large to his own dark designs,
That with reiterated crimes he might
Heap on himself damnation, while he sought
Evil to others, and enraged might see
How all his malice served but to bring forth
Infinite goodness, grace and mercy shown
On man by him seduced, but on himself
Treble confusion, wrath and vengeance poured.   220
Forthwith upright he rears from off the pool
His mighty stature; on each hand the flames

Read Providence

Then flies to "land".

197–199. The classical fables of the war of the Titans against
Uranus and the war of the earth-born Giants against Jove provided Renaissance poets and mythographers with analogies to
Satan's ambitious war against God. The Titan *Briareos* had a
hundred arms; the Giant *Typhon* a hundred heads.

201. *Leviathan* in the Bible means any huge monster, but Milton's contemporaries usually took it to mean "whale." The associa-
tion of the Leviathan with Satan stems from such passages as
Isaiah 27:1, "In that day the Lord . . . shall punish leviathan the
piercing serpent, even leviathan that crooked serpent; and he shall
slay the dragon that is in the sea." Cf. Job 41:1–9.

Driv'n backward slope their pointing spires, and rolled
In billows, leave i' th' midst a horrid vale.
Then with expanded wings he steers his flight
Aloft, incumbent on the dusky air
That felt unusual weight, till on dry land
He lights, if it were land that ever burned
With solid, as the lake with liquid fire;
And such appeared in hue, as when the force   230
Of subterranean wind transports a hill
Torn from Pelorus, or the shattered side
Of thundering Etna, whose combustible
And fueled entrails thence conceiving fire,
Sublimed with mineral fury, aid the winds,
And leave a singéd bottom all involved
With stench and smoke: such resting found the sole
Of unblest feet. Him followed his next mate,
Both glorying to have 'scaped the Stygian flood
As gods, and by their own recovered strength,   240
Not by the sufferance of supernal power.
  "Is this the region, this the soil, the clime,"
Said then the lost Archangel, "this the seat
That we must change for Heav'n, this mournful gloom
For that celestial light? Be it so, since he
Who now is sovran can dispose and bid
What shall be right: farthest from him is best
Whom reason hath equaled, force hath made supreme
Above his equals. Farewell happy fields
Where joy forever dwells: hail horrors, hail   250
Infernal world, and thou profoundest Hell
Receive thy new possessor: one who brings
A mind not to be changed by place or time.

---

226. *incumbent:* leaning, resting.
230. Earthquakes were thought to be caused by the escape of
underground winds.
232–233. Mount *Etna* is on the Sicilian promontory *Pelorus.*
235. *sublimed:* kindled into a very hot flame.
236. *involved:* wrapped in.
248. Satan claims to be equal to God in reason, inferior only
in might.

The mind is its own place, and in itself
Can make a Heav'n of Hell, a Hell of Heav'n.
What matter where, if I be still the same,
And what I should be, all but less than he
Whom thunder hath made greater? Here at least
We shall be free; th' Almighty hath not built
Here for his envy, will not drive us hence:
Here we may reign secure, and in my choice   260
To reign is worth ambition though in Hell:
Better to reign in Hell, than serve in Heav'n.
But wherefore let we then our faithful friends,
Th' associates and copartners of our loss
Lie thus astonished on th' oblivious pool,
And call them not to share with us their part
In this unhappy mansion, or once more
With rallied arms to try what may be yet
Regained in Heav'n, or what more lost in Hell?"   270
    So Satan spake, and him Beëlzebub
Thus answered. "Leader of those armies bright,
Which but th' Omnipotent none could have foiled,
If once they hear that voice, their liveliest pledge
Of hope in fears and dangers, heard so oft
In worst extremes, and on the perilous edge
Of battle when it raged, in all assaults
Their surest signal, they will soon resume
New courage and revive, though now they lie
Groveling and prostrate on yon lake of fire,   280
As we erewhile, astounded and amazed,
No wonder, fall'n such a pernicious highth."
    He scarce had ceased when the superior Fiend
Was moving toward the shore; his ponderous shield
Ethereal temper, massy, large and round,

___

254–255. Later (IV, 75) Satan sees that only half of this proud
boast is true.
257. *all but less than:* nearly equal to.
276. *edge:* front line (of battle).
281. *amazed:* cf. II, 561, "in wandering mazes lost" and many
other passages; a much stronger word than it is now.
282. *pernicious:* death-dealing.

Behind him cast; the broad circumference
Hung on his shoulders like the moon, whose orb
Through optic glass the Tuscan artist views
At evening from the top of Fesole,
Or in Valdarno, to descry new lands,   290
Rivers or mountains in her spotty globe.
His spear, to equal which the tallest pine
Hewn on Norwegian hills, to be the mast
Of some great ammiral, were but a wand,
He walked with to support uneasy steps
Over the burning marl, not like those steps
On Heaven's azure, and the torrid clime
Smote on him sore besides, vaulted with fire;
Nathless he so endured, till on the beach
Of that inflaméd sea, he stood and called   300
His legions, angel forms, who lay entranced
Thick as autumnal leaves that strow the brooks
In Vallombrosa, where th' Etrurian shades
High overarched embow'r; or scattered sedge
Afloat, when with fierce winds Orion armed
Hath vexed the Red Sea coast, whose waves o'erthrew
Busiris and his Memphian chivalry,
While with perfidious hatred they pursued
The sojourners of Goshen, who beheld

288–290. In *Areopagitica* M. says he visited Galileo (*the Tuscan artist*), who resided both at *Fiesole,* a hill near Florence, and at a villa on the banks of the Arno (*Valdarno*-valley of the Arno), also near Florence.

294. *ammiral:* flagship, admiral's ship.

296. *marl:* rich, moist earth (here, of course, used ironically).

299. *nathless:* not the less.

303. *Vallombrosa:* a shady valley (as its name implies) not far from Florence.

304. *sedge:* seaweed.

307–311. The simile, which began by comparing the great number and abject condition of the fallen angels to leaves and seaweed, characteristically develops into an allusion to the escape of the Jews from Goshen, the passing of the Red Sea, and the destruction of the Pharaoh and his army (*Busiris and his Memphian chivalry*).

From the safe shore their floating carcasses   310
And broken chariot wheels, so thick bestrown
Abject and lost lay these, covering the flood,
Under amazement of their hideous change.
He called so loud, that all the hollow deep
Of Hell resounded. "Princes, Potentates,
Warriors, the flow'r of Heav'n, once yours, now lost,
If such astonishment as this can seize
Eternal spirits; or have ye chos'n this place
After the toil of battle to repose
Your wearied virtue, for the ease you find   320
To slumber here, as in the vales of Heav'n?
Or in this abject posture have ye sworn
To adore the conqueror? who now beholds
Cherub and Seraph rolling in the flood
With scattered arms and ensigns, till anon
His swift pursuers from Heav'n gates discern
Th' advantage, and descending tread us down
Thus drooping, or with linkéd thunderbolts
Transfix us to the bottom of this gulf.
Awake, arise, or be for ever fall'n."   330
    They heard, and were abashed, and up they sprung
Upon the wing, as when men wont to watch
On duty, sleeping found by whom they dread,
Rouse and bestir themselves ere well awake.
Nor did they not perceive the evil plight
In which they were, or the fierce pains not feel;
Yet to their general's voice they soon obeyed
Innumerable. As when the potent rod
Of Amram's son in Egypt's evil day
Waved round the coast, up called a pitchy cloud   340
Of locusts, warping on the eastern wind,
That o'er the realm of impious Pharaoh hung
Like night, and darkened all the land of Nile:
So numberless were those bad angels seen

338–343. The fallen angels, risen from the lake, are now compared to the locusts called up by Moses (*Amram's son*) to plague
the Egyptians (Exodus 10:12–15).

Hovering on wing under the cope of Hell
'Twixt upper, nether, and surrounding fires;
Till, as a signal giv'n, th' uplifted spear
Of their great Sultan waving to direct
Their course, in even balance down they light
On the firm brimstone, and fill all the plain;   35
A multitude, like which the populous North
Poured never from her frozen loins, to pass
Rhene or the Danaw, when her barbarous sons
Came like a deluge on the South, and spread
Beneath Gibraltar to the Lybian sands.
Forthwith from every squadron and each band
The heads and leaders thither haste where stood
Their great commander; godlike shapes and forms
Excelling human, princely dignities,
And powers that erst in Heaven sat on thrones;   36
Though of their names in heav'nly records now
Be no memorial blotted out and razed
By their rebellion, from the Books of Life.
Nor had they yet among the sons of Eve
Got them new names, till wandering o'er the earth
Through God's high sufferance for the trial of man,
By falsities and lies the greatest part
Of mankind they corrupted to forsake
God their Creator, and th' invisible
Glory of him that made them, to transform   37
Oft to the image of a brute, adorned
With gay religions full of pomp and gold,
And devils to adore for deities:
Then were they known to men by various names,
And various idols through the heathen world.

351–355. The series of similes which began in line 302 now ends
with an image of even greater destruction, the inundation of the
Roman Empire by barbarians from north of the Rhine and
Danube.

363. The *Books of Life* contain the names of those angels and
men who are saved. Cf. Revelation 13:8.

Say, Muse, their names then known, who first, who last,
Roused from the slumber, on that fiery couch,
At their great emperor's call, as next in worth
Came singly where he stood on the bare strand,
While the promiscuous crowd stood yet aloof?   380
The chief were those who from the pit of Hell
Roaming to seek their prey on earth, durst fix
Their seats long after next the seat of God,
Their altars by his altar, gods adored
Among the nations round, and durst abide
Jehovah thundering out of Sion, throned
Between the Cherubim; yea, often placed
Within his sanctuary itself their shrines,
Abominations; and with cursèd things
His holy rites, and solemn feasts profaned,   390
And with their darkness durst affront his light.
First Moloch, horrid king besmeared with blood
Of human sacrifice, and parents' tears,
Though for the noise of drums and timbrels loud
Their children's cries unheard, that passed through fire
To his grim idol. Him the Ammonite
Worshipped in Rabba and her wat'ry plain,
In Argob and in Basan, to the stream
Of utmost Arnon. Nor content with such
Audacious neighborhood, the wisest heart   400
Of Solomon he led by fraud to build
His temple right against the temple of God
On that opprobrious hill, and made his grove
The pleasant valley of Hinnom, Tophet thence
And black Gehenna called, the type of Hell.

376–521. This catalogue of devils, which is like Homer's list of
ships in Book II of the *Iliad* and Virgil's list of warriors in Book
VII of the *Aeneid*, may be read without a precise knowledge of all
the proper names, since M. provides the essential information in
the text. Biblical and other references are provided in the notes
for those who wish to pursue them.

392. *Moloch:* 1 Kings 11:7, 2 Kings 23:10, Jeremiah 32:35.

Next Chemos, th' obscene dread of Moab's sons,
From Aroar to Nebo, and the wild
Of southmost Abarim; in Hesebon
And Horonaim, Seon's realm, beyond
The flow'ry dale of Sibma clad with vines,   410
And Eleale to th' asphaltic pool.
Peor his other name, when he enticed
Israel in Sittim on their march from Nile
To do him wanton rites, which cost them woe.
Yet thence his lustful orgies he enlarged
Ev'n to that hill of scandal, by the grove
Of Moloch homicide, lust hard by hate;
Till good Josiah drove them thence to Hell.
With these came they, who from the bordering flood
Of old Euphrates to the brook that parts   420
Egypt from Syrian ground, had general names
Of Baalim and Ashtaroth, those male,
These feminine. For spirits when they please
Can either sex assume, or both; so soft
And uncompounded is their essence pure,
Not tied or manacled with joint or limb,
Nor founded on the brittle strength of bones,
Like cumbrous flesh; but in what shape they choose
Dilated or condensed, bright or obscure,
Can execute their aery purposes,   430
And works of love or enmity fulfill.
For those the race of Israel oft forsook
Their living strength, and unfrequented left

406–411. The place names identify the land of the Moabites, which was assigned to the tribe of Reuben in Numbers 32. See Jeremiah 48 for the judgment of the Moabites and their god Chemosh. The *asphaltic pool* is the Dead Sea.

412–414. Numbers 25:1–3.

415–418. Cf. 1 Kings 11:7, "Then did Solomon build an high place for Chemosh, the abomination of Moab, in the hill that is before Jerusalem, and for Molech, the abomination of the children of Ammon." For *Josiah* see 2 Kings 23:5–16.

422. *Baalim and Ashtaroth* are plurals. Baal means "lord" (cf. Beëlzebub, a variant of Baalzebub).

His righteous altar, bowing lowly down
To bestial gods; for which their heads as low
Bowed down in battle, sunk before the spear
Of despicable foes. With these in troop
Came Astoreth, whom the Phoenicians called
Astarte, queen of heav'n, with crescent horns;
To whose bright image nightly by the moon   440
Sidonian virgins paid their vows and songs,
In Sion also not unsung, where stood
Her temple on th' offensive mountain, built
By that uxorious king, whose heart though large,
Beguiled by fair idolatresses, fell
To idols foul. Thammuz came next behind,
Whose annual wound in Lebanon allured
The Syrian damsels to lament his fate
In amorous ditties all a summer's day,
While smooth Adonis from his native rock   450
Ran purple to the sea, supposed with blood
Of Thammuz yearly wounded: the love-tale
Infected Sion's daughters with like heat,
Whose wanton passions in the sacred porch
Ezekiel saw, when by the vision led
His eye surveyed the dark idolatries
Of alienated Judah. Next came one
Who mourned in earnest, when the captive ark
Maimed his brute image, head and hands lopped off
In his own temple, on the grunsel edge,   460
Where he fell flat, and shamed his worshippers:
Dagon his name, sea monster, upward man
And downward fish: yet had his temple high
Reared in Azotus, dreaded through the coast

The Goddess

440–446. 1 Kings 11:4–5. This is the third allusion to the idolatry of Solomon, whose "wives turned away his heart after other gods," as Eve turned away the heart of another uxorious king.

446–457. Ezekiel 8:5–18. The River Adonis, which rises in Lebanon and flows into the Mediterranean, gets its red color from the earth in spring floods.

457–466. 1 Samuel 5:1–4. The five cities mentioned in lines 464–466 were the chief cities of the Philistines.

Of Palestine, in Gath and Ascalon
And Accaron and Gaza's frontier bounds.
Him followed Rimmon, whose delightful seat
Was fair Damascus, on the fertile banks
Of Abbana and Pharphar, lucid streams.
He also against the house of God was bold: 470
A leper once he lost and gained a king,
Ahaz his sottish conqueror, whom he drew
God's altar to disparage and displace
For one of Syrian mode, whereon to burn
His odious offerings, and adore the gods
Whom he had vanquished. After these appeared
A crew who under names of old renown,
Osiris, Isis, Orus and their train
With monstrous shapes and sorceries abused
Fanatic Egypt and her priests, to seek   480
Their wandering gods disguised in brutish forms
Rather than human. Nor did Israel scape
Th' infection when their borrowed gold composed
The calf in Oreb: and the rebel king
Doubled that sin in Bethel and in Dan,
Likening his Maker to the grazéd ox,
Jehovah, who in one night when he passed
From Egypt marching, equaled with one stroke
Both her first-born and all her bleating gods.
Belial came last, than whom a spirit more lewd   490
Fell not from Heaven, or more gross to love

---

467. *Rimmon:* 2 Kings 5:18.

471–476. The *leper* is Naaman (2 Kings 5:8–14). For King *Ahaz* see 2 Kings 16:10–18.

479. *abused:* deluded.

482–484. Exodus 32:1–4.

484–485. The *rebel king* is Jeroboam, who doubled the sin by setting up two calves of gold, one in *Bethel* and one in *Dan* (1 Kings 12:28–29).

487–489. Exodus 12:29.

490. *Belial* is an abstract noun meaning "worthlessness." The phrase "sons of Belial" (lines 501–502) occurs in Judges 19:22, where the story of the matron in Gibeah (lines 503–505) is recounted.

Vice for itself. To him no temple stood
Or altar smoked; yet who more oft than he
In temples and at altars, when the priest
Turns atheist, as did Eli's sons, who filled
With lust and violence the house of God.
In courts and palaces he also reigns
And in luxurious cities, where the noise
Of riot ascends above their loftiest tow'rs,
And injury and outrage: and when night   500
Darkens the streets, then wander forth the sons
Of Belial, flown with insolence and wine.
Witness the streets of Sodom, and that night
In Gibeah, when the hospitable door
Exposed a matron to avoid worse rape.
These were the prime in order and in might;
The rest were long to tell, though far renowned,
Th' Ionian gods, of Javan's issue held
Gods, yet confessed later than heav'n and earth
Their boasted parents; Titan heav'n's first-born   510
With his enormous brood, and birthright seized
By younger Saturn, he from mightier Jove
His own and Rhea's son like measure found;
So Jove usurping reigned: these first in Crete
And Ida known, thence on the snowy top
Of cold Olympus ruled the middle air
Their highest heav'n; or on the Delphian cliff,
Or in Dodona, and through all the bounds
Of Doric land; or who with Saturn old
Fled over Adria to th' Hesperian fields,   520
And o'er the Celtic roamed the utmost isles.

---

495. "Now the sons of Eli were sons of Belial; they knew not the Lord" (1 Samuel 2:12).

502. *flown:* flushed.

508. *Javan* was one of the sons of Japhet. Javan's sons divided "the isles of the Gentiles" (Genesis 10:5). After the lengthy account of the false gods worshipped by the Chosen People, M. dismisses the Greek gods in a few contemptuous lines.

509. *confessed later:* admitted to be of later origin.

511. *enormous:* monstrous.

All these and more came flocking; but with looks
Downcast and damp, yet such wherein appeared
Obscure some glimpse of joy, to have found their chief
Not in despair, to have found themselves not lost
In loss itself; which on his count'nance cast
Like doubtful hue: but he his wonted pride
Soon recollecting, with high words, that bore
Semblance of worth, not substance, gently raised
Their fainting courage, and dispelled their fears.   530
Then straight commands that at the warlike sound
Of trumpets loud and clarions upreared
His mighty standard; that proud honor claimed
Azazel as his right, a Cherub tall:
Who forthwith from the glittering staff unfurled
Th' imperial ensign, which full high advanced
Shone like a meteor streaming to the wind
With gems and golden luster rich emblazed,
Seraphic arms and trophies: all the while
Sonorous metal blowing martial sounds: 540
At which the universal host upsent
A shout that tore Hell's concave, and beyond
Frighted the reign of Chaos and old Night.
All in a moment through the gloom were seen
Ten thousand banners rise into the air
With orient colors waving: with them rose
A forest huge of spears: and thronging helms
Appeared, and serried shields in thick array
Of depth immeasurable: anon they move
In perfect phalanx to the Dorian mood   550

---

523. *damp:* damped, depressed.

534. *Azazel* is the Hebrew appellation of the scapegoat in Leviticus 16:8.

538. *emblazed:* emblazoned (with heraldic devices).

550. In Plato's *Republic,* III, 399, the *Dorian mode* is described as a "warlike" harmony that sounds "the note or accent which a brave man utters in the hour of danger and stern resolve, or when his cause is failing, and he is going to wounds or death or is overtaken by some other evil, and at every such crisis meets the blows of fortune with firm step and a determination to endure."

Of flutes and soft recorders; such as raised
To highth of noblest temper heroes old
Arming to battle, and instead of rage
Deliberate valor breathed, firm and unmoved
With dread of death to flight or foul retreat,
Nor wanting power to mitigate and swage
With solemn touches, troubled thoughts, and chase
Anguish and doubt and fear and sorrow and pain
From mortal or immortal minds. Thus they
Breathing united force with fixéd thought   560
Moved on in silence to soft pipes that charmed
Their painful steps o'er the burnt soil; and now
Advanced in view, they stand, a horrid front
Of dreadful length and dazzling arms, in guise
Of warriors old with ordered spear and shield,
Awaiting what command their mighty chief
Had to impose: he through the arméd files
Darts his experienced eye, and soon traverse
The whole battalion views, their order due,
Their visages and stature as of gods,   570
Their number last he sums. And now his heart
Distends with pride, and hardening in his strength
Glories: for never since created man,
Met such embodied force, as named with these
Could merit more than that small infantry
Warred on by cranes: though all the giant brood
Of Phlegra with th' heroic race were joined
That fought at Thebes and Ilium, on each side
Mixed with auxiliar gods; and what resounds
In fable or romance of Uther's son   580
Begirt with British and Armoric knights;

---

556. *swage:* assuage.
563. *horrid:* bristling.
573. *created man:* the creation of man.
574–587. "Compared to Satan's followers the great armies of
epic and romance are no better than pygmies." M. alludes to the
Thebaid of Statius, the *Iliad,* the Arthurian romances (Arthur is
Uther's son), Italian romances such as Ariosto's *Orlando Furioso,*
and the *Song of Roland.*

And all who since, baptized or infidel
Jousted in Aspramont or Montalban,
Damasco, or Marocco, or Trebisond,
Or whom Biserta sent from Afric shore
When Charlemain with all his peerage fell
By Fontarabbia. Thus far these beyond
Compare of mortal prowess, yet observed
Their dread commander: he above the rest
In shape and gesture proudly eminent   5
Stood like a tow'r; his form had yet not lost
All her original brightness, nor appeared
Less than Archangel ruined, and th' excess
Of glory obscured: as when the sun new ris'n
Looks through the horizontal misty air
Shorn of his beams, or from behind the moon
In dim eclipse disastrous twilight sheds
On half the nations, and with fear of change
Perplexes monarchs. Darkened so, yet shone
Above them all th' Archangel: but his face   6
Deep scars of thunder had entrenched, and care
Sat on his faded cheek, but under brows
Of dauntless courage, and considerate pride
Waiting revenge: cruel his eye, but cast
Signs of remorse and passion to behold
The fellows of his crime, the followers rather
(Far other once beheld in bliss) condemned
For ever now to have their lot in pain,
Millions of spirits for his fault amerced
Of Heav'n, and from eternal splendors flung   6
For his revolt, yet faithful how they stood,
Their glory withered. As when heaven's fire
Hath scathed the forest oaks, or mountain pines,
With singéd top their stately growth though bare

---

588. *observed:* obeyed.
603. *considerate:* conscious, full of thought.
609. *amerced:* a legal term meaning "fined with the loss of."
613. *scathed:* damaged.

Stands on the blasted heath. He now prepared
To speak; whereat their doubled ranks they bend
From wing to wing, and half enclose him round
With all his peers: attention held them mute.
Thrice he assayed, and thrice in spite of scorn,
Tears such as angels weep, burst forth: at last   620
Words interwove with sighs found out their way.

    "O myriads of immortal spirits, O Powers
Matchless, but with th' Almighty, and that strife
Was not inglorious, though th' event was dire,
As this place testifies, and this dire change
Hateful to utter: but what power of mind
Foreseeing or presaging, from the depth
Of knowledge past or present, could have feared,
How such united force of gods, how such
As stood like these, could ever know repulse?   630
For who can yet believe, though after loss,
That all these puissant legions, whose exile
Hath emptied Heav'n, shall fail to re-ascend
Self-raised, and repossess their native seat?
For me be witness all the host of Heav'n,
If counsels different, or danger shunned
By me, have lost our hopes. But he who reigns
Monarch in Heav'n, till then as one secure
Sat on his throne, upheld by old repute,
Consent or custom, and his regal state   640
Put forth at full, but still his strength concealed,
Which tempted our attempt, and wrought our fall.
Henceforth his might we know, and know our own
So as not either to provoke, or dread
New war, provoked; our better part remains
To work in close design, by fraud or guile
What force effected not: that he no less

---

  624. *event:* outcome.

  642. *tempted our attempt:* Such plays on words (cf. IV, 181; V, 869; and IX, 648), much admired by Renaissance rhetoricians, are usually associated with the Satanic mind in *PL*.

At length from us may find, who overcomes
By force, hath overcome but half his foe.
Space may produce new worlds; whereof so rife   650
There went a fame in Heav'n that he ere long
Intended to create, and therein plant
A generation, whom his choice regard
Should favor equal to the sons of Heav'n:
Thither, if but to pry, shall be perhaps
Our first eruption, thither or elsewhere:
For this infernal pit shall never hold
Celestial spirits in bondage, nor th' abyss
Long under darkness cover. But these thoughts
Full counsel must mature: peace is despaired,   660
For who can think submission? War then, war
Open or understood must be resolved."

    He spake: and to confirm his words, outflew
Millions of flaming swords, drawn from the thighs
Of mighty Cherubim; the sudden blaze
Far round illumined Hell: highly they raged
Against the Highest, and fierce with graspéd arms
Clashed on their sounding shields the din of war,
Hurling defiance toward the vault of Heav'n.

    There stood a hill not far whose grisly top   670
Belched fire and rolling smoke; the rest entire
Shone with a glossy scurf, undoubted sign
That in his womb was hid metallic ore,
The work of sulphur. Thither winged with speed
A numerous brigad hastened. As when bands
Of pioners with spade and pickaxe armed
Forerun the royal camp, to trench a field,
Or cast a rampart. Mammon led them on,

650–651. Although Satan here speaks of a rumor about the creation of man, it is not until after the expulsion of the rebel angels
that God announces his plan (VII, 150 ff.). Like Shakespeare, M.
allows himself inconsistencies for dramatic purposes.
651. *fame:* rumor.
675. *brigad:* brigade (accented on first syllable).
676. *pioners:* pioneers, military engineers.
678. *Mammon:* an abstract word meaning "wealth."

Mammon, the least erected spirit that fell
From Heav'n, for ev'n in Heav'n his looks and
    thoughts   680
Were always downward bent, admiring more
The riches of Heav'n's pavement, trodden gold,
Than aught divine or holy else enjoyed
In vision beatific; by him first
Men also, and by his suggestion taught,
Ransacked the center, and with impious hands
Rifled the bowels of their mother earth
For treasures better hid. Soon had his crew
Opened into the hill a spacious wound
And digged out ribs of gold. Let none admire   690
That riches grow in Hell; that soil may best
Deserve the precious bane. And here let those
Who boast in mortal things, and wondering tell
Of Babel, and the works of Memphian kings
Learn how their greatest monuments of fame,
And strength and art are easily outdone
By spirits reprobate, and in an hour
What in an age they with incessant toil
And hands innumerable scarce perform.
Nigh on the plain in many cells prepared,   700
That underneath had veins of liquid fire
Sluiced from the lake, a second multitude
With wondrous art founded the massy ore,
Severing each kind, and scummed the bullion dross.
A third as soon had formed within the ground
A various mold, and from the boiling cells
By strange conveyance filled each hollow nook,

---

679. *erected:* cf. IV, 289, "godlike erect." Man's erect stature, which enabled him to look up to Heaven, was often contrasted to that of the beasts.

690. *admire:* wonder.

691. *grow:* a grim metaphor; nothing grows in Hell except "barren metal," as Antonio calls it in *The Merchant of Venice* (I, iii).

703. *founded:* The 1674 ed. has "found out." "Founded," taken from the 1667 ed., seems preferable, though it is not clear what process is referred to.

As in an organ from one blast of wind
To many a row of pipes the sound-board breathes.
Anon out of the earth a fabric huge   710
Rose like àn exhalation, with the sound
Of dulcet symphonies and voices sweet,
Built like a temple, where pilasters round
Were set, and Doric pillars overlaid
With golden architrave; nor did there want
Cornice or frieze, with bossy sculptures grav'n,
The roof was fretted gold. Not Babylon,
Nor great Alcairo such magnificence
Equaled in all their glories, to enshrine
Belus or Serapis their gods, or seat   720
Their kings, when Egypt with Assyria strove
In wealth and luxury. Th' ascending pile
Stood fixed her stately highth, and straight the doors
Opening their brazen folds discover wide
Within, her ample spaces, o'er the smooth
And level pavement: from the archéd roof
Pendant by subtle magic many a row
Of starry lamps and blazing cressets fed
With naphtha and asphaltus yielded light
As from a sky. The hasty multitude   730
Admiring entered, and the work some praise
And some the architect: his hand was known
In Heav'n by many a towered structure high,
Where sceptered angels held their residence,
And sat as princes, whom the supreme King
Exalted to such power, and gave to rule,
Each in his hierarchy, the orders bright.
Nor was his name unheard or unadored
In ancient Greece; and in Ausonian land

717–722. As before in physical prowess, so now the devils outdo
man in physical splendor. The Spirit of God prefers "Before all
temples th' upright heart and pure" (I, 18).

728–729. Liquid *naphtha* was burned in the lamps, solid *asphaltus* (bitumen) in the cressets, a kind of iron basket.

738–740. In Greece *his name* was Hephaestus, in Italy (*Ausonian
land*) *Mulciber* or Vulcan.

Men called him Mulciber; and how he fell   740
From Heav'n, they fabled, thrown by angry Jove
Sheer o'er the crystal battlements; from morn
To noon he fell, from noon to dewy eve,
A summer's day; and with the setting sun
Dropped from the zenith like a falling star,
On Lemnos th' Aegean isle: thus they relate,
Erring; for he with this rebellious rout
Fell long before; nor aught availed him now
To have built in Heav'n high tow'rs; nor did he scape
By all his engines, but was headlong sent   750
With his industrious crew to build in Hell.
Meanwhile the wingéd heralds by command
Of sovran power, with awful ceremony
And trumpets' sound throughout the host proclaim
A solemn council forthwith to be held
At Pandemonium, the high capitol   *Monarchy - No.*
Of Satan and his peers: their summons called
From every band and squaréd regiment
By place or choice the worthiest; they anon
With hundreds and with thousands trooping came   760
Attended: all access was thronged, the gates
And porches wide, but chief the spacious hall
(Though like a covered field, where champions bold
Wont ride in armed, and at the Soldan's chair
Defied the best of paynim chivalry
To mortal combat or career with lance)
Thick swarmed, both on the ground and in the air,
Brushed with the hiss of rustling wings. As bees
In springtime, when the sun with Taurus rides,

---

750. *engines:* contrivances.
764. *wont:* were wont to. *Soldan:* Sultan.
765. *paynim:* pagan.
766. *career:* a short gallop at high speed as a test of skill, not a
fight to the death as in mortal combat.
768–775. Defenders of monarchy tried to find a natural (and
hence God-given) sanction for kingship in the government of the
bees, as in the well-known speech of Canterbury in *Henry V,* I, ii.
M. sardonically puts the comparison where he thinks it belongs.

Pour forth their populous youth about the hive   770
In clusters; they among fresh dews and flowers
Fly to and fro, or on the smoothéd plank,
The suburb of their straw-built citadel,
New rubbed with balm, expatiate and confer
Their state affairs. So thick the aery crowd
Swarmed and were straitened; till the signal giv'n,
Behold a wonder! they but now who seemed
In bigness to surpass Earth's giant sons
Now less than smallest dwarfs, in narrow room
Throng numberless, like that Pygmean race   780
Beyond the Indian mount, or fairy elves,
Whose midnight revels, by a forest side
Or fountain some belated peasant sees,
Or dreams he sees, while overhead the moon
Sits arbitress, and nearer to the earth
Wheels her pale course, they on their mirth and dance
Intent, with jocund music charm his ear;
At once with joy and fear his heart rebounds.
Thus incorporeal spirits to smallest forms
Reduced their shapes immense, and were at large,   790
Though without number still amidst the hall
Of that infernal court. But far within
And in their own dimensions like themselves
The great Seraphic lords and Cherubim
In close recess and secret conclave sat
A thousand demi-gods on golden seats,
Frequent and full. After short silence then
And summons read, the great consult began.

---

774. *expatiate:* walk abroad. *confer:* discuss.

776. *straitened:* crowded in.

790–791. "Though numberless, they still had room to move
around (*were at large*)."

795. *conclave:* probably a sarcastic allusion to the Conclave of
Cardinals in the Catholic Church. Cf. the use of "pontifical" in
X, 313.

797. *frequent:* crowded.

BOOK II ❧

THE ARGUMENT

The consultation begun, Satan debates whether another battle be to be hazarded for the recovery of Heaven: some advise it, others dissuade: a third proposal is preferred, mentioned before by Satan, to search the truth of that prophecy or tradition in Heaven concerning another world, and another kind of creature equal or not much inferior to themselves, about this time to be created: their doubt who shall be sent on this difficult search: Satan their chief undertakes alone the voyage, is honored and applauded. The council thus ended, the rest betake them several ways and to several employments, as their inclinations lead them, to entertain the time till Satan return. He passes on his journey to Hell gates, finds them shut, and who sat there to guard them, by whom at length they are opened, and discover to him the great gulf between Hell and Heaven; with what difficulty he passes through, directed by Chaos, the power of that place, to the sight of this new world which he sought.

High on a throne of royal state, which far
Outshone the wealth of Ormus and of Ind,

---

2. *Ormus:* an island town at the mouth of the Persian Gulf, a seventeenth-century byword for wealth.

Or where the gorgeous East with richest hand
Show'rs on her kings barbaric pearl and gold,
Satan exalted sat, by merit raised
To that bad eminence; and from despair
Thus high uplifted beyond hope, aspires
Beyond thus high, insatiate to pursue
Vain war with Heav'n, and by success untaught
His proud imaginations thus displayed.   10
     "Powers and Dominions, deities of Heav'n,
For since no deep within her gulf can hold
Immortal vigor, though oppressed and fall'n,
I give not Heav'n for lost. From this descent
Celestial Virtues rising, will appear
More glorious and more dread than from no fall,
And trust themselves to fear no second fate:
Me though just right, and the fixed laws of Heav'n
Did first create your leader, next free choice,
With what besides, in counsel or in fight,   20
Hath been achieved of merit, yet this loss
Thus far at least recovered, hath much more
Established in a safe unenvied throne
Yielded with full consent. The happier state
In Heav'n, which follows dignity, might draw
Envy from each inferior; but who here
Will envy whom the highest place exposes
Foremost to stand against the Thunderer's aim
Your bulwark, and condemns to greatest share
Of endless pain? Where there is then no good   30
For which to strive, no strife can grow up there
From faction; for none sure will claim in Hell
Precedence, none, whose portion is so small
Of present pain, that with ambitious mind
Will covet more. With this advantage then
To union, and firm faith, and firm accord,
More than can be in Heav'n, we now return
To claim our just inheritance of old,
Surer to prosper than prosperity

----

9. *success:* outcome (whether good or bad).

Could have assured us; and by what best way,   40
Whether of open war or covert guile,
We now debate; who can advise, may speak."
    He ceased, and next him Moloch, sceptered king
Stood up, the strongest and the fiercest spirit
That fought in Heav'n; now fiercer by despair:
His trust was with th' Eternal to be deemed
Equal in strength, and rather than be less
Cared not to be at all; with that care lost
Went all his fear: of God, or Hell, or worse
He recked not, and these words thereafter spake.   50
    "My sentence is for open war: of wiles,
More unexpert, I boast not: them let those
Contrive who need, or when they need, not now.
For while they sit contriving, shall the rest,
Millions that stand in arms, and longing wait
The signal to ascend, sit lingering here
Heav'n's fugitives, and for their dwelling place
Accept this dark opprobrious den of shame,
The prison of his tyranny who reigns
By our delay? No, let us rather choose   60
Armed with hell flames and fury all at once
O'er Heav'n's high tow'rs to force resistless way,
Turning our tortures into horrid arms
Against the torturer; when to meet the noise
Of his almighty engine he shall hear
Infernal thunder, and for lightning see
Black fire and horror shot with equal rage
Among his angels; and his throne itself
Mixed with Tartarean sulphur, and strange fire,
His own invented torments. But perhaps   70
The way seems difficult and steep to scale
With upright wing against a higher foe.
Let such bethink them, if the sleepy drench
Of that forgetful lake benumb not still,
That in our proper motion we ascend

---

51. *sentence:* opinion, judgment.
52. *more unexpert:* less experienced.

Up to our native seat: descent and fall
To us is adverse. Who but felt of late
When the fierce foe hung on our broken rear
Insulting, and pursued us through the deep
With what compulsion and laborious flight   80
We sunk thus low? Th' ascent is easy then;
Th' event is feared; should we again provoke
Our stronger, some worse way his wrath may find
To our destruction: if there be in Hell
Fear to be worse destroyed: what can be worse
Than to dwell here, driv'n out from bliss, condemned
In this abhorréd deep to utter woe;
Where pain of unextinguishable fire
Must exercise us without hope of end
The vassals of his anger, when the scourge   90
Inexorably, and the torturing hour
Calls us to penance? More destroyed than thus
We should be quite abolished and expire.
What fear we then? what doubt we to incense
His utmost ire? which to the highth enraged,
Will either quite consume us, and reduce
To nothing this essential, happier far
Than miserable to have eternal being:
Or if our substance be indeed divine,
And cannot cease to be, we are at worst   100
On this side nothing; and by proof we feel
Our power sufficient to disturb his Heav'n,
And with perpetual inroads to alarm,
Though inaccessible, his fatal throne:
Which if not victory is yet revenge."
    He ended frowning, and his look denounced
Desperate revenge, and battle dangerous
To less than gods. On th' other side up rose

----

89. *exercise:* torment.

97. *essential:* essence; an example of M.'s frequent use of adjective for noun.

104. *fatal:* another example of the sophistry already encountered in I, 116 and 133.

Belial, in act more graceful and humane;
A fairer person lost not Heav'n; he seemed   110
For dignity composed and high exploit:
But all was false and hollow; though his tongue
Dropped manna, and could make the worse appear
The better reason, to perplex and dash
Maturest counsels: for his thoughts were low;
To vice industrious, but to nobler deeds
Timorous and slothful: yet he pleased the ear,
And with persuasive accent thus began.
    "I should be much for open war, O peers,
As not behind in hate; if what was urged   120
Main reason to persuade immediate war,
Did not dissuade me most, and seem to cast
Ominous conjecture on the whole success:
When he who most excels in fact of arms,
In what he counsels and in what excels
Mistrustful, grounds his courage on despair
And utter dissolution, as the scope
Of all his aim, after some dire revenge.
First, what revenge? The tow'rs of Heav'n are filled
With arméd watch, that render all access   130
Impregnable; oft on the bordering deep
Encamp their legions, or with obscure wing
Scout far and wide into the realm of night,
Scorning surprise. Or could we break our way
By force, and at our heels all Hell should rise
With blackest insurrection, to confound
Heav'n's purest light, yet our great enemy
All incorruptible would on his throne
Sit unpolluted, and th' ethereal mold
Incapable of stain would soon expel   140
Her mischief, and purge off the baser fire
Victorious. Thus repulsed, our final hope

---

124. *fact:* feat, exploits.
127. *scope:* aim.
142–146. *Thus . . . more:* a sarcastic resumé of Moloch's point
of view.

Is flat despair: we must exasperate
Th' almighty victor to spend all his rage,
And that must end us, that must be our cure,
To be no more; sad cure; for who would lose,
Though full of pain, this intellectual being,
Those thoughts that wander through eternity,
To perish rather, swallowed up and lost
In the wide womb of uncreated night,   150
Devoid of sense and motion? And who knows,
Let this be good, whether our angry foe
Can give it, or will ever? How he can
Is doubtful; that he never will is sure.
Will he, so wise, let loose at once his ire,
Belike through impotence, or unaware,
To give his enemies their wish, and end
Them in his anger, whom his anger saves
To punish endless? 'Wherefore cease we then?'
Say they who counsel war, 'we are decreed,   160
Reserved and destined to eternal woe;
Whatever doing, what can we suffer more,
What can we suffer worse?' Is this then worst,
Thus sitting, thus consulting, thus in arms?
What when we fled amain, pursued and strook
With Heav'n's afflicting thunder, and besought
The deep to shelter us? This Hell then seemed
A refuge from those wounds: or when we lay
Chained on the burning lake? That sure was worse.
What if the breath that kindled those grim fires   170
Awaked should blow them into sevenfold rage
And plunge us in the flames? Or from above
Should intermitted vengeance arm again
His red right hand to plague us? What if all
Her stores were opened, and this firmament
Of Hell should spout her cataracts of fire,
Impendent horrors, threatening hideous fall
One day upon our heads; while we perhaps

159–163. Belial once again paraphrases Moloch's point of view.
165. *What . . . amain:* What about the time we hastily fled?

Designing or exhorting glorious war,
Caught in a fiery tempest shall be hurled   180
Each on his rock transfixed, the sport and prey
Of racking whirlwinds, or for ever sunk
Under yon boiling ocean, wrapped in chains;
There to converse with everlasting groans,
Unrespited, unpitied, unreprieved,
Ages of hopeless end; this would be worse.
War therefore, open or concealed, alike
My voice dissuades; for what can force or guile
With him, or who deceive his mind, whose eye   189
Views all things at one view? He from Heav'n's highth
All these our motions vain, sees and derides;
Not more almighty to resist our might
Than wise to frustrate all our plots and wiles.
Shall we then live thus vile, the race of Heav'n
Thus trampled, thus expelled to suffer here
Chains and these torments? Better these than worse
By my advice; since fate inevitable
Subdues us, and omnipotent decree,
The victor's will. To suffer, as to do,
Our strength is equal, nor the law unjust   200
That so ordains: this was at first resolved,
If we were wise, against so great a foe
Contending, and so doubtful what might fall.
I laugh, when those who at the spear are bold
And vent'rous, if that fail them, shrink and fear
What yet they know must follow, to endure
Exile, or ignominy, or bonds, or pain,
The sentence of their conqueror: This is now
Our doom; which if we can sustain and bear,
Our súpreme foe in time may much remit   210
His anger, and perhaps thus far removed
Not mind us not offending, satisfied
With what is punished; whence these raging fires

---

182. *racking:* sweeping along, like clouds.
184. *converse:* dwell.
194–196. Belial recognizes a possible objection to his proposal.

Will slacken, if his breath stir not their flames.
Our purer essence then will overcome
Their noxious vapor, or enured not feel,
Or changed at length, and to the place conformed
In temper and in nature, will receive
Familiar the fierce heat, and void of pain;
This horror will grow mild, this darkness light,   220
Besides what hope the never-ending flight
Of future days may bring, what chance, what change
Worth waiting, since our present lot appears
For happy though but ill, for ill not worst,
If we procure not to ourselves more woe."
    Thus Belial with words clothed in reason's garb
Counseled ignoble ease, and peaceful sloth,
Not peace: and after him thus Mammon spake.
    "Either to disenthrone the King of Heav'n
We war, if war be best, or to regain   230
Our own right lost: him to unthrone we then
May hope when everlasting fate shall yield
To fickle chance, and Chaos judge the strife:
The former vain to hope argues as vain
The latter: for what place can be for us
Within Heav'n's bound, unless Heav'n's Lord supreme
We overpower? Suppose he should relent
And publish grace to all, on promise made
Of new subjection; with what eyes could we
Stand in his presence humble, and receive   240
Strict laws imposed, to celebrate his throne
With warbled hymns, and to his godhead sing
Forced halleluiahs; while he lordly sits
Our envied sovran, and his altar breathes
Ambrosial odors and ambrosial flowers,
Our servile offerings. This must be our task
In Heav'n, this our delight; how wearisome
Eternity so spent in worship paid

---

218. *temper:* temperament.
224. *for happy:* regarded as happiness.
234. *argues:* proves.

To whom we hate. Let us not then pursue
By force impossible, by leave obtained   250
Unáccaptáble, though in Heav'n, our state
Of splendid vassalage, but rather seek
Our own good from ourselves, and from our own
Live to ourselves, though in this vast recess,
Free, and to none accountable, preferring
Hard liberty before the easy yoke
Of servile pomp. Our greatness will appear
Then most conspicuous, when great things of small,
Useful of hurtful, prosperous of adverse
We can create, and in what place so e'er   260
Thrive under evil, and work ease out of pain
Through labor and endurance. This deep world
Of darkness do we dread? How oft amidst
Thick clouds and dark doth Heav'n's all-ruling Sire
Choose to reside, his glory unobscured,
And with the majesty of darkness round
Covers his throne; from whence deep thunders roar
Mustering their rage, and Heav'n resembles Hell?
As he our darkness, cannot we his light
Imitate when we please? This desert soil   270
Wants not her hidden luster, gems and gold;
Nor want we skill or art, from whence to raise
Magnificence; and what can Heav'n show more?
Our torments also may in length of time
Become our elements, these piercing fires
As soft as now severe, our temper changed
Into their temper; which must needs remove
The sensible of pain. All things invite
To peaceful counsels, and the settled state
Of order, how in safety best we may   280
Compose our present evils, with regard

---

249. *pursue:* try to regain ("our state," line 251).
269. God's darkness, however, is the excess of light. Cf. III, 380,
and V, 599.
271. *wants not:* does not lack.
281. *compose:* adjust to.

Of what we are and were, dismissing quite
All thoughts of war: ye have what I advise."
   He scarce had finished, when such murmur filled
Th' assembly, as when hollow rocks retain
The sound of blustering winds, which all night long
Had roused the sea, now with hoarse cadence lull
Seafaring men o'erwatched, whose bark by chance
Or pinnace anchors in a craggy bay
After the tempest: such applause was heard   2⫶
As Mammon ended, and his sentence pleased,
Advising peace: for such another field
They dreaded worse than Hell: so much the fear
Of thunder and the sword of Michaël
Wrought still within them; and no less desire
To found this nether empire, which might rise
By policy, and long process of time,
In emulation opposite to Heav'n.
Which when Beëlzebub perceived, than whom,
Satan except, none higher sat, with grave   3⫶
Aspect he rose, and in his rising seemed
A pillar of state; deep on his front engrav'n
Deliberation sat and public care;
And princely counsel in his face yet shone,
Majestic though in ruin: sage he stood
With Atlantean shoulders fit to bear
The weight of mightiest monarchies; his look
Drew audience and attention still as night
Or summer's noontide air, while thus he spake.   3⫶
   "Thrones and imperial Powers, offspring of Heav'n,
Ethereal Virtues; or these titles now
Must we renounce, and changing style be called
Princes of Hell? For so the popular vote

---

282. *were:* ed. 2 (1674); ed. 1 (1667) reads "where."
288. *o'erwatched:* tired from watching.
297. *policy:* statecraft; used pejoratively, as in Shakespeare.
302. *front:* forehead.
306. *Atlantean:* like those of Atlas, the Titan who was con
demned by Zeus to hold up heaven on his shoulders.
312. *style:* title.

Inclines, here to continue, and build up here
A growing empire; doubtless; while we dream
And know not that the King of Heav'n hath doomed
This place our dungeon, not our safe retreat
Beyond his potent arm, to live exempt
From Heav'n's high jurisdiction, in new league
Banded against his throne, but to remain　　　　　320
In strictest bondage, though thus far removed,
Under th' inevitable curb, reserved
His captive multitude: for he, be sure
In highth or depth, still first and last will reign
Sole king, and of his kingdom lose no part
By our revolt, but over Hell extend
His empire, and with iron scepter rule
Us here, as with his golden those in Heav'n.
What sit we then projecting peace and war?
War hath determined us, and foiled with loss　　　　　330
Irreparable; terms of peace yet none
Vouchsafed or sought; for what peace will be giv'n
To us enslaved, but custody severe,
And stripes, and arbitrary punishment
Inflicted? And what peace can we return,
But to our power hostility and hate,
Untamed reluctance, and revenge though slow,
Yet ever plotting how the conqueror least
May reap his conquest, and may least rejoice
In doing what we most in suffering feel?　　　　　340
Nor will occasion want, nor shall we need
With dangerous expedition to invade
Heav'n, whose high walls fear no assault or siege,
Or ambush from the deep. What if we find
Some easier enterprise? There is a place
(If ancient and prophetic fame in Heav'n
Err not) another world, the happy seat

------

327. Cf. Psalm 2:9, "Thou shalt break them with a rod of iron."
336. *to our power:* to the best of our power.
337. *untamed:* not to be tamed.
346. *fame:* rumor, report.

Of some new race called man, about this time
To be created like to us, though less
In power and excellence, but favored more   350
Of him who rules above; so was his will
Pronounced among the gods, and by an oath,
That shook Heav'n's whole circumference, confirmed.
Thither let us bend all our thoughts, to learn
What creatures there inhabit, of what mold,
Or substance, how endued, and what their power,
And where their weakness, how attempted best,
By force or subtlety. Though Heav'n be shut,
And Heav'n's high arbitrator sit secure
In his own strength, this place may lie exposed   360
The utmost border of his kingdom, left
To their defense who hold it: here perhaps
Some advantageous act may be achieved
By sudden onset, either with Hell fire
To waste his whole creation, or possess
All as our own, and drive as we were driv'n,
The puny habitants, or if not drive,
Seduce them to our party, that their God
May prove their foe, and with repenting hand
Abolish his own works. This would surpass   370
Common revenge, and interrupt his joy
In our confusion, and our joy upraise
In his disturbance; when his darling sons
Hurled headlong to partake with us, shall curse
Their frail original, and faded bliss,
Faded so soon. Advise if this be worth
Attempting, or to sit in darkness here
Hatching vain empires." Thus Beëlzebub
Pleaded his devilish counsel, first devised

---

356. *endued:* gifted, endowed.
367. *puny:* weak, small; born later, inferior.
375. *original:* original parent (Adam), or original state of innocence.
376. *advise:* consider.

By Satan, and in part proposed: for whence, 380
But from the author of all ill could spring
So deep a malice, to confound the race
Of mankind in one root, and earth with Hell
To mingle and involve, done all to spite
The great Creator? But their spite still serves
His glory to augment. The bold design
Pleased highly those infernal States, and joy
Sparkled in all their eyes; with full assent
They vote: whereat his speech he thus renews.

"Well have ye judged, well ended long debate, 390
Synod of gods, and like to what ye are,
Great things resolved, which from the lowest deep
Will once more lift us up, in spite of fate,
Nearer our ancient seat; perhaps in view
Of those bright confines, whence with neighboring arms
And opportune excursion we may chance
Re-enter Heav'n; or else in some mild zone
Dwell not unvisited of Heav'n's fair light
Secure, and at the brightening orient beam
Purge off this gloom; the soft delicious air, 400
To heal the scar of these corrosive fires
Shall breathe her balm. But first whom shall we send
In search of this new world, whom shall we find
Sufficient? Who shall tempt with wandering feet
The dark unbottomed infinite abyss
And through the palpable obscure find out
His uncouth way, or spread his aery flight
Upborne with indefatigable wings
Over the vast abrupt, ere he arrive
The happy isle; what strength, what art can then 410
Suffice, or what evasion bear him safe

---

387. *States:* members of a representative body.
404. *tempt:* try.
407. *uncouth:* unknown.
409. *abrupt:* the gulf between Hell and the created world; like "obscure," an adjective used as a noun.

Through the strict senteries and stations thick
Of angels watching round? Here he had need
All circumspection, and we now no less
Choice in our suffrage; for on whom we send,
The weight of all and our last hope relies."
    This said, he sat; and expectation held
His look suspense, awaiting who appeared
To second, or oppose, or undertake
The perilous attempt: but all sat mute,   420
Pondering the danger with deep thoughts; and each
In other's count'nance read his own dismay
Astonished: none among the choice and prime
Of those Heav'n-warring champions could be found
So hardy as to proffer or accept
Alone the dreadful voyage; till at last
Satan, whom now transcendent glory raised
Above his fellows, with monarchal pride
Conscious of highest worth, unmoved thus spake.
    "O progeny of Heav'n, empyreal Thrones,   430
With reason hath deep silence and demur
Seized us, though undismayed: long is the way
And hard, that out of Hell leads up to light;
Our prison strong, this huge convex of fire,
Outrageous to devour, immures us round
Ninefold, and gates of burning adamant
Barred over us prohibit all egress.
These passed, if any pass, the void profound
Of unessential Night receives him next
Wide gaping, and with utter loss of being   440
Threatens him, plunged in that abortive gulf.
If thence he scape into whatever world,
Or unknown region, what remains him less
Than unknown dangers and as hard escape.

413–415. "We need no less circumspection in choosing someone
than he will need in making the journey."

423. *astonished:* struck with dismay. *prime:* chief.

439. *unessential Night:* i.e., Night is without essence or being.

441. *abortive:* not only "monstrous" but also "rendering abortive."

But I should ill become this throne, O peers,
And this imperial sovranty, adorned
With splendor, armed with power, if aught proposed
And judged of public moment, in the shape
Of difficulty or danger could deter
Me from attempting. Wherefore do I assume   450
These royalties, and not refuse to reign,
Refusing to accept as great a share
Of hazard as of honor, due alike
To him who reigns, and so much to him due
Of hazard more, as he above the rest
High honored sits? Go therefore mighty Powers,
Terror of Heav'n, though fall'n; intend at home,
While here shall be our home, what best may ease
The present misery, and render Hell
More tolerable; if there be cure or charm   460
To respite or deceive, or slack the pain
Of this ill mansion: intermit no watch
Against a wakeful foe, while I abroad
Through all the coasts of dark destruction seek
Deliverance for us all: this enterprise
None shall partake with me." Thus saying rose
The monarch, and prevented all reply,
Prudent, lest from his resolution raised
Others among the chief might offer now
(Certain to be refused) what erst they feared;   470
And so refused might in opinion stand
His rivals, winning cheap the high repute
Which he through hazard huge must earn. But they
Dreaded not more th' adventure than his voice
Forbidding; and at once with him they rose;
Their rising all at once was as the sound
Of thunder heard remote. Towards him they bend
With awful reverence prone; and as a god

---

448. *moment:* importance.
457. *intend:* consider.
461. *deceive:* beguile.
467. *prevented:* forestalled.
478. *awful:* full of awe.

Extol him equal to the Highest in Heav'n:
Nor failed they to express how much they praised,   480
That for the general safety he despised
His own: for neither do the spirits damned
Lose all their virtue; lest bad men should boast
Their specious deeds on earth, which glory excites,
Or close ambition varnished o'er with zeal.
Thus they their doubtful consultations dark
Ended rejoicing in their matchless chief:
As when from mountain tops the dusky clouds
Ascending, while the north wind sleeps, o'erspread
Heav'n's cheerful face, the lowering element   490
Scowls o'er the darkened landscape snow, or show'r;
If chance the radiant sun with farewell sweet
Extend his evening beam, the fields revive,
The birds their notes renew, and bleating herds
Attest their joy, that hill and valley rings.
O shame to men! Devil with devil damned
Firm concord holds, men only disagree
Of creatures rational, though under hope
Of heav'nly grace: and God proclaiming peace,
Yet live in hatred, enmity, and strife   500
Among themselves, and levy cruel wars,
Wasting the earth, each other to destroy:
As if (which might induce us to accord)
Man had not hellish foes enow besides,
That day and night for his destruction wait.
    The Stygian council thus dissolved; and forth
In order came the grand infernal peers,
Midst came their mighty paramount, and seemed
Alone th' antagonist of Heav'n, nor less
Than Hell's dread emperor with pomp supreme,   510

482–485. "Evil men who perform outwardly virtuous deeds
from motives of glory or secret ambition masquerading as zeal
should remember that devils also possess this kind of virtue."

490. *element:* sky.

508. *paramount:* chief.

And godlike imitated state; him round
A globe of fiery Seraphim enclosed
With bright emblazonry, and horrent arms.
Then of their session ended they bid cry
With trumpets' regal sound the great result:
Toward the four winds four speedy Cherubim
Put to their mouths the sounding alchemy
By herald's voice explained: the hollow abyss
Heard far and wide, and all the host of Hell
With deafening shout, returned them loud acclaim.   520
Thence more at ease their minds and somewhat raised
By false presumptuous hope, the rangéd powers
Disband, and wandering, each his several way
Pursues, as inclination or sad choice
Leads him perplexed, where he may likeliest find
Truce to his restless thoughts, and entertain
The irksome hours, till his great chief return.
Part on the plain, or in the air sublime
Upon the wing, or in swift race contend,
As at th' Olympian games or Pythian fields;   530
Part curb their fiery steeds, or shun the goal
With rapid wheels, or fronted brigads form.
As when to warn proud cities war appears
Waged in the troubled sky, and armies rush
To battle in the clouds, before each van
Prick forth the aery knights, and couch their spears
Till thickest legions close; with feats of arms
From either end of heav'n the welkin burns.
Others with vast Typhoean rage more fell
Rend up both rocks and hills, and ride the air   540
In whirlwind; Hell scarce holds the wild uproar.

---

512. *globe:* compact band.
513. *emblazonry:* shields with coats of arms. *horrent:* bristling.
522. *rangéd powers:* armies assembled in ranks.
526. *entertain:* while away.
528. *sublime:* uplifted.
539. *Typhoean:* cf. I, 199.

As when Alcides from Oechalia crowned
With conquest, felt th' envenomed robe, and tore
Through pain up by the roots Thessalian pines,
And Lichas from the top of Oeta threw
Into th' Euboic Sea. Others more mild,
Retreated in a silent valley, sing
With notes angelical to many a harp
Their own heroic deeds and hapless fall
By doom of battle; and complain that fate   550
Free virtue should enthrall to force or chance.
Their song was partial, but the harmony
(What could it less when spirits immortal sing?)
Suspended Hell, and took with ravishment
The thronging audience. In discourse more sweet
(For eloquence the soul, song charms the sense,)
Others apart sat on a hill retired,
In thoughts more elevate, and reasoned high
Of providence, foreknowledge, will and fate,
Fixed fate, free will, foreknowledge absolute,   560
And found no end, in wandering mazes lost.
Of good and evil much they argued then,
Of happiness and final misery,
Passion and apathy, and glory and shame,
Vain wisdom all, and false philosophy:
Yet with a pleasing sorcery could charm
Pain for a while or anguish, and excite
Fallacious hope, or arm th' obduréd breast
With stubborn patience as with triple steel.
Another part in squadrons and gross bands,   570

---

542. The story of the death of Hercules (*Alcides*) is told in Ovid's *Metamorphoses*, Book IX, and is the subject of Seneca's tragedy *Hercules Furens*.

552. *partial:* prejudiced, one-sided.

554. *suspended:* held in rapt suspense.

564. *apathy:* the Stoic ideal of freedom from all passion, condemned by M. in *Paradise Regained*, IV, 300 ff.

569. Their patience is *stubborn* and hence false, not the true Christian patience mentioned in IX, 32, and XII, 583.

570. *gross:* compact.

On bold adventure to discover wide
That dismal world, if any clime perhaps
Might yield them easier habitation, bend
Four ways their flying march, along the banks
Of four infernal rivers that disgorge
Into the burning lake their baleful streams;
Abhorréd Styx the flood of deadly hate,
Sad Acheron of sorrow, black and deep;
Cocytus, named of lamentation loud
Heard on the rueful stream; fierce Phlegeton　　580
Whose waves of torrent fire inflame with rage.
Far off from these a slow and silent stream,
Lethe the river of oblivion rolls
Her wat'ry labyrinth, whereof who drinks
Forthwith his former state and being forgets,
Forgets both joy and grief, pleasure and pain.
Beyond this flood a frozen continent
Lies dark and wild, beat with perpetual storms
Of whirlwind and dire hail, which on firm land
Thaws not, but gathers heap, and ruin seems　　590
Of ancient pile; all else deep snow and ice,
A gulf profound as that Serbonian bog
Betwixt Damiata and Mount Casius old,
Where armies whole have sunk: the parching air
Burns frore, and cold performs th' effect of fire.
Thither by harpy-footed Furies haled,
At certain revolutions all the damned
Are brought: and feel by turns the bitter change
Of fierce extremes, extremes by change more fierce,
From beds of raging fire to starve in ice　　600
Their soft ethereal warmth, and there to pine
Immovable, infixed, and frozen round,

---

591. *pile:* building.
592. Lake Serbonis, on the coast of Lower Egypt, had treacherous shores of sand.
595. *frore:* frosty.
596. *harpy-footed:* with claws like those of the Harpies. *haled:* dragged.
600. *starve:* die.

Periods of time, thence hurried back to fire.
They ferry over this Lethean sound
Both to and fro, their sorrow to augment,
And wish and struggle, as they pass, to reach
The tempting stream, with one small drop to lose
In sweet forgetfulness all pain and woe,
All in one moment, and so near the brink;
But fate withstands, and to oppose th' attempt   610
Medusa with Gorgonian terror guards
The ford, and of itself the water flies
All taste of living wight, as once it fled
The lip of Tantalus. Thus roving on
In cónfused march forlorn, th' advent'rous bands
With shuddering horror pale, and eyes aghast
Viewed first their lamentable lot, and found
No rest: through many a dark and dreary vale
They passed, and many a region dolorous,
O'er many a frozen, many a fiery Alp,   620
Rocks, caves, lakes, fens, bogs, dens, and shades of
    death,
A universe of death, which God by curse
Created evil, for evil only good,
Where all life dies, death lives, and nature breeds,
Perverse, all monstrous, all prodigious things,
Abominable, inutterable, and worse
Than fables yet have feigned, or fear conceived,
Gorgons and Hydras, and Chimeras dire.
    Meanwhile the Adversary of God and man,
Satan with thoughts inflamed of highest design,   630
Puts on swift wings, and toward the gates of Hell

611. *Medusa:* one of the three Gorgons. Her hair had been
changed into serpents, and her appearance was so hideous that
one look at her turned a man into stone.
614. In the classical myth *Tantalus* was so punished for his
greed when he dined with the gods.
615. *forlorn:* utterly lost; a much stronger word than it is now.
625. *prodigious:* monstrous.
628. *Hydra:* a serpent with nine heads. *Chimera:* a fire-breath-
ing monster.

Explores his solitary flight; sometimes
He scours the right hand coast, sometimes the left,
Now shaves with level wing the deep, then soars
Up to the fiery concave towering high.
As when far off at sea a fleet descried
Hangs in the clouds, by equinoctial winds
Close sailing from Bengala, or the isles
Of Ternate and Tidore, whence merchants bring
Their spicy drugs: they on the trading flood   640
Through the wide Ethiopian to the Cape
Ply stemming nightly toward the Pole. So seemed
Far off the flying Fiend: at last appear
Hell bounds high reaching to the horrid roof,
And thrice threefold the gates; three folds were brass,
Three iron, three of adamantine rock,
Impenetrable, impaled with circling fire,
Yet unconsumed. Before the gates there sat
On either side a formidable shape;
The one seemed woman to the waist, and fair,   650
But ended foul in many a scaly fold
Voluminous and vast, a serpent armed
With mortal sting: about her middle round
A cry of hell hounds never ceasing barked
With wide Cerberean mouths full loud, and rung
A hideous peal: yet, when they list, would creep,
If aught disturbed their noise, into her womb,
And kennel there, yet there still barked and howled,
Within unseen. Far less abhorred than these

---

632. *explores:* tests.
638. *close:* close together. *Bengala:* Bay of Bengal.
639. *Ternate and Tidore:* the best known of the Moluccas or
Spice Islands in the Malay Archipelago.
641. *Ethiopian:* the Indian Ocean. *Cape:* Cape of Good Hope.
642. *stemming:* pressing forward (toward the South Pole).
648. The allegory of Sin and Death is based primarily on James
1:15, "Then when lust hath conceived, it bringeth forth sin: and
sin, when it is finished, bringeth forth death." The description of
Sin owes much to classical accounts of Scylla like Ovid's (*Metamorphoses,* XIV, 40–74) and Virgil's (*Aeneid,* III, 424 ff.).

Vexed Scylla bathing in the sea that parts   660
Calabria from the hoarse Trinacrian shore:
Nor uglier follow the night-hag, when called
In secret, riding through the air she comes
Lured with the smell of infant blood, to dance
With Lapland witches, while the laboring moon
Eclipses at their charms. The other shape,
If shape it might be called that shape had none
Distinguishable in member, joint, or limb,
Or substance might be called that shadow seemed,
For each seemed either; black it stood as night,   670
Fierce as ten furies, terrible as Hell,
And shook a dreadful dart; what seemed his head
The likeness of a kingly crown had on.
Satan was now at hand, and from his seat
The monster moving onward came as fast
With horrid strides, Hell trembled as he strode.
Th' undaunted Fiend what this might be admired,
Admired, not feared; God and his Son except,
Created thing naught valued he nor shunned;
And with disdainful look thus first began.   680
   "Whence and what art thou, execrable shape,
That dar'st, though grim and terrible, advance
Thy miscreated front athwart my way
To yonder gates? Through them I mean to pass,
That be assured, without leave asked of thee:
Retire, or taste thy folly, and learn by proof,
Hell-born, not to contend with spirits of Heav'n."
   To whom the goblin full of wrath replied.
"Art thou that traitor angel, art thou he,
Who first broke peace in Heav'n and faith, till then   690
Unbroken, and in proud rebellious arms
Drew after him the third part of Heav'n's sons

---

662. *night-hag:* Hecate.
667–69. Death has no shape or substance because it is merely
the absence of life.
677. *admired:* wondered.

Conjured against the Highest, for which both thou
And they outcast from God, are here condemned
To waste eternal days in woe and pain?
And reckon'st thou thyself with spirits of Heav'n,
Hell-doomed, and breath'st defiance here and scorn
Where I reign king, and to enrage thee more,
Thy king and lord? Back to thy punishment,
False fugitive, and to thy speed add wings,   700
Lest with a whip of scorpions I pursue
Thy lingering, or with one stroke of this dart
Strange horror seize thee, and pangs unfelt before."
　So spake the grisly terror, and in shape,
So speaking and so threatening, grew tenfold
More dreadful and deform: on th' other side
Incensed with indignation Satan stood
Unterrified, and like a comet burned,
That fires the length of Ophiucus huge
In th' arctic sky, and from his horrid hair   710
Shakes pestilence and war. Each at the head
Leveled his deadly aim; their fatal hands
No second stroke intend, and such a frown
Each cast at th' other, as when two black clouds
With heav'n's artillery fraught, come rattling on
Over the Caspian, then stand front to front
Hovering a space, till winds the signal blow
To join their dark encounter in mid air:
So frowned the mighty combatants, that Hell
Grew darker at their frown, so matched they stood;   720
For never but once more was either like
To meet so great a foe: and now great deeds
Had been achieved, whereof all Hell had rung,
Had not the snaky sorceress that sat
Fast by Hell gate, and kept the fatal key,

---

693. *conjured:* sworn together.
709. *Ophiucus:* the "serpent-holder," a northern constellation.
716. The *Caspian* Sea was traditionally stormy.
722. *foe:* i.e., Christ.

Ris'n, and with hideous outcry rushed between.
   "O father, what intends thy hand," she cried,
"Against thy only son? What fury O son,
Possesses thee to bend that mortal dart
Against thy father's head? And know'st for whom;   730
For him who sits above and laughs the while
At thee ordained his drudge, to execute
Whate'er his wrath, which he calls justice, bids,
His wrath which one day will destroy ye both."
   She spake, and at her words the hellish pest
Forbore, then these to her Satan returned:
   "So strange thy outcry, and thy words so strange
Thou interposest, that my sudden hand
Prevented spares to tell thee yet by deeds
What it intends; till first I know of thee,   740
What thing thou art, thus double-formed, and why
In this infernal vale first met thou call'st
Me father, and that phantasm call'st my son?
I know thee not, nor ever saw till now
Sight more detestable than him and thee."
   T' whom thus the portress of Hell gate replied.
"Hast thou forgot me then, and do I seem
Now in thine eye so foul, once deemed so fair
In Heav'n, when at th' assembly, and in sight
Of all the Seraphim with thee combined   750
In bold conspiracy against Heav'n's King,
All on a sudden miserable pain
Surprised thee, dim thine eyes, and dizzy swum
In darkness, while thy head flames thick and fast
Threw forth, till on the left side opening wide,
Likest to thee in shape and count'nance bright,
Then shining heav'nly fair, a goddess armed
Out of thy head I sprung: amazement seized

727–728. Satan, Sin, and Death make up a kind of infernal Trinity. Cf. line 869 below.

739. *spares to:* refrains from.

752–758. The birth of Sin ironically parallels that of the goddess of wisdom, Minerva, who sprang fully armed from the head of Jupiter. There is also an allusion to the birth of Eve.

All th' host of Heav'n; back they recoiled afraid
At first, and called me Sin, and for a sign   760
Portentous held me; but familiar grown,
I pleased, and with attractive graces won
The most averse, thee chiefly, who full oft
Thyself in me thy perfect image viewing
Becam'st enamored, and such joy thou took'st
With me in secret, that my womb conceived
A growing burden. Meanwhile war arose,
And fields were fought in Heav'n; wherein remained
(For what could else) to our almighty foe
Clear victory, to our part loss and rout   770
Through all the empyrean: down they fell
Driv'n headlong from the pitch of Heaven, down
Into this deep, and in the general fall
I also; at which time this powerful key
Into my hand was giv'n, with charge to keep
These gates forever shut, which none can pass
Without my opening. Pensive here I sat
Alone, but long I sat not, till my womb
Pregnant by thee, and now excessive grown
Prodigious motion felt and rueful throes.   780
At last this odious offspring whom thou seest
Thine own begotten, breaking violent way
Tore through my entrails, that with fear and pain
Distorted, all my nether shape thus grew
Transformed: but he my inbred enemy
Forth issued, brandishing his fatal dart
Made to destroy: I fled, and cried out 'Death';
Hell trembled at the hideous name, and sighed
From all her caves, and back resounded 'Death.'
I fled, but he pursued (though more, it seems,   790
Inflamed with lust than rage) and swifter far,
Me overtook his mother all dismayed,
And in embraces forcible and foul
Engendering with me, of that rape begot
These yelling monsters that with ceaseless cry
Surround me, as thou saw'st, hourly conceived
And hourly born, with sorrow infinite

To me, for when they list into the womb
That bred them they return, and howl and gnaw
My bowels, their repast; then bursting forth   8
Afresh with conscious terrors vex me round,
That rest or intermission none I find.
Before mine eyes in opposition sits
Grim Death my son and foe, who sets them on,
And me his parent would full soon devour
For want of other prey, but that he knows
His end with mine involved; and knows that I
Should prove a bitter morsel, and his bane,
Whenever that shall be; so fate pronounced.
But thou O father, I forewarn thee, shun   8
His deadly arrow; neither vainly hope
To be invulnerable in those bright arms,
Though tempered heav'nly, for that mortal dint,
Save he who reigns above, none can resist."
    She finished, and the subtle Fiend his lore
Soon learned, now milder, and thus answered smooth.
"Dear daughter, since thou claim'st me for thy sire,
And my fair son here show'st me, the dear pledge
Of dalliance had with thee in Heav'n, and joys   81
Then sweet, now sad to mention through dire change
Befall'n us unforeseen, unthought of, know
I come no enemy, but to set free
From out this dark and dismal house of pain,
Both him and thee, and all the heav'nly host
Of spirits that in our just pretenses armed
Fell with us from on high: from them I go
This uncouth errand sole, and one for all
Myself expose, with lonely steps to tread
Th' unfounded deep, and through the void immense
To search with wandering quest a place foretold   83
Should be, and, by concurring signs, ere now
Created vast and round, a place of bliss
In the purlieus of Heav'n, and therein placed

---

813. *mortal dint:* deadly blow.
825. *pretenses:* claims (a legal term).

A race of upstart creatures, to supply
Perhaps our vacant room, though more removed,
Lest Heav'n surcharged with potent multitude
Might hap to move new broils. Be this or aught
Than this more secret now designed, I haste
To know, and this once known, shall soon return,
And bring ye to the place where thou and Death   840
Shall dwell at ease, and up and down unseen
Wing silently the buxom air, embalmed
With odors; there ye shall be fed and filled
Immeasurably, all things shall be your prey."
He ceased, for both seemed highly pleased, and Death
Grinned horrible a ghastly smile to hear
His famine should be filled, and blessed his maw
Destined to that good hour: no less rejoiced
His mother bad, and thus bespake her sire.

    "The key of this infernal pit by due,   850
And by command of Heav'n's all-powerful King
I keep, by him forbidden to unlock
These adamantine gates; against all force
Death ready stands to interpose his dart,
Fearless to be o'ermatched by living might.
But what owe I to his commands above
Who hates me, and hath hither thrust me down
Into this gloom of Tartarus profound,
To sit in hateful office here confined,
Inhabitant of Heav'n, and heav'nly-born   860
Here in perpetual agony and pain,
With terrors and with clamors compassed round
Of mine own brood, that on my bowels feed:
Thou art my father, thou my author, thou
My being gav'st me; whom should I obey
But thee, whom follow? Thou wilt bring me soon
To that new world of light and bliss, among

---

836. *surcharged*: overfull.
837. *broils*: conflicts.
842. *buxom*: unresisting. *embalmed*: made balmy or fragrant.
847. *famine*: insatiable hunger.

The gods who live at ease, where I shall reign
At thy right hand voluptuous, as beseems
Thy daughter and thy darling, without end."   870
    Thus saying, from her side the fatal key,
Sad instrument of all our woe, she took;
And towards the gate rolling her bestial train,
Forthwith the huge portcullis high up drew,
Which but herself not all the Stygian powers
Could once have moved; then in the keyhole turns
Th' intricate wards, and every bolt and bar
Of massy iron or solid rock with ease
Unfastens: on a sudden open fly
With impetuous recoil and jarring sound   880
Th' infernal doors, and on their hinges grate
Harsh thunder, that the lowest bottom shook
Of Erebus. She opened, but to shut
Excelled her power; the gates wide open stood,
That with extended wings a bannered host
Under spread ensigns marching might pass through
With horse and chariots ranked in loose array;
So wide they stood, and like a furnace mouth
Cast forth redounding smoke and ruddy flame.
Before their eyes in sudden view appear   890
The secrets of the hoary deep, a dark
Illimitable ocean without bound,
Without dimension, where length, breadth, and highth,
And time and place are lost; where eldest Night
And Chaos, ancestors of nature, hold
Eternal anarchy, amidst the noise
Of endless wars, and by confusion stand.
For hot, cold, moist, and dry, four champions fierce
Strive here for mast'ry, and to battle bring
Their embryon atoms; they around the flag   900

879–894. Cf. VII, 205–223.
    883. In Hesiod's *Theogony* (123) *Erebus* is the first child of
Chaos, and Night (line 894) is the second.
    895. *Chaos,* like the Ptolemaic spheres, is largely a symbol in
M.'s poetic universe. It need not be taken as a literal description
of reality.

Of each his faction, in their several clans,
Light-armed or heavy, sharp, smooth, swift or slow,
Swarm populous, unnumbered as the sands
Of Barca or Cyrene's torrid soil,
Levied to side with warring winds, and poise
Their lighter wings. To whom these most adhere,
He rules a moment; Chaos umpire sits,
And by decision more embroils the fray
By which he reigns: next him high arbiter
Chance governs all. Into this wild abyss,   910
The womb of nature and perhaps her grave,
Of neither sea, nor shore, nor air, nor fire,
But all these in their pregnant causes mixed
Confus'dly, and which thus must ever fight,
Unless th' Almighty Maker them ordain
His dark materials to create more worlds,
Into this wild abyss the wary Fiend
Stood on the brink of Hell and looked a while,
Pondering his voyage; for no narrow frith
He had to cross. Nor was his ear less pealed   920
With noises loud and ruinous (to compare
Great things with small) than when Bellona storms,
With all her battering engines bent to raze
Some capital city; or less than if this frame
Of heav'n were falling, and these elements
In mutiny had from her axle torn
The steadfast earth. At last his sail-broad vans
He spreads for flight, and in the surging smoke
Uplifted spurns the ground, thence many a league
As in a cloudy chair ascending rides   930
Audacious, but that seat soon failing, meets
A vast vacuity: all unawares

---

904. *Barca* and *Cyrene* were cities of Cyrenaica, a region of
N. Africa just west of Egypt.
911. *womb of nature:* cf. VII, 224–242.
919. *frith:* firth, estuary.
922. *Bellona:* the Roman goddess of war.
927. *vans:* wings.

Fluttering his pennons vain plumb down he drops
Ten thousand fadom deep, and to this hour
Down had been falling, had not by ill chance
The strong rebuff of some tumultuous cloud
Instinct with fire and nitre hurried him
As many miles aloft: that fury stayed,
Quenched in a boggy Syrtis, neither sea,
Nor good dry land: nigh foundered on he fares,   940
Treading the crude consistence, half on foot,
Half flying; behoves him now both oar and sail.
As when a griffin through the wilderness
With wingéd course o'er hill or moory dale,
Pursues the Arimaspian, who by stealth
Had from his wakeful custody purloined
The guarded gold: so eagerly the Fiend
O'er bog or steep, through strait, rough, dense, or rare,
With head, hands, wings or feet pursues his way,
And swims or sinks, or wades, or creeps, or flies.   950
At length a universal hubbub wild
Of stunning sounds and voices all confused
Borne through the hollow dark assaults his ear
With loudest vehemence: thither he plies,
Undaunted to meet there whatever power
Or spirit of the nethermost abyss
Might in that noise reside, of whom to ask
Which way the nearest coast of darkness lies
Bordering on light; when straight behold the throne
Of Chaos, and his dark pavilion spread   960
Wide on the wasteful deep; with him enthroned
Sat sable-vested Night, eldest of things,
The consort of his reign; and by them stood

---

933. *pennons:* pinions.

934. *fadom:* fathom.

939. *Syrtis:* a sandy gulf near which lay Barca and Cyrene (cf. line 904 above).

945. In Herodotus, III, 116, the *Arimaspians* are a one-eyed people who steal from the griffins, mythical monsters part eagle, part lion.

Orcus and Ades, and the dreaded name
Of Demogorgon; Rumor next and Chance,
And Tumult and Confusion all embroiled,
And Discord with a thousand various mouths.
   T' whom Satan turning boldly, thus. "Ye powers
And spirits of this nethermost abyss,
Chaos and ancient Night, I come no spy,   970
With purpose to explore or to disturb
The secrets of your realm, but by constraint
Wandering this darksome desert, as my way
Lies through your spacious empire up to light,
Alone, and without guide, half lost, I seek
What readiest path leads where your gloomy bounds
Confine with Heav'n; or if some other place
From your dominion won, th' ethereal King
Possesses lately, thither to arrive
I travel this profound, direct my course;   980
Directed, no mean recompense it brings
To your behoof, if I that region lost,
All usurpation thence expelled, reduce
To her original darkness and your sway
(Which is my present journey) and once more
Erect the standard there of ancient Night;
Yours be th' advantage all, mine the revenge."
   Thus Satan; and him thus the Anarch old
With faltering speech and visage incomposed
Answered. "I know thee, stranger, who thou art,   990
That mighty leading angel, who of late
Made head against Heav'n's King, though overthrown.

---

964. *Orcus* and *Ades* are Roman and Greek names for Pluto or
Hades, god of hell.
   964–965. *name of Demogorgon:* i.e., Demogorgon himself. In
Boccaccio's *Genealogy of the Gods* he is the progenitor of all the
pagan gods.
   977. *confine with:* border on.
   982. *that region lost:* i.e., that region lost by Chaos when God
created the world.
   988. *Anarch:* i.e., Chaos, here personified.

I saw and heard, for such a numerous host
Fled not in silence through the frighted deep
With ruin upon ruin, rout on rout,
Confusion worse confounded; and Heav'n gates
Poured out by millions her victorious bands
Pursuing. I upon my frontiers here
Keep residence; if all I can will serve,
That little which is left so to defend,   1000
Encroached on still through our intestine broils
Weakening the scepter of old Night: first Hell
Your dungeon stretching far and wide beneath;
Now lately heav'n and earth, another world
Hung o'er my realm, linked in a golden chain
To that side Heav'n from whence your legions fell.
If that way be your walk, you have not far;
So much the nearer danger; go and speed;
Havoc and spoil and ruin are my gain."

    He ceased; and Satan stayed not to reply,   1010
But glad that now his sea should find a shore,
With fresh alacrity and force renewed
Springs upward like a pyramid of fire
Into the wild expanse, and through the shock
Of fighting elements, on all sides round
Environed wins his way; harder beset
And more endangered, than when Argo passed
Through Bosporus betwixt the justling rocks:
Or when Ulysses on the larboard shunned
Charybdis, and by th' other whirlpool steered.   1020
So he with difficulty and labor hard
Moved on, with difficulty and labor he;
But he once passed, soon after when man fell,
Strange alteration! Sin and Death amain
Following his track, such was the will of Heav'n,
Paved after him a broad and beaten way

_____

    1008. Chaos speeds Satan on his journey. Cf. Satan's lying account in X, 474–480. *danger:* mischief, harm.
    1017. *Argo:* the ship in which Jason and the Argonauts sailed.
    1026. Cf. X, 293–320.

Over the dark abyss, whose boiling gulf
Tamely endured a bridge of wondrous length
From Hell continued reaching th' utmost orb
Of this frail world; by which the spirits perverse   1030
With easy intercourse pass to and fro
To tempt or punish mortals, except whom
God and good angels guard by special grace.
But now at last the sacred influence
Of light appears, and from the walls of Heav'n
Shoots far into the bosom of dim Night
A glimmering dawn; here nature first begins
Her farthest verge, and Chaos to retire
As from her outmost works a broken foe
With tumult less and with less hostile din,   1040
That Satan with less toil, and now with ease
Wafts on the calmer wave by dubious light
And like a weather-beaten vessel holds
Gladly the port, though shrouds and tackle torn;
Or in the emptier waste, resembling air,
Weighs his spread wings, at leisure to behold
Far off th' empyreal Heav'n, extended wide
In circuit, undetermined square or round,
With opal tow'rs and battlements adorned
Of living sapphire, once his native seat;   1050
And fast by hanging in a golden chain
This pendent world, in bigness as a star
Of smallest magnitude close by the moon.
Thither full fraught with mischievous revenge,
Accursed, and in a curséd hour he hies.

1043. *holds:* holds for, makes for.
1052. *this pendent world:* the whole universe, not just the earth.

BOOK III

THE ARGUMENT

God sitting on his throne sees Satan flying towards this world, then newly created; shows him to the Son who sat at his right hand; foretells the success of Satan in perverting mankind; clears his own justice and wisdom from all imputation, having created man free and able enough to have withstood his tempter; yet declares his purpose of grace towards him, in regard he fell not of his own malice, as did Satan, but by him seduced. The Son of God renders praises to his Father for the manifestation of his gracious purpose towards man; but God again declares, that grace cannot be extended towards man without the satisfaction of divine justice; man hath offended the majesty of God by aspiring to Godhead, and therefore with all his progeny devoted to death must die, unless someone can be found sufficient to answer for his offence, and undergo his punishment. The Son of God freely offers himself a ransom for man: the Father accepts him, ordains his incarnation, pronounces his exaltation above all names in Heaven and earth; commands all the angels to adore him; they obey, and hymning to their harps in full choir, celebrate the Father and the Son. Meanwhile Satan alights upon the bare convex of this world's outermost orb; where wandering he first finds a place since called the Limbo of Vanity; what persons and things fly up thither; thence

comes to the gate of Heaven, described ascending by
stairs, and the waters above the firmament that flow
about it. His passage thence to the orb of the sun; he
finds there Uriel the regent of that orb, but first changes
himself into the shape of a meaner angel; and pretending a zealous desire to behold the new creation and man
whom God had placed here, inquires of him the place
of his habitation, and is directed; alights first on Mount
Niphates.

Hail holy light, offspring of Heav'n first-born
Or of th' Eternal coeternal beam
May I express thee unblamed? Since God is light,
And never but in unapproachéd light
Dwelt from eternity, dwelt then in thee,
Bright effluence of bright essence increate.
Or hear'st thou rather pure ethereal stream,
Whose fountain who shall tell? Before the sun,
Before the heav'ns thou wert, and at the voice
Of God, as with a mantle didst invest   10
The rising world of waters dark and deep,
Won from the void and formless infinite.
Thee I revisit now with bolder wing
Escaped the Stygian pool, though long detained
In that obscure sojourn, while in my flight

1–8. M. is aware that *light* is both the name of a physical phe-
nomenon and a biblical metaphor (cf. the next two notes). In
keeping with his belief that "those have acquired the truest apprehension of the nature of God who submit their understandings
to his word; considering that he has accommodated his word to
their understandings, and has shown what he wishes their notion
of the Deity should be" (*Christian Doctrine*, I, ii), M. refuses to
conceptualize the metaphor. The human understanding must remain content with God's metaphorical descriptions of himself in
Scripture.
   3. Cf. 1 John 1:5, "God is light."
   4. Cf. 1 Timothy 6:16, "dwelling in the light which no man can
approach."
   7. *hear'st thou rather:* do you prefer to be called.
   9–10. Cf. VII, 243–249.

Through utter and through middle darkness borne
With other notes than to th' Orphean lyre
I sung of Chaos and eternal Night,
Taught by the heav'nly Muse to venture down
The dark descent, and up to reascend,   20
Though hard and rare: thee I revisit safe,
And feel thy sovran vital lamp; but thou
Revisit'st not these eyes, that roll in vain
To find thy piercing ray, and find no dawn;
So thick a drop serene hath quenched their orbs,
Or dim suffusion veiled. Yet not the more
Cease I to wander where the Muses haunt
Clear spring, or shady grove, or sunny hill,
Smit with the love of sacred song; but chief
Thee Sion and the flow'ry brooks beneath   30
That wash thy hallowed feet, and warbling flow,
Nightly I visit: nor sometimes forget
Those other two equaled with me in fate,
So were I equaled with them in renown,
Blind Thamyris and blind Maeonides,
And Tiresias and Phineus prophets old.
Then feed on thoughts, that voluntary move
Harmonious numbers; as the wakeful bird
Sings darkling, and in shadiest covert hid

---

16. *utter* (outer) and *middle darkness* are Hell and Chaos.

17. *Orphean lyre:* M. once again asserts the superiority of his inspiration. Here he refers to the Orphic *Hymn to Night*.

25-26. *drop serene . . . suffusion:* technical terms, the former being the more specific, referring to disease of the optic nerve in which the outward appearance of the eye does not change.

26-32. He still loves classical literature, whose Muses haunted Mount Helicon with its fountains Aganippe and Hippocrene and Mount Parnassus with the Castalian fountain, but he prefers Hebrew literature such as that of David, whose palace was on Mount Sion, beneath which flowed the brooks Siloa and Kidron.

35. *Thamyris:* a Thracian bard mentioned by Homer (*Iliad*, II, 595-600) and Plato. *Maeonides:* Homer.

36. *Tiresias:* the blind seer of *Oedipus Rex*. *Phineus:* a king of Thrace blinded by the gods.

38. *numbers:* verse. *wakeful bird:* the nightingale.

Tunes her nocturnal note. Thus with the year   40
Seasons return, but not to me returns
Day, or the sweet approach of ev'n or morn,
Or sight of vernal bloom, or summer's rose,
Or flocks, or herds, or human face divine;
But cloud instead, and ever-during dark
Surrounds me, from the cheerful ways of men
Cut off, and for the book of knowledge fair
Presented with a universal blank
Of Nature's works to me expunged and razed,
And wisdom at one entrance quite shut out.   50
So much the rather thou celestial light
Shine inward, and the mind through all her powers
Irradiate, there plant eyes, all mist from thence
Purge and disperse, that I may see and tell
Of things invisible to mortal sight.
   Now had th' Almighty Father from above,
From the pure empyrean where he sits
High throned above all highth, bent down his eye,
His own works and their works at once to view:
About him all the sanctities of Heav'n   60
Stood thick as stars, and from his sight received
Beatitude past utterance; on his right
The radiant image of his glory sat,
His only Son; on earth he first beheld
Our two first parents, yet the only two
Of mankind, in the happy garden placed,
Reaping immortal fruits of joy and love,
Uninterrupted joy, unrivaled love
In blissful solitude; he then surveyed
Hell and the gulf between, and Satan there   70

---

60. *sanctities:* angels.

62–63. Cf. Hebrews 1:3, "Who being the brightness of his glory,
and the express image of his person . . . sat down on the right
hand of the Majesty on high."

70–74. Satan is still aloft (*sublime*) in Chaos, coasting the wall
of Heaven (the "empyrean" of line 57), the abode of God and the
angels. The air is dusky (*dun*) because lit by a "glimmering dawn"
(II, 1037) from the light of Heaven. He is about to pounce (*stoop*)
on the universe (*this world*).

Coasting the wall of Heav'n on this side night
In the dun air sublime, and ready now
To stoop with wearied wings, and willing feet
On the bare outside of this world, that seemed
Firm land imbosomed without firmament,
Uncertain which, in ocean or in air.
Him God beholding from his prospect high,
Wherein past, present, future he beholds,
Thus to his only Son foreseeing spake.

   "Only begotten Son, seest thou what rage   80
Transports our adversary, whom no bounds
Prescribed, no bars of Hell, nor all the chains
Heaped on him there, nor yet the main abyss
Wide interrupt can hold; so bent he seems
On desperate revenge, that shall redound
Upon his own rebellious head. And now
Through all restraint broke loose he wings his way
Not far off Heav'n, in the precincts of light,
Directly towards the new created world,
And man there placed, with purpose to assay   90
If him by force he can destroy, or worse,
By some false guile pervert; and shall pervert,
For man will hearken to his glozing lies,
And easily transgress the sole command,
Sole pledge of his obedience: so will fall,
He and his faithless progeny: whose fault?
Whose but his own? Ingrate, he had of me

---

76. *uncertain which:* it is uncertain which.

78. The eternity that is God's mode of existence is not an endless succession of moments, but the simultaneous apprehension of
all time at once. Notice the frequent shifts in tense in God's
speeches.

80–84. God is being ironical. Cf. V, 719–737.

83–84. *abyss:* Chaos, as in I, 21, and II, 405. *wide interrupt:* i.e.,
Chaos forms a wide breach between Heaven and Hell; *interrupt*
is a past participle meaning "broken open."

94. *sole command:* i.e., not to eat of the Tree of Knowledge.

96–99. The temptation to read these lines as an expression of
petulance must be resisted. God is tonelessly stating the facts.

All he could have; I made him just and right,
Sufficient to have stood, though free to fall.
Such I created all th' ethereal Powers   100
And spirits, both them who stood and them who failed;
Freely they stood who stood, and fell who fell.
Not free, what proof could they have giv'n sincere
Of true allegiance, constant faith or love,
Where only what they needs must do, appeared,
Not what they would? What praise could they receive?
What pleasure I from such obedience paid,
When will and reason (reason also is choice)
Useless and vain, of freedom both despoiled,
Made passive both, had served necessity,   110
Not me. They therefore as to right belonged,
So were created, nor can justly accuse
Their maker, or their making, or their fate,
As if predestination overruled
Their will, disposed by absolute decree
Or high foreknowledge; they themselves decreed
Their own revolt, not I: if I foreknew,
Foreknowledge had no influence on their fault,
Which had no less proved certain unforeknown.
So without least impulse or shadow of fate,   120
Or aught by me immutably foreseen,
They trespass, authors to themselves in all
Both what they judge and what they choose; for so
I formed them free, and free they must remain,
Till they enthrall themselves: I else must change
Their nature, and revoke the high decree
Unchangeable, eternal, which ordained
Their freedom, they themselves ordained their fall.
The first sort by their own suggestion fell,
Self-tempted, self-depraved: man falls deceived   130
By th' other first: man therefore shall find grace,

---

108. Man has freedom of the will precisely because his reason
enables him to discriminate among various goods and weigh the
consequences of his actions. Cf. IX, 351–356.
129. *the first sort:* the fallen angels. *suggestion:* temptation.

The other none: in mercy and justice both,
Through Heav'n and earth, so shall my glory excel,
But mercy first and last shall brightest shine."
   Thus while God spake, ambrosial fragrance filled
All Heav'n, and in the blessèd spirits elect
Sense of new joy ineffable diffused.
Beyond compare the Son of God was seen
Most glorious, in him all his Father shone
Substantially expressed, and in his face   140
Divine compassion visibly appeared,
Love without end, and without measure grace,
Which uttering thus he to his Father spake.
   "O Father, gracious was that word which closed
Thy sovran sentence, that man should find grace;
For which both Heav'n and earth shall high extol
Thy praises, with th' innumerable sound
Of hymns and sacred songs, wherewith thy throne
Encompassed shall resound thee ever blest.
For should man finally be lost, should man   150
Thy creature late so loved, thy youngest son
Fall circumvented thus by fraud, though joined
With his own folly? That be from thee far,
That far be from thee, Father, who art judge
Of all things made, and judgest only right.
Or shall the adversary thus obtain
His end, and frustrate thine, shall he fulfill
His malice, and thy goodness bring to naught,
Or proud return though to his heavier doom,
Yet with revenge accomplished and to Hell   160
Draw after him the whole race of mankind,
By him corrupted? Or wilt thou thyself
Abolish thy creation, and unmake,
For him, what for thy glory thou has made?

153–155. Cf. Genesis 18:25, where Abraham pleads with God
for the inhabitants of Sodom: "That be far from thee to do after
this manner, to slay the righteous with the wicked: and that
the righteous should be as the wicked, that be far from thee:
Shall not the Judge of all the earth do right?"

So should thy goodness and thy greatness both
Be questioned and blasphemed without defense."
     To whom the great Creator thus replied.
"O Son, in whom my soul hath chief delight,
Son of my bosom, Son who art alone
My word, my wisdom, and effectual might,   170
All hast thou spoken as my thoughts are, all
As my eternal purpose hath decreed:
Man shall not quite be lost, but saved who will,
Yet not of will in him, but grace in me
Freely vouchsafed; once more I will renew
His lapséd powers, though forfeit and enthralled
By sin to foul exorbitant desires;
Upheld by me, yet once more he shall stand
On even ground against his mortal foe,
By me upheld, that he may know how frail   180
His fall'n condition is, and to me owe
All his deliverance, and to none but me.
Some I have chosen of peculiar grace
Elect above the rest; so is my will:
The rest shall hear me call, and oft be warned
Their sinful state, and to appease betimes
Th' incenséd Deity, while offered grace
Invites; for I will clear their senses dark,
What may suffice, and soften stony hearts
To pray, repent, and bring obedience due.   190
To prayer, repentance, and obedience due,
Though but endeavored with sincere intent,
Mine ear shall not be slow, mine eye not shut.
And I will place within them as a guide
My umpire conscience, whom if they will hear,

174–177. So Adam and Eve's repentance at the end of Book X is made possible by "prevenient grace descending" (XI, 3).

183–184. Those of *peculiar grace* are probably such chosen vessels as the prophets and apostles. That others who are not *elect above the rest* may be saved is made clear in lines 195–197. This is not the Calvinist doctrine of predestination and reprobation.

189. Cf. XI, 4 and Ezekiel 36:26.

Light after light well used they shall attain,
And to the end persisting, safe arrive.
This my long sufferance and my day of grace
They who neglect and scorn, shall never taste;
But hard be hardened, blind be blinded more,   2◄
That they may stumble on, and deeper fall;
And none but such from mercy I exclude.
But yet all is not done; man disobeying,
Disloyal breaks his fealty, and sins
Against the high supremacy of Heav'n,
Affecting Godhead, and so losing all,
To expiate his treason hath naught left,
But to destruction sacred and devote,
He with his whole posterity must die,
Die he or justice must; unless for him   2◄
Some other able, and as willing, pay
The rigid satisfaction, death for death.
Say heav'nly Powers, where shall we find such love,
Which of ye will be mortal to redeem
Man's mortal crime, and just th' unjust to save,
Dwells in all Heaven charity so dear?"

      He asked, but all the heav'nly choir stood mute,
And silence was in Heav'n: on man's behalf
Patron or intercessor none appeared,
Much less that durst upon his own head draw   2◄
The deadly forfeiture, and ransom set.
And now without redemption all mankind
Must have been lost, adjudged to death and Hell
By doom severe, had not the Son of God,
In whom the fulness dwells of love divine,

---

208. *Sacred* and *devote* both have their Latin meaning c
"dedicated or set apart as by a vow to a deity for destruction.
215. *just th' unjust:* i.e., so just as to save the unjust. Cf.
Peter 3:18.
216. *charity:* love.
217. Cf. II, 420–421.
219. *patron:* defender, advocate (in a court of law). Cf.
John 2:1.
224. *doom:* judgment.

His dearest mediation thus renewed.
   "Father, thy word is passed, man shall find grace;
And shall grace not find means, that finds her way,
The speediest of thy wingéd messengers,
To visit all thy creatures, and to all   230
Comes unprevented, unimplored, unsought,
Happy for man, so coming; he her aid
Can never seek, once dead in sins and lost;
Atonement for himself or offering meet,
Indebted and undone, hath none to bring:
Behold me then, me for him, life for life
I offer, on me let thine anger fall;
Account me man; I for his sake will leave
Thy bosom, and this glory next to thee
Freely put off, and for him lastly die   240
Well pleased, on me let Death wreck all his rage;
Under his gloomy power I shall not long
Lie vanquished; thou hast giv'n me to possess
Life in myself forever, by thee I live,
Though now to Death I yield, and am his due
All that of me can die, yet that debt paid,
Thou wilt not leave me in the loathsome grave
His prey, nor suffer my unspotted soul
Forever with corruption there to dwell;
But I shall rise victorious, and subdue   250
My vanquisher, spoiled of his vaunted spoil;
Death his death's wound shall then receive, and stoop
Inglorious, of his mortal sting disarmed.
I through the ample air in triumph high
Shall lead Hell captive maugre Hell, and show
The powers of darkness bound. Thou at the sight
Pleased, out of Heaven shalt look down and smile,
While by thee raised I ruin all my foes,
Death last, and with his carcass glut the grave:
Then with the multitude of my redeemed   260

---

231. *unprevented:* unanticipated.
235. *hath:* the subject is "he" (line 232).
255. *maugre:* in spite of.

Shall enter Heav'n long absent, and return,
Father, to see thy face, wherein no cloud
Of anger shall remain, but peace assured,
And reconcilement; wrath shall be no more
Thenceforth, but in thy presence joy entire."
   His words here ended, but his meek aspect
Silent yet spake, and breathed immortal love
To mortal men, above which only shone
Filial obedience: as a sacrifice
Glad to be offered, he attends the will   270
Of his great Father. Admiration seized
All Heav'n, what this might mean, and whither tend
Wondering; but soon th' Almighty thus replied.
   "O thou in Heav'n and earth the only peace
Found out for mankind under wrath, O thou
My sole complacence! well thou know'st how dear
To me are all my works, nor man the least
Though last created, that for him I spare
Thee from my bosom and right hand, to save,
By losing thee a while, the whole race lost.   280
Thou therefore whom thou only canst redeem,
Their nature also to thy nature join;
And be thyself man among men on earth,
Made flesh, when time shall be, of virgin seed,
By wondrous birth: be thou in Adam's room
The head of all mankind, though Adam's son.
As in him perish all men, so in thee
As from a second root shall be restored,
As many as are restored, without thee none.
His crime makes guilty all his sons, thy merit   290
Imputed shall absolve them who renounce
Their own both righteous and unrighteous deeds,
And live in thee transplanted, and from thee

---

270. *attends:* awaits.
271. *admiration:* wonder.
287. Cf. 1 Corinthians 15:22, "For as in Adam all die, even
so in Christ shall all be made alive."
288. Cf. Revelation 22:16, "I am the root and the offspring
of David."

Receive new life. So man, as is most just,
Shall satisfy for man, be judged and die,
And dying rise, and rising with him raise
His brethren, ransomed with his own dear life.
So heav'nly love shall outdo hellish hate,
Giving to death, and dying to redeem,
So dearly to redeem what hellish hate   300
So easily destroyed, and still destroys
In those who, when they may, accept not grace.
Nor shalt thou by descending to assume
Man's nature, lessen or degrade thine own.
Because thou hast, though throned in highest bliss
Equal to God, and equally enjoying
Godlike fruition, quitted all to save
A world from utter loss, and hast been found
By merit more than birthright Son of God,
Found worthiest to be so by being good,   310
Far more than great or high; because in thee
Love hath abounded more than glory abounds,
Therefore thy humiliation shall exalt
With thee thy manhood also to this throne;
Here shalt thou sit incarnate, here shalt reign
Both God and Man, Son both of God and Man,
Anointed universal King; all power
I give thee, reign forever, and assume
Thy merits; under thee as head supreme
Thrones, Princedoms, Powers, Dominions I reduce: 320
All knees to thee shall bow, of them that bide
In Heav'n, or earth, or under earth in Hell;
When thou attended gloriously from Heav'n
Shalt in the sky appear, and from thee send
The summoning Archangels to proclaim
Thy dread tribunal: forthwith from all winds
The living, and forthwith the cited dead
Of all past ages to the general doom
Shall hasten, such a peal shall rouse their sleep.

---

327. *cited:* summoned.
328. *general doom:* Last Judgment.

Then all thy saints assembled, thou shalt judge   330
Bad men and angels, they arraigned shall sink
Beneath thy sentence; Hell, her numbers full,
Thenceforth shall be forever shut. Meanwhile
The world shall burn, and from her ashes spring
New heav'n and earth, wherein the just shall dwell,
And after all their tribulations long
See golden days, fruitful of golden deeds,
With joy and love triumphing, and fair truth.
Then thou thy regal scepter shalt lay by,
For regal scepter then no more shall need,   340
God shall be all in all. But all ye gods,
Adore him, who to compass all this dies,
Adore the Son, and honor him as me."
    No sooner had th' Almighty ceased, but all
The multitude of angels with a shout
Loud as from numbers without number, sweet
As from blest voices, uttering joy, Heav'n rung
With jubilee, and loud hosannas filled
Th' eternal regions: lowly reverent
Towards either throne they bow, and to the ground   350
With solemn adoration down they cast
Their crowns inwove with amarant and gold,
Immortal amarant, a flow'r which once
In Paradise, fast by the Tree of Life
Began to bloom, but soon for man's offense
To Heav'n removed where first it grew, there grows,
And flow'rs aloft shading the fount of life,
And where the river of bliss through midst of Heav'n
Roll o'er Elysian flow'rs her amber stream;
With these that never fade the spirits elect   360
Bind their resplendent locks inwreathed with beams,
Now in loose garlands thick thrown off, the bright
Pavement that like a sea of jasper shone

---

341. Cf. 1 Corinthians 15:28.
350 ff. This passage owes many of its details to the Book of
Revelation.
353. *amarant:* unwithering.

Impurpled with celestial roses smiled.
Then crowned again their golden harps they took,
Harps ever tuned, that glittering by their side
Like quivers hung, and with preamble sweet
Of charming symphony they introduce
Their sacred song, and waken raptures high;
No voice exempt, no voice but well could join　　370
Melodious part, such concord is in Heav'n.
　　Thee Father first they sung omnipotent,
Immutable, immortal, infinite,
Eternal King; thee Author of all being,
Fountain of light, thyself invisible
Amidst the glorious brightness where thou sit'st
Throned inaccessible, but when thou shad'st
The full blaze of thy beams, and through a cloud
Drawn round about thee like a radiant shrine,
Dark with excessive bright thy skirts appear,　　380
Yet dazzle Heav'n, that brightest Seraphim
Approach not, but with both wings veil their eyes.
Thee next they sang, of all creation first,
Begotten Son, divine similitude,
In whose conspicuous count'nance, without cloud
Made visible, th' Almighty Father shines,
Whom else no creature can behold; on thee
Impressed th' effulgence of his glory abides,
Transfused on thee his ample spirit rests.
He Heav'n of Heav'ns and all the Powers therein　　390
By thee created, and by thee threw down
Th' aspiring Dominations: thou that day
Thy Father's dreadful thunder didst not spare,
Nor stop thy flaming chariot wheels, that shook
Heav'n's everlasting frame, while o'er the necks
Thou drov'st of warring angels disarrayed.
Back from pursuit thy Powers with loud acclaim
Thee only extolled, Son of thy Father's might,
To execute fierce vengeance on his foes,
Not so on man; him through their malice fall'n,　　400
Father of mercy and grace, thou didst not doom
So strictly, but much more to pity incline:

No sooner did thy dear and only Son
Perceive thee purposed not to doom frail man
So strictly, but much more to pity inclined,
He to appease thy wrath, and end the strife
Of mercy and justice in thy face discerned,
Regardless of the bliss wherein he sat
Second to thee, offered himself to die
For man's offense. O unexampled love,   41◖
Love nowhere to be found less than divine!
Hail Son of God, Saviour of men, thy Name
Shall be the copious matter of my song
Henceforth, and never shall my harp thy praise
Forget, nor from thy Father's praise disjoin.

 Thus they in Heav'n, above the starry sphere,
Their happy hours in joy and hymning spent.
Meanwhile upon the firm opacous globe
Of this round world, whose first convex divides
The luminous inferior orbs, enclosed   420
From Chaos and th' inroad of darkness old,
Satan alighted walks: a globe far off
It seemed, now seems a boundless continent
Dark, waste, and wild, under the frown of Night
Starless exposed, and ever-threatening storms
Of Chaos blustering round, inclement sky;
Save on that side which from the wall of Heav'n
Though distant far some small reflection gains
Of glimmering air less vexed with tempest loud:
Here walked the Fiend at large in spacious field.   430
As when a vulture on Imaus bred,
Whose snowy ridge the roving Tartar bounds,
Dislodging from a region scarce of prey

---

409. *offered:* the subject is "He" (line 406 above).
418. *opacous:* opaque.
423. *now seems:* To Satan, who is now standing on it, the
outside sphere of the universe seems like a vast plain.
431. *Imaus:* the name given by Ptolemy to the great north-
south dividing range of Central Asia. A vulture flying from the
northern part to the Ganges and Hydaspes in India would pass
over the northwest plains of China (*Sericana,* line 438).

To gorge the flesh of lambs or yeanling kids
On hills where flocks are fed, flies toward the springs
Of Ganges or Hydaspes, Indian streams;
But in his way lights on the barren plains
Of Sericana, where Chineses drive
With sails and wind their cany wagons light:
So on this windy sea of land, the Fiend   440
Walked up and down alone bent on his prey,
Alone, for other creature in this place
Living or lifeless to be found was none,
None yet, but store hereafter from the earth
Up hither like aërial vapors flew
Of all things transitory and vain, when Sin
With vanity had filled the works of men:
Both all things vain, and all who in vain things
Built their fond hopes of glory or lasting fame,
Or happiness in this or th' other life;   450
All who have their reward on earth, the fruits
Of painful superstition and blind zeal,
Naught seeking but the praise of men, here find
Fit retribution, empty as their deeds;
All th' unaccomplished works of nature's hand,
Abortive, monstrous, or unkindly mixed,
Dissolved on earth, fleet hither, and in vain,
Till final dissolution, wander here,
Not in the neighboring moon, as some have dreamed;
Those argent fields more likely habitants,   460
Translated saints, or middle spirits hold
Betwixt th' angelical and human kind:
Hither of ill-joined sons and daughters born
First from the ancient world those giants came
With many a vain exploit, though then renowned:
The builders next of Babel on the plain
Of Sennaär, and still with vain design
New Babels, had they wherewithal, would build:

_____

449. *fond:* foolish.
456. *unkindly:* unnaturally.
463–465. Cf. XI, 573–592.

Others came single; he who to be deemed
A god, leaped fondly into Etna flames,   470
Empedocles, and he who to enjoy
Plato's Elysium, leaped into the sea,
Cleombrotus, and many more too long,
Embryos and idiots, eremites and friars
White, Black and Gray, with all their trumpery.
Here pilgrims roam, that strayed so far to seek
In Golgotha him dead, who lives in Heav'n;
And they who to be sure of Paradise
Dying put on the weeds of Dominic,
Or in Franciscan think to pass disguised;   480
They pass the planets sev'n, and pass the fixed,
And that crystalline sphere whose balance weighs
The trepidation talked, and that first moved;
And now Saint Peter at Heav'n's wicket seems
To wait them with his keys, and now at foot
Of Heav'n's ascent they lift their feet, when lo
A violent cross wind from either coast
Blows them transverse ten thousand leagues awry
Into the devious air; then might ye see
Cowls, hoods and habits with their wearers tossed   490
And fluttered into rags, then relics, beads,
Indulgences, dispenses, pardons, bulls,
The sport of winds: all these upwhirled aloft
Fly o'er the backside of the world far off
Into a limbo large and broad, since called
The Paradise of Fools, to few unknown
Long after, now unpeopled, and untrod;

---

474. *eremites:* hermits.

475. The White, Black, and Gray friars are the Carmelites,
Dominicans, and Franciscans respectively.

477. *Golgotha* was the scene of the Crucifixion. As Michael tells
Adam, "God attributes to place/ No sanctity" (XI, 836–837).

481. *the fixed:* the sphere of the fixed stars (as opposed to the
wandering stars or planets).

483. *trepidation:* the supposed oscillation of the ninth or
crystalline sphere, a theory of early medieval astronomers designed to account for the precession of the equinoxes.

All this dark globe the fiend found as he passed,
And long he wandered, till at last a gleam
Of dawning light turned thitherward in haste   500
His traveled steps; far distant he descries
Ascending by degrees magnificent
Up to the wall of Heav'n a structure high,
At top whereof, but far more rich appeared
The work as of a kingly palace gate
With frontispiece of diamond and gold
Imbellished, thick with sparkling orient gems
The portal shone, inimitable on earth
By model, or by shading pencil drawn.
The stairs were such as whereon Jacob saw   510
Angels ascending and descending, bands
Of guardians bright, when he from Esau fled
To Padan-Aram in the field of Luz,
Dreaming by night under the open sky,
And waking cried, "This is the gate of Heav'n."
Each stair mysteriously was meant, nor stood
There always, but drawn up to Heav'n sometimes
Viewless, and underneath a bright sea flowed
Of jasper, or of liquid pearl, whereon
Who after came from earth, sailing arrived,   520
Wafted by angels, or flew o'er the lake
Rapt in a chariot drawn by fiery steeds.
The stairs were then let down, whether to dare
The Fiend by easy ascent, or aggravate
His sad exclusion from the doors of bliss.
Direct against which opened from beneath,

---

501. *traveled:* tired.
502. *degrees:* steps.
510–515. Cf. Genesis 28:11–17.
516. *mysteriously was meant:* had a mystic significance.
518–519. The *sea of jasper* is the waters above the firmament of the universe described in VII, 261–271, as a "crystalline ocean." In Revelation 21:11 the light of the heavenly Jerusalem is "like a jasper stone, clear as crystal."
521–522. Lazarus (Luke 16:22) and Elijah (2 Kings 2:11) are alluded to.

Just o'er the blissful seat of Paradise,
A passage down to th' earth, a passage wide,
Wider by far than that of aftertimes
Over Mount Sion, and, though that were large,   530
Over the Promised Land to God so dear,
By which, to visit oft those happy tribes,
On high behests his angels to and fro
Passed frequent, and his eye with choice regard
From Paneas the fount of Jordan's flood
To Beërsaba, where the Holy Land
Borders on Egypt and th' Arabian shore;
So wide the opening seemed, where bounds were set
To darkness, such as bound the ocean wave.
Satan from hence now on the lower stair   540
That scaled by steps of gold to Heaven gate
Looks down with wonder at the sudden view
Of all this world at once. As when a scout
Through dark and desert ways with peril gone
All night; at last by break of cheerful dawn
Obtains the brow of some high-climbing hill,
Which to his eye discovers unaware
The goodly prospect of some foreign land
First seen, or some renowned metropolis
With glistering spires and pinnacles adorned,   550
Which now the rising sun gilds with his beams.
Such wonder seized, though after Heaven seen,
The spirit malign, but much more envy seized
At sight of all this world beheld so fair.
Round he surveys, and well might, where he stood
So high above the circling canopy
Of Night's extended shade; from eastern point
Of Libra to the fleecy star that bears

---

534. *choice regard:* careful look.

535–536. From Paneas . . . to Beërsaba: i.e., from north to south of Palestine.

552. *though after Heaven seen:* even though he had seen Heaven.

558. *fleecy star:* the constellation of the Ram (Aries), below Andromeda at the opposite or western end of the Zodiac from Libra.

Andromeda far off Atlantic seas
Beyond th' horizon; then from pole to pole   560
He views in breadth, and without longer pause
Down right into the world's first region throws
His flight precipitant, and winds with ease
Through the pure marble air his oblique way
Amongst innumerable stars, that shone
Stars distant, but nigh hand seemed other worlds,
Or other worlds they seemed, or happy isles,
Like those Hesperian gardens famed of old,
Fortunate fields, and groves and flow'ry vales,
Thrice happy isles, but who dwelt happy there   570
He stayed not to inquire: above them all
The golden sun in splendor likest Heav'n
Allured his eye. Thither his course he bends
Through the calm firmament; but up or down
By center, or eccentric, hard to tell,
Or longitude, where the great luminary
Aloof the vulgar constellations thick,
That from his lordly eye keep distance due,
Dispenses light from far; they as they move
Their starry dance in numbers that compute   580
Days, months, and years, towards his all-cheering lamp
Turn swift their various motions, or are turned
By his magnetic beam, that gently warms
The universe, and to each inward part
With gentle penetration, though unseen,
Shoots invisible virtue even to the deep:

---

567. *happy isles:* the "Fortunate Isles" of Greek mythology, later identified by some as the Canary Islands.

568. *Hesperian gardens:* the gardens where the Hesperides guarded the tree with the golden apples.

571. *above:* greater (in splendor), not above in place, since the sphere of the stars is higher than that of the sun.

574-576. M. finds it *hard to tell* the direction of Satan's journey toward the sun because he does not want to commit himself to either the Ptolemaic system, where the earth is the center of the universe and the sun is *eccentric*, or the Copernican, where the sun is the center.

So wondrously was set his station bright.
There lands the Fiend, a spot like which perhaps
Astronomer in the sun's lucent orb
Through his glazed optic tube yet never saw.   590
The place he found beyond expression bright,
Compared with aught on earth, metal or stone;
Not all parts like, but all alike informed
With radiant light, as glowing iron with fire;
If metal, part seemed gold, part silver clear;
If stone, carbuncle most or chrysolite,
Ruby or topaz, to the twelve that shone
In Aaron's breastplate, and a stone besides
Imagined rather oft than elsewhere seen,
That stone, or like to that which here below   600
Philosophers in vain so long have sought,
In vain, though by their powerful art they bind
Volatile Hermes, and call up unbound
In various shapes old Proteus from the sea,
Drained through a limbec to his native form.
What wonder then if fields and regions here
Breathe forth elixir pure, and rivers run
Potable gold, when with one virtuous touch
Th' arch-chemic sun so far from us remote
Produces with terrestrial humor mixed   610
Here in the dark so many precious things
Of color glorious and effect so rare?
Here matter new to gaze the Devil met

589–590. Another allusion to Galileo and the telescope.

600. *that stone:* the philosopher's stone or "elixir" (line 607),
by which alchemists ("philosophers") sought to transmute baser
metals into gold.

603. *Hermes:* Mercury (i.e., the metal).

604. *Proteus:* the "old man of the sea," who could assume
various shapes.

605. *limbec:* alembic, distilling apparatus.

606. *here:* i.e., on the sun.

610. *humor:* moisture.

611. *here:* i.e., on earth. *precious things:* precious stones,
thought to be produced by the sun's influence.

Undazzled, far and wide his eye commands,
For sight no obstacle found here, nor shade,
But all sunshine, as when his beams at noon
Culminate from th' equator, as they now
Shot upward still direct, whence no way round
Shadow from body opaque can fall, and th' air,
Nowhere so clear, sharpened his visual ray   620
To objects distant far, whereby he soon
Saw within ken a glorious angel stand,
The same whom John saw also in the sun:
His back was turned, but not his brightness hid;
Of beaming sunny rays, a golden tiar
Circled his head, nor less his locks behind
Illustrious on his shoulders fledge with wings
Lay waving round; on some great charge employed
He seemed, or fixed in cogitation deep.
Glad was the spirit impure as now in hope   630
To find who might direct his wandering flight
To Paradise the happy seat of man,
His journey's end and our beginning woe.
But first he casts to change his proper shape,
Which else might work him danger or delay:
And now a stripling Cherub he appears,
Not of the prime, yet such as in his face
Youth smiled celestial, and to every limb
Suitable grace diffused, so well he feigned;
Under a coronet his flowing hair   640
In curls on either cheek played, wings he wore
Of many a colored plume sprinkled with gold,
His habit fit for speed succinct, and held
Before his decent steps a silver wand.
He drew not nigh unheard; the angel bright,

---

617. *culminate:* The position of the sun when it reaches the
meridian over the equator is called its culmination.

620. *his visual ray:* Satan's sight.

623. Cf. Revelation 19:17.

625. *tiar:* crown, tiara.

643. *succinct:* girded up.

644. *decent:* graceful, becoming.

Ere he drew nigh, his radiant visage turned,
Admonished by his ear, and straight was known
Th' Archangel Uriel, one of the sev'n
Who in God's presence, nearest to his throne
Stand ready at command, and are his eyes   650
That run through all the heav'ns, or down to th' earth
Bear his swift errands over moist and dry,
O'er sea and land: him Satan thus accosts.
   "Uriel, for thou of those sev'n spirits that stand
In sight of God's high throne, gloriously bright,
The first art wont his great authentic will
Interpreter through highest Heav'n to bring,
Where all his sons thy embassy attend;
And here art likeliest by supreme decree
Like honor to obtain, and as his eye   660
To visit oft this new creation round;
Unspeakable desire to see, and know
All these his wondrous works, but chiefly man,
His chief delight and favor, him for whom
All these his works so wondrous he ordained,
Hath brought me from the choirs of Cherubim
Alone thus wandering. Brightest Seraph tell
In which of all these shining orbs hath man
His fixéd seat, or fixéd seat hath none,
But all these shining orbs his choice to dwell;   670
That I may find him, and with secret gaze,
Or open admiration him behold
On whom the great Creator hath bestowed
Worlds, and on whom hath all these graces poured;
That both in him and all things, as is meet,
The Universal Maker we may praise;
Who justly hath driv'n out his rebel foes
To deepest Hell, and to repair that loss
Created this new happy race of men

---

648. The name *Uriel* appears in 1 Chronicles 6:24. It means "fire of God."

654. The "seven spirits" are mentioned in Revelation 1:4 and Zechariah 4:10.

To serve him better: wise are all his ways." 680
  So spake the false dissembler unperceived;
For neither man nor angel can discern
Hypocrisy, the only evil that walks
Invisible, except to God alone,
By his permissive will, through Heav'n and earth:
And oft though wisdom wake, suspicion sleeps
At wisdom's gate, and to simplicity
Resigns her charge, while goodness thinks no ill
Where no ill seems: which now for once beguiled
Uriel, though regent of the sun, and held 690
The sharpest-sighted spirit of all in Heav'n;
Who to the fraudulent impostor foul
In his uprightness answer thus returned.
"Fair angel, thy desire which tends to know
The works of God, thereby to glorify
The great Work-Master, leads to no excess
That reaches blame, but rather merits praise
The more it seems excess, that led thee hither
From thy empyreal mansion thus alone,
To witness with thine eyes what some perhaps 700
Contented with report hear only in Heav'n:
For wonderful indeed are all his works,
Pleasant to know, and worthiest to be all
Had in remembrance always with delight;
But what created mind can comprehend
Their number, or the wisdom infinite
That brought them forth, but hid their causes deep.
I saw when at his Word the formless mass,
This world's material mold, came to a heap:
Confusion heard his voice, and wild uproar 710
Stood ruled, stood vast infinitude confined;
Till at his second bidding darkness fled,
Light shone, and order from disorder sprung:
Swift to their several quarters hasted then
The cumbrous elements, earth, flood, air, fire,
And this ethereal quintessence of heav'n
Flew upward, spirited with various forms,
That rolled orbicular, and turned to stars

Numberless, as thou seest, and how they move;
Each had his place appointed, each his course, 720
The rest in circuit walls this universe.
Look downward on that globe whose hither side
With light from hence, though but reflected, shines;
That place is earth the seat of man, that light
His day, which else as th' other hemisphere
Night would invade, but there the neighboring **moon**
(So call that opposite fair star) her aid
Timely interposes, and her monthly round
Still ending, still renewing, through mid heav'n,
With borrowed light her countenance triform 73
Hence fills and empties to enlighten th' earth,
And in her pale dominion checks the night.
That spot to which I point is Paradise,
Adam's abode, those lofty shades his bow'r.
Thy way thou canst not miss, me mine requires."
    Thus said, he turned, and Satan bowing low,
As to superior spirits is wont in Heav'n,
Where honor due and reverence none neglects,
Took leave, and toward the coast of earth beneath,
Down from th' ecliptic, sped with hoped success, 74
Throws his steep flight in many an aery wheel,
Nor stayed, till on Niphates' top he lights.

---

740. *ecliptic:* the path of the sun.
742. Mount *Niphates* is part of the Taurus range in Armeni
near the border of Assyria.

BOOK IV

THE ARGUMENT

Satan now in prospect of Eden, and nigh the place where he must now attempt the bold enterprise which he undertook alone against God and man, falls into many doubts with himself, and many passions, fear, envy, and despair; but at length confirms himself in evil, journeys on to Paradise, whose outward prospect and situation is described, overleaps the bounds, sits in the shape of a cormorant on the Tree of Life, as highest in the Garden to look about him. The Garden described; Satan's first sight of Adam and Eve; his wonder at their excellent form and happy state, but with resolution to work their fall; overhears their discourse, thence gathers that the Tree of Knowledge was forbidden them to eat of, under penalty of death; and thereon intends to found his temptation, by seducing them to transgress: then leaves them a while, to know further of their state by some other means. Meanwhile Uriel descending on a sunbeam warns Gabriel, who had in charge the gate of Paradise, that some evil spirit had escaped the deep, and passed at noon by his sphere in the shape of a good angel down to Paradise, discovered after by his furious gestures in the mount. Gabriel promises to find him ere morning. Night coming on, Adam and Eve discourse of going to their rest: their bower described; their evening worship. Gabriel drawing forth his bands of night-watch to walk the round of Paradise, appoints two strong angels to Adam's bower, lest the evil spirit should be there doing some harm to Adam or Eve sleeping; there they find him at the ear of Eve, tempting her in a dream, and bring him, though unwilling, to Gabriel; by whom questioned, he scornfully answers, prepares resistance, but hindered by a sign from Heaven, flies out of Paradise.

O for that warning voice, which he who saw
Th' Apocalypse, heard cry in Heav'n aloud,
Then when the Dragon, put to second rout,
Came furious down to be revenged on men,
"Woe to th' inhabitants on Earth!" that now,
While time was, our first parents had been warned
The coming of their secret foe, and scaped
Haply so scaped his mortal snare; for now
Satan, now first inflamed with rage, came down,
The tempter ere th' accuser of mankind,   10
To wreak on innocent frail man his loss
Of that first battle, and his flight to Hell:
Yet not rejoicing in his speed, though bold,
Far off and fearless, nor with cause to boast,
Begins his dire attempt, which nigh the birth
Now rolling, boils in his tumultuous breast,
And like a devilish engine back recoils
Upon himself; horror and doubt distract
His troubled thoughts, and from the bottom stir
The Hell within him, for within him Hell   20
He brings, and round about him, nor from Hell
One step no more than from himself can fly
By change of place: Now conscience wakes despair
That slumbered, wakes the bitter memory
Of what he was, what is, and what must be

---

5. Cf. Revelation 12:12, "Woe to the inhabiters of the earth and of the sea! for the devil is come down unto you, having great wrath, because he knoweth that he hath but a short time."

17. *engine:* the cannon, invented by Satan (VI, 482–491).

Worse; of worse deeds worse sufferings must ensue.
Sometimes towards Eden which now in his view
Lay pleasant, his grieved look he fixes sad,
Sometimes towards Heav'n and the full-blazing sun,
Which now sat high in his meridian tow'r: 30
Then much revolving, thus in sighs began.
   "O thou that with surpassing glory crowned,
Look'st from thy sole dominion like the god
Of this new world; at whose sight all the stars
Hide their diminished heads; to thee I call,
But with no friendly voice, and add thy name
O sun, to tell thee how I hate thy beams
That bring to my remembrance from what state
I fell, how glorious once above thy sphere;
Till pride and worse ambition threw me down   40
Warring in Heav'n against Heav'n's matchless King:
Ah wherefore! he deserved no such return
From me, whom he created what I was
In that bright eminence, and with his good
Upbraided none; nor was his service hard.
What could be less than to afford him praise,
The easiest recompense, and pay him thanks,
How due! Yet all his good proved ill in me,
And wrought but malice; lifted up so high
I sdained subjection, and thought one step higher   50
Would set me highest, and in a moment quit
The debt immense of endless gratitude,
So burdensome still paying, still to owe;
Forgetful what from him I still received,

---

31. *much revolving:* turning many things over in his mind.

32–41. M.'s nephew Edward Phillips says in his *Life of Milton* that these lines were written "several years" before *PL* was begun and were designed for the very beginning of M.'s projected tragedy *Adam Unparadized.*

43. Elsewhere Satan denies that he was created by God. Since this is a soliloquy Satan has no need to lie, as he does when he is exhorting his followers.

50. *sdained:* disdained.

53. *still:* continually.

And understood not that a grateful mind
By owing owes not, but still pays, at once
Indebted and discharged; what burden then?
O had his powerful destiny ordained
Me some inferior angel, I had stood
Then happy; no unbounded hope had raised   60
Ambition. Yet why not? Some other power
As great might have aspired, and me though mean
Drawn to his part; but other powers as great
Fell not, but stand unshaken, from within
Or from without, to all temptations armed.
Hadst thou the same free will and power to stand?
Thou hadst: whom hast thou then or what to accuse,
But Heav'n's free love dealt equally to all?
Be then his love accurst, since love or hate,
To me alike, it deals eternal woe.   70
Nay cursed be thou; since against his thy will
Chose freely what it now so justly rues.
Me miserable! which way shall I fly
Infinite wrath, and infinite despair?
Which way I fly is Hell; myself am Hell;
And in the lowest deep a lower deep
Still threatening to devour me opens wide,
To which the Hell I suffer seems a Heav'n.
O then at last relent: is there no place
Left for repentance, none for pardon left?   80
None left but by submission; and that word
Disdain forbids me, and my dread of shame
Among the spirits beneath, whom I seduced
With other promises and other vaunts
Than to submit, boasting I could subdue
Th' Omnipotent. Ay me, they little know
How dearly I abide that boast so vain,

55–57. Gratitude itself discharges an obligation, and at the same
time a grateful person is always conscious of a sense of indebted-
ness.

75. This is Satan's moment of recognition. Cf. his boast in I,
254–255.

Under what torments inwardly I groan;
While they adore me on the throne of Hell,
With diadem and scepter high advanced   90
The lower still I fall, only supreme
In misery; such joy ambition finds.
But say I could repent and could obtain
By act of grace my former state; how soon
Would highth recall high thoughts, how soon unsay
What feigned submission swore: ease would recant
Vows made in pain, as violent and void.
For never can true reconcilement grow
Where wounds of deadly hate have pierced so deep:
Which would but lead me to a worse relapse   100
And heavier fall: so should I purchase dear
Short intermission bought with double smart.
This knows my punisher; therefore as far
From granting he, as I from begging peace:
All hope excluded thus, behold instead
Of us outcast, exiled, his new delight,
Mankind created, and for him this world.
So farewell hope, and with hope farewell fear,
Farewell remorse: all good to me is lost;
Evil be thou my good; by thee at least   110
Divided empire with Heav'n's King I hold
By thee, and more than half perhaps will reign;
As man ere long, and this new world shall know."

    Thus while he spake, each passion dimmed his face
Thrice changed with pale, ire, envy and despair,
Which marred his borrowed visage, and betrayed
Him counterfeit, if any eye beheld.
For heav'nly minds from such distempers foul
Are ever clear. Whereof he soon aware,
Each perturbation smoothed with outward calm,   120
Artificer of fraud; and was the first
That practised falsehood under saintly show,

115–116. Satan's *borrowed visage*, that of a stripling Cherub
(III, 636), three times turns pale with the passions of *ire, envy,*
and *despair.*

Deep malice to conceal, couched with revenge:
Yet not enough had practised to deceive
Uriel once warned; whose eye pursued him down
The way he went, and on th' Assyrian mount
Saw him disfigured, more than could befall
Spirit of happy sort: his gestures fierce
He marked and mad demeanor, then alone,
As he supposed, all unobserved, unseen.   130
So on he fares, and to the border comes
Of Eden, where delicious Paradise,
Now nearer, crowns with her enclosure green,
As with a rural mound the champaign head
Of a steep wilderness, whose hairy sides
With thicket overgrown, grotesque and wild,
Access denied; and over head up grew
Insuperable highth of loftiest shade,
Cedar, and pine, and fir, and branching palm,
A silvan scene, and as the ranks ascend   140
Shade above shade, a woody theater
Of stateliest view. Yet higher than their tops
The verdurous wall of Paradise up sprung:
Which to our general sire gave prospect large
Into his nether empire neighboring round.
And higher than that wall a circling row
Of goodliest trees loaden with fairest fruit,
Blossoms and fruits at once of golden hue
Appeared, with gay enameled colors mixed:
On which the sun more glad impressed his beams   150
Than in fair evening cloud, or humid bow,
When God hath show'red the earth; so lovely seemed
That landscape: and of pure now purer air

---

123. *couched:* lying hid.
132. *Eden* is the whole region of which *Paradise* is a part.
134. *champaign head:* open, level summit.
136. *grotesque:* It. *grottesca* (=*pittura grottesca*) was defined
by Florio in 1611 as "anticke or landskip worke of Painters" (OED).
The word carried connotations of fantastic extravagance.
151. *humid bow:* the rainbow.
153. *of:* after.

Meets his approach, and to the heart inspires
Vernal delight and joy, able to drive
All sadness but despair: now gentle gales
Fanning their odoriferous wings dispense
Native perfumes, and whisper whence they stole
Those balmy spoils. As when tó them who sail
Beyond the Cape of Hope, and now are passed　　160
Mozambic, off at sea northeast winds blow
Sabean odors from the spicy shore
Of Araby the blest, with such delay
Well pleased they slack their course, and many a league
Cheered with the grateful smell old Ocean smiles.
So entertained those odorous sweets the Fiend
Who came their bane, though with them better pleased
Than Asmodeus with the fishy fume,
That drove him, though enamored, from the spouse
Of Tobit's son, and with a vengeance sent　　170
From Media post to Egypt, there fast bound.
　Now to th' ascent of that steep savage hill
Satan had journeyed on, pensive and slow;
But further way found none, so thick entwined,
As one continued brake, the undergrowth
Of shrubs and tangling bushes had perplexed
All path of man or beast that passed that way:
One gate there only was, and that looked east
On th' other side: which when th' Archfelon saw
Due entrance he disdained, and in contempt,　　180
At one slight bound high overleaped all bound
Of hill or highest wall, and sheer within
Lights on his feet. As when a prowling wolf,

---

158. *native:* natural, not artificial.

162. *Sabean:* referring to Saba, or Sheba as the Bible has it.

168–171. The story is told in the Book of Tobit.

172. *Savage* may mean simply "wooded," but since the sides of the hill seem to foreshadow the "wilderness of this world" into which Adam and Eve are expelled after the Fall, it is easy to hear the overtones that are clearly present when the word reappears in IX, 1085.

183–193. The whole of the parable of the good shepherd (John 10) should be read in connection with this passage.

Whom hunger drives to seek new haunt for prey,
Watching where shepherds pen their flocks at eve
In hurdled cotes amid the field secure,
Leaps o'er the fence with ease into the fold:
Or as a thief bent to unhoard the cash
Of some rich burgher, whose substantial doors,
Cross-barred and bolted fast, fear no assault,   190
In at the window climbs, or o'er the tiles;
So clomb this first grand thief into God's fold:
So since into his Church lewd hirelings climb.
Thence up he flew, and on the Tree of Life,
The middle tree and highest there that grew,
Sat like a cormorant; yet not true life
Thereby regained, but sat devising death
To them who lived; nor on the virtue thought
Of that life-giving plant, but only used
For prospect, what well used had been the pledge   200
Of immortality. So little knows
Any, but God alone, to value right
The good before him, but perverts best things
To worst abuse, or to their meanest use.
Beneath him with new wonder now he views
To all delight of human sense exposed
In narrow room Nature's whole wealth, yea more,
A Heav'n on earth, for blissful paradise
Of God the garden was, by him in th' east
Of Eden planted; Eden stretched her line   210
From Auran eastward to the royal tow'rs
Of great Seleucia, built by Grecian kings,

---

186. *hurdled cotes:* wattled sheep-pens. *secure:* (foolishly) free
from care; it modifies *shepherds.*

194. *Tree of Life:* Genesis 2:9.

196. *cormorant:* a voracious sea-bird; figuratively, an insatiably
greedy person.

211–212. *From Auran . . . to . . . Seleucia:* If by Auran the
Syrian district called Hauran in Ezekiel 47:18 is meant, the area
referred to lies roughly between modern Damascus and modern
Baghdad. If the city Haran is meant, the area lies between the
upper reaches of the Euphrates and modern Baghdad.

Or where the sons of Eden long before
Dwelt in Telassar: in this pleasant soil
His far more pleasant garden God ordained;
Out of the fertile ground he caused to grow
All trees of noblest kind for sight, smell, taste;
And all amid them stood the Tree of Life,
High eminent, blooming ambrosial fruit
Of vegetable gold; and next to Life   220
Our death the Tree of Knowledge grew fast by,
Knowledge of good bought dear by knowing ill.
Southward through Eden went a river large,
Nor changed his course, but through the shaggy hill
Passed underneath ingulfed, for God had thrown
That mountain as his garden mold high raised
Upon the rapid current, which through veins
Of porous earth with kindly thirst updrawn,
Rose a fresh fountain, and with many a rill
Watered the garden; thence united fell   230
Down the steep glade, and met the nether flood,
Which from his darksome passage now appears,
And now divided into four main streams,
Runs diverse, wandering many a famous realm
And country whereof here needs no account,
But rather to tell how, if art could tell,
How from that sapphire fount the crispéd brooks,
Rolling on orient pearl and sands of gold,
With mazy error under pendant shades
Ran nectar, visiting each plant, and fed   240
Flow'rs worthy of Paradise which not nice art
In beds and curious knots, but Nature boon
Poured forth profuse on hill and dale and plain,
Both where the morning sun first warmly smote
The open field, and where th' unpierced shade

213–214. Since he is not sure where Eden was, M. provides an
even vaguer alternative. The "children of Eden which were in
Telassar" are mentioned in Isaiah 37:12.

228. *kindly:* natural.

239. *error:* wandering.

Imbrowned the noontide bow'rs: Thus was this place,
A happy rural seat of various view;
Groves whose rich trees wept odorous gums and balm,
Others whose fruit burnished with golden rind
Hung amiable, Hesperian fables true,   250
I^f true, here only, and of delicious taste.
Betwixt them lawns, or level downs, and flocks
Grazing the tender herb, were interposed,
Or palmy hillock, or the flow'ry lap
Of some irriguous valley spread her store,
Flow'rs of all hue, and without thorn the rose.
Another side, umbrageous grots and caves
Of cool recess, o'er which the mantling vine
Lays forth her purple grape, and gently creeps
Luxuriant; meanwhile murmuring waters fall   260
Down the slope hills, dispersed, or in a lake,
That to the fringéd bank with myrtle crowned,
Her crystal mirror holds, unite their streams.
The birds their choir apply; airs, vernal airs,
Breathing the smell of field and grove, attune
The trembling leaves, while universal Pan
Knit with the Graces and the Hours in dance
Led on th' eternal spring. Not that fair field
Of Enna, where Proserpin gathering flow'rs
Herself a fairer flow'r by gloomy Dis   270
Was gathered, which cost Ceres all that pain
To seek her through the world; nor that sweet grove
Of Daphne by Orontes, and th' inspired
Castalian spring, might with this paradise
Of Eden strive; nor that Nyseian isle

---

246. *imbrowned:* darkened.
250. *amiable:* lovely.
258. *mantling:* covering as with a mantle.
266. *Pan:* here, the god of all nature.
267. *Graces:* the sisters Euphrosyne, Aglaia, and Thalia, personifications of grace and beauty. *Hours:* goddesses of the seasons.
268–272. The story is told by Ovid, *Metamorphoses*, V, 385–571.
275–284. These gardens are described by Diodorus Siculus, *Library*, III, 68–69, and Peter Heylin, *Cosmographie*, IV, lxiv.

Girt with the river Triton, where old Cham,
Whom Gentiles Ammon call and Lybian Jove,
Hid Amalthea and her florid son
Young Bacchus from his stepdame Rhea's eye;
Nor where Abassin kings their issue guard, 280
Mount Amara, though this by some supposed
True Paradise under the Ethiop line
By Nilus head, enclosed with shining rock,
A whole day's journey high, but wide remote
From this Assyrian garden where the Fiend
Saw undelighted all delight, all kind
Of living creatures new to sight and strange:
Two of far nobler shape erect and tall,
Godlike erect, with native honor clad
In naked majesty seemed lords of all, 290
And worthy seemed, for in their looks divine
The image of their glorious Maker shone,
Truth, wisdom, sanctitude severe and pure,
Severe, but in true filial freedom placed;
Whence true authority in men; though both
Not equal, as their sex not equal seemed;
For contemplation he and valor formed,
For softness she and sweet attractive grace,
He for God only, she for God in him:
His fair large front and eye sublime declared 300
Absolute rule; and hyacinthine locks
Round from his parted forelock manly hung
Clustering, but not beneath his shoulders broad.
She as a veil down to the slender waist
Her unadornéd golden tresses wore
Disheveled, but in wanton ringlets waved
As the vine curls her tendrils, which implied
Subjection, but required with gentle sway,
And by her yielded, by him best received,
Yielded with coy submission, modest pride, 310

---

288. *erect:* Cf. I, 679*n.*
301. *hyacinthine:* like the hyacinth in some respect; a Homeric
epithet (*Odyssey*, VI, 231).
310. *coy:* modest, shy.

And sweet reluctant amorous delay.
Nor those mysterious parts were then concealed,
Then was not guilty shame, dishonest shame
Of nature's works, honor dishonorable,
Sin-bred, how have ye troubled all mankind
With shows instead, mere shows of seeming pure,
And banished from man's life his happiest life,
Simplicity and spotless innocence.
So passed they naked on, nor shunned the sight
Of God or angel, for they thought no ill: 320
So hand in hand they passed, the loveliest pair
That ever since in love's embraces met,
Adam the goodliest man of men since born
His sons, the fairest of her daughters Eve.
Under a tuft of shade that on a green
Stood whispering soft, by a fresh fountain side
They sat them down, and after no more toil
Of their sweet gard'ning labor than sufficed
To recommend cool Zephyr, and made ease
More easy, wholesome thirst and appetite   330
More grateful, to their supper fruits they fell,
Nectarine fruits which the compliant boughs
Yielded them, sidelong as they sat recline
On the soft downy bank damasked with flow'rs.
The savory pulp they chew, and in the rind
Still as they thirsted scoop the brimming stream;
Nor gentle purpose, nor endearing smiles
Wanted, nor youthful dalliance as beseems
Fair couple, linked in happy nuptial league,
Alone as they. About them frisking played   340

---

313. *dishonest:* unchaste.

324–325. This idiom is found both in Elizabethan English and
in Greek. It telescopes the comparative ("Eve was fairer than all
her daughters") and the superlative ("Eve was the fairest of all
women").

329. *recommend:* make pleasant. *Zephyr:* the west wind.

333. *recline:* reclining.

337. *purpose:* conversation.

338. *wanted:* were lacking.

All beasts of th' earth, since wild, and of all chase
In wood or wilderness, forest or den;
Sporting the lion ramped, and in his paw
Dandled the kid; bears, tigers, ounces, pards,
Gamboled before them, th' unwieldy elephant
To make them mirth used all his might, and wreathed
His lithe proboscis; close the serpent sly
Insinuating, wove with Gordian twine
His braided train, and of his fatal guile
Gave proof unheeded; others on the grass   350
Couched, and now filled with pasture gazing sat,
Or bedward ruminating: for the sun
Declined was hasting now with prone career
To th' ocean isles, and in th' ascending scale
Of heav'n the stars that usher evening rose.
When Satan still in gaze, as first he stood,
Scarce thus at length failed speech recovered sad.
    "O Hell! What do mine eyes with grief behold,
Into our room of bliss thus high advanced
Creatures of other mold, earth-born perhaps,   360
Not spirits, yet to heav'nly spirits bright
Little inferior; whom my thoughts pursue
With wonder, and could love, so lively shines
In them divine resemblance, and such grace
The hand that formed them on their shape hath poured.
Ah gentle pair, ye little think how nigh
Your change approaches, when all these delights
Will vanish and deliver ye to woe,
More woe, the more your taste is now of joy;
Happy, but for so happy ill secured   370
Long to continue, and this high seat your heav'n
Ill fenced to Heav'n to keep out such a foe
As now is entered; yet no purposed foe

---

344. *ounces:* lynxes.
348. *insinuating:* coiling.
352. *ruminating:* chewing the cud.
361–362. Cf. Psalm 8:5, "For thou has made [man] a little lower
than the angels."
370. *for so happy:* considering how happy you are.

To you whom I could pity thus forlorn
Though I unpitied: league with you I seek,
And mutual amity so strait, so close,
That I with you must dwell, or you with me
Henceforth; my dwelling haply may not please
Like this fair Paradise, your sense, yet such
Accept your Maker's work; he gave it me,   380
Which I as freely give; Hell shall unfold,
To entertain you two, her widest gates,
And send forth all her kings; there will be room,
Not like these narrow limits, to receive
Your numerous offspring; if no better place,
Thank him who puts me loath to this revenge
On you who wrong me not for him who wronged.
And should I at your harmless innocence
Melt, as I do, yet public reason just,
Honor and empire with revenge enlarged,   390
By conquering this new world, compels me now
To do what else though damned I should abhor."
    So spake the Fiend, and with necessity,
The tyrant's plea, excused his devilish deeds.
Then from his lofty stand on that high tree
Down he alights among the sportful herd
Of those fourfooted kinds, himself now one,
Now other, as their shape served best his end
Nearer to view his prey, and unespied
To mark what of their state he more might learn   400
By word or action marked: about them round
A lion now he stalks with fiery glare,
Then as a tiger, who by chance hath spied
In some purlieu two gentle fawns at play,
Straight couches close, then rising changes oft
His couchant watch, as one who chose his ground
Whence rushing he might surest seize them both
Gripped in each paw: when Adam first of men
To first of women Eve thus moving speech,

---

398. *end:* purpose.
404. *purlieu:* the outskirts of a forest.

Turned him all ear to hear new utterance flow.   410
   "Sole partner and sole part of all these joys,
Dearer thyself than all; needs must the power
That made us, and for us this ample world
Be infinitely good, and of his good
As liberal and free as infinite,
That raised us from the dust and placed us here
In all this happiness, who at his hand
Have nothing merited, nor can perform
Aught whereof he hath need, he who requires
From us no other service than to keep   420
This one, this easy charge, of all the trees
In Paradise that bear delicious fruit
So various, not to taste that only Tree
Of Knowledge, planted by the Tree of Life,
So near grows death to life, whate'er death is,
Some dreadful thing no doubt; for well thou know'st
God hath pronounced it death to taste that tree,
The only sign of our obedience left
Among so many signs of power and rule
Conferred upon us, and dominion giv'n   430
Over all other creatures that possess
Earth, air, and sea. Then let us not think hard
One easy prohibition, who enjoy
Free leave so large to all things else, and choice
Unlimited of manifold delights:
But let us ever praise him, and extol
His bounty, following our delightful task
To prune these growing plants, and tend these flow'rs,
Which were it toilsome, yet with thee were sweet."
   To whom thus Eve replied. "O thou for whom   440
And from whom I was formed flesh of thy flesh,
And without whom am to no end, my guide
And head, what thou hast said is just and right.
For we to him indeed all praises owe,
And daily thanks, I chiefly who enjoy
So far the happier lot, enjoying thee
Preeminent by so much odds, while thou
Like consort to thyself canst nowhere find.

That day I oft remember, when from sleep
I first awaked, and found myself reposéd   4⬤
Under a shade on flow'rs, much wondering where
And what I was, whence thither brought, and how.
Not distant far from thence a murmuring sound
Of waters issued from a cave and spread
Into a liquid plain, then stood unmoved
Pure as th' expanse of heav'n; I thither went
With unexperienced thought, and laid me down
On the green bank, to look into the clear
Smooth lake, that to me seemed another sky.
As I bent down to look, just opposite,   46
A shape within the wat'ry gleam appeared
Bending to look on me, I started back,
It started back, but pleased I soon returned,
Pleased it returned as soon with answering looks
Of sympathy and love; there I had fixed
Mine eyes till now, and pined with vain desire,
Had not a voice thus warned me, 'What thou seest,
What there thou seest fair creature is thyself,
With thee it came and goes: but follow me,
And I will bring thee where no shadow stays   47
Thy coming, and thy soft embraces, he
Whose image thou art, him thou shall enjoy
Inseparably thine, to him shalt bear
Multitudes like thyself, and thence be called
Mother of human race.' What could I do,
But follow straight, invisibly thus led?
Till I espied thee, fair indeed and tall,
Under a platan, yet methought less fair,
Less winning soft, less amiably mild,
Than that smooth wat'ry image; back I turned,   48
Thou following cried'st aloud, 'Return fair Eve;
Whom fli'st thou? Whom thou fli'st, of him thou art,
His flesh, his bone; to give thee being I lent
Out of my side to thee, nearest my heart

---

470. *stays:* awaits.
478. *platan:* plane tree.

Substantial life, to have thee by my side
Henceforth an individual solace dear;
Part of my soul I seek thee, and thee claim
My other half.' With that thy gentle hand
Seized mine, I yielded, and from that time see
How beauty is excelled by manly grace　　　　　　490
And wisdom, which alone is truly fair."

So spake our general mother, and with eyes
Of conjugal attraction unreproved,
And meek surrender, half embracing leaned
On our first father, half her swelling breast
Naked met his under the flowing gold
Of her loose tresses hid: he in delight
Both of her beauty and submissive charms
Smiled with superior love, as Jupiter
On Juno smiles, when he impregns the clouds ·　　500
That shed May flow'rs; and pressed her matron lip
With kisses pure: aside the Devil turned
For envy, yet with jealous leer malign
Eyed them askance, and to himself thus plained.

"Sight hateful, sight tormenting! thus these two
Imparadised in one another's arms
The happier Eden, shall enjoy their fill
Of bliss on bliss, while I to Hell am thrust,
Where neither joy nor love, but fierce desire,
Among our other torments not the least,　　　　　510
Still unfulfilled with pain of longing pines;
Yet let me not forget what I have gained
From their own mouths; all is not theirs it seems:
One fatal tree there stands of knowledge called,
Forbidden them to taste: Knowledge forbidd'n?

---

　486. *individual:* not to be divided.
　493. *unreproved:* unprovable, blameless.
　500. *impregns:* impregnates.
　511. *pines:* makes me pine.
　515. In III, 95, God speaks of the prohibition as "sole pledge of [man's] obedience." It is only Satan (and later, of course, Eve) who thinks, or pretends to think, that the fruit has the magical power of giving knowledge.

Suspicious, reasonless. Why should their Lord
Envy them that? Can it be sin to know,
Can it be death? And do they only stand
By ignorance, is that their happy state,
The proof of their obedience and their faith?   520
O fair foundation laid whereon to build
Their ruin! Hence I will excite their minds
With more desire to know, and to reject
Envious commands, invented with design
To keep them low whom knowledge might exalt
Equal with gods; aspiring to be such,
They taste and die: what likelier can ensue?
But first with narrow search I must walk round
This garden, and no corner leave unspied;
A chance but chance may lead where I may meet   530
Some wandering spirit of Heav'n, by fountain side,
Or in thick shade retired, from him to draw
What further would be learnt. Live while ye may,
Yet happy pair; enjoy, till I return,
Short pleasures, for long woes are to succeed."
    So saying, his proud step he scornful turned,
But with sly circumspection, and began
Through wood, through waste, o'er hill, o'er dale his
        roam.
Meanwhile in utmost longitude, where heav'n
With earth and ocean meets, the setting sun   540
Slowly descended, and with right aspect
Against the eastern gate of Paradise
Leveled his evening rays: it was a rock
Of alablaster, piled up to the clouds,
Conspicuous far, winding with one ascent
Accessible from earth, one entrance high;
The rest was craggy cliff, that overhung
Still as it rose, impossible to climb.

_____

    530. *a chance but chance:* there is just a possibility that chance.
    539. *in utmost longitude:* in the farthest west.
    541-542. The sun shines directly (*with right aspect*) on the in-
ner side of the eastern gate of Paradise.

Betwixt these rocky pillars Gabriel sat
Chief of th' angelic guards, awaiting night;   550
About him exercised heroic games
Th' unarméd youth of Heav'n, but nigh at hand
Celestial armory, shields, helms, and spears,
Hung high with diamond flaming, and with gold.
Thither came Uriel, gliding through the ev'n
On a sunbeam, swift as a shooting star
In autumn thwarts the night, when vapors fired
Impress the air, and shows the mariner
From what point of his compass to beware
Impetuous winds: he thus began in haste.   560
   "Gabriel, to thee thy course by lot hath giv'n
Charge and strict watch that to this happy place
No evil thing approach or enter in;
This day at highth of noon came to my sphere
A spirit, zealous, as he seemed, to know
More of th' Almighty's works, and chiefly man
God's latest image: I described his way
Bent all on speed, and marked his aery gait;
But in the mount that lies from Eden north,
Where he first lighted, soon discerned his looks   570
Alien from Heav'n, with passions foul obscured:
Mine eye pursued him still, but under shade
Lost sight of him; one of the banished crew
I fear, hath ventured from the deep, to raise
New troubles; him thy care must be to find."
   To whom the wingéd warrior thus returned:
"Uriel, no wonder if thy perfect sight,
Amid the sun's bright circle where thou sit'st,
See far and wide: in at this gate none pass
The vigilance here placed, but such as come   580
Well known from Heav'n; and since meridian hour
No creature thence: if spirit of other sort,
So minded, have o'erleaped these earthy bounds

---

557. *thwarts:* crosses, shoots across.
567. *latest image:* man (the first being Christ).
568. *aery gait:* course through the air.

On purpose, hard thou know'st it to exclude
Spiritual substance with corporeal bar.
But if within the circuit of these walks,
In whatsoever shape he lurk, of whom
Thou tell'st, by morrow dawning I shall know."
  So promised he, and Uriel to his charge
Returned on that bright beam, whose point now
    raised   590
Bore him slope downward to the sun now fall'n
Beneath th' Azores; whether the prime orb,
Incredible how swift, had thither rolled
Diurnal, or this less volúble earth
By shorter flight to th' east, had left him there
Arraying with reflected purple and gold
The clouds that on his western throne attend.
Now came still evening on, and twilight gray·
Had in her sober livery all things clad;
Silence accompanied, for beast and bird,   600
They to their grassy couch, these to their nests
Were slunk, all but the wakeful nightingale;
She all night long her amorous descant sung;
Silence was pleased: now glowed the firmament
With living sapphires: Hesperus that led
The starry host, rode brightest, till the moon
Rising in clouded majesty, at length
Apparent queen unveiled her peerless light,
And o'er the dark her silver mantle threw.
    When Adam thus to Eve: "Fair consort, th' hour   610
Of night, and all things now retired to rest
Mind us of like repose, since God hath set
Labor and rest, as day and night to men
Successive, and the timely dew of sleep

592–597. M. does not commit himself to either the Ptolemaic
or the Copernican system.
   594. *volúble:* turning.
   603. *descant:* a song with variations.
   605. *Hesperus:* the evening star.
   608. *apparent:* visible, manifest.

Now falling with soft slumbrous weight inclines
Our eyelids; other creatures all day long
Rove idle unemployed, and less need rest;
Man hath his daily work of body or mind
Appointed, which declares his dignity,
And the regard of Heav'n on all his ways;   620
While other animals unactive range,
And of their doings God takes no account.
Tomorrow ere fresh morning streak the east
With first approach of light, we must be ris'n,
And at our pleasant labor, to reform
Yon flow'ry arbors, yonder alleys green,
Our walk at noon, with branches overgrown,
That mock our scant manuring, and require
More hands than ours to lop their wanton growth:
Those blossoms also, and those dropping gums,   630
That lie bestrown unsightly and unsmooth,
Ask riddance, if we mean to tread with ease;
Meanwhile, as nature wills, night bids us rest."
    To whom thus Eve with perfect beauty adorned.
"My author and disposer, what thou bid'st
Unargued I obey; so God ordains,
God is thy law, thou mine: to know no more
Is woman's happiest knowledge and her praise.
With thee conversing I forget all time,
All seasons and their change, all please alike.   640
Sweet is the breath of morn, her rising sweet,
With charm of earliest birds; pleasant the sun
When first on this delightful land he spreads
His orient beams, on herb, tree, fruit, and flow'r,
Glistering with dew; fragrant the fertile earth
After soft show'rs; and sweet the coming on
Of grateful evening mild, then silent night

---

628. *manuring:* cultivating (literally, working with the hands).
632. *ask:* require.
640. *seasons:* times of the day.
642. *charm:* song.

With this her solemn bird and this fair moon,
And these the gems of heav'n, her starry train:
But neither breath of morn when she ascends   650
With charm of earliest birds, nor rising sun
On this delightful land, nor herb, fruit, flow'r,
Glistering with dew, nor fragrance after show'rs,
Nor grateful evening mild, nor silent night
With this her solemn bird, nor walk by moon,
Or glittering starlight without thee is sweet.
But wherefore all night long shine these, for whom
This glorious sight, when sleep hath shut all eyes?"
    To whom our general ancestor replied.
"Daughter of God and man, accomplished Eve,   660
Those have their course to finish, round the earth,
By morrow evening, and from land to land
In order, though to nations yet unborn,
Ministering light prepared, they set and rise;
Lest total darkness should by night regain
Her old possession, and extinguish life
In nature and all things, which these soft fires
Not only enlighten, but with kindly heat
Of various influence foment and warm,
Temper or nourish, or in part shed down   670
Their stellar virtue on all kinds that grow
On earth, made hereby apter to receive
Perfection from the sun's more potent ray.
These then, though unbeheld in deep of night,
Shine not in vain, nor think, though men were none,
That heav'n would want spectators, God want praise;
Millions of spiritual creatures walk the earth
Unseen, both when we wake, and when we sleep:
All these with ceaseless praise his works behold
Both day and night: how often from the steep   680
Of echoing hill or thicket have we heard
Celestial voices to the midnight air,
Sole, or responsive each to other's note

---

668. *kindly:* natural.

Singing their great Creator: oft in bands
While they keep watch, or nightly rounding walk
With heav'nly touch of instrumental sounds
In full harmonic number joined, their songs
Divide the night, and lift our thoughts to Heav'n."
    Thus talking hand in hand alone they passed
On to their blissful bow'r; it was a place   690
Chos'n by the sovran Planter, when he framed
All things to man's delightful use; the roof
Of thickest covert was inwoven shade
Laurel and myrtle, and what higher grew
Of firm and fragrant leaf; on either side
Acanthus, and each odorous bushy shrub
Fenced up the verdant wall; each beauteous flow'r,
Iris all hues, roses, and jessamine
Reared high their flourished heads between, and
      wrought
Mosaic; underfoot the violet,   700
Crocus, and hyacinth with rich inlay
Broidered the ground, more colored than with stone
Of costliest emblem: other creature here
Beast, bird, insect, or worm durst enter none;
Such was their awe of man. In shadier bow'r
More sacred and sequestered, though but feigned,
Pan or Silvanus never slept, nor nymph,
Nor Faunus haunted. Here in close recess
With flowers, garlands, and sweet-smelling herbs
Espoused Eve decked first her nuptial bed,   710
And heav'nly choirs the hymenean sung,
What day the genial angel to our sire
Brought her in naked beauty more adorned,

---

688. *divide the night:* i.e., into watches, marked by trumpet
calls in the Roman army.
699. *flourished:* laden with flowers.
703. *emblem:* inlay.
711. *hymenean:* marriage song.
712. *genial:* nuptial.

More lovely than Pandora, whom the gods
Endowed with all their gifts, and O too like
In sad event, when to th' unwiser son
Of Japhet brought by Hermes, she ensnared
Mankind with her fair looks, to be avenged
On him who had stole Jove's authentic fire.
   Thus at their shady lodge arrived, both stood,   720
Both turned, and under open sky adored
The God that made both sky, air, earth and heav'n
Which they beheld, the moon's resplendent globe
And starry pole: "Thou also mad'st the night,
Maker omnipotent, and thou the day,
Which we in our appointed work employed
Have finished happy in our mutual help
And mutual love, the crown of all our bliss
Ordained by thee, and this delicious place
For us too large, where thy abundance wants   730
Partakers, and uncropped falls to the ground.
But thou hast promised from us two a race
To fill the earth, who shall with us extol
Thy goodness infinite, both when we wake,
And when we seek, as now, thy gift of sleep."
   This said unanimous, and other rites
Observing none, but adoration pure
Which God likes best, into their inmost bow'r
Handed they went; and eased the putting off
These troublesome disguises which we wear,   740
Straight side by side were laid, nor turned I ween

714–719. In order to revenge himself on Prometheus ("fore-thought") for stealing his fire, Jove fashioned a woman endowed with all gifts (*Pandora*) and gave her a box which she was to present to the man she married. *Hermes* conducted her to Prometheus, who was too crafty to accept her. His unwiser brother Epimetheus ("afterthought") married her and opened the box, out of which flew all the evils that afflict mankind. The brothers were the sons of the Titan Iapetos, sometimes identified with Noah's son Japhet.

724–725. Cf. Psalm 74:16, "The day is thine, the night also is thine: thou hast prepared the light and the sun."

Adam from his fair spouse, nor Eve the rites
Mysterious of connubial love refused:
Whatever hypocrites austerely talk
Of purity and place and innocence,
Defaming as impure what God declares
Pure, and commands to some, leaves free to all.
Our Maker bids increase, who bids abstain
But our destroyer, foe to God and man?
Hail wedded love, mysterious law, true source   750
Of human offspring, sole propriety,
In Paradise of all things common else.
By thee adulterous lust was driv'n from men
Among the bestial herds to range, by thee
Founded in reason, loyal, just, and pure,
Relations dear, and all the charities
Of father, son, and brother first were known.
Far be it, that I should write thee sin or blame,
Or think thee unbefitting holiest place,
Perpetual fountain of domestic sweets,   760
Whose bed is undefiled and chaste pronounced,
Present, or past, as saints and patriarchs used.
Here Love his golden shafts employs, here lights
His constant lamp, and waves his purple wings,
Reigns here and revels; not in the bought smile
Of harlots, loveless, joyless, unendeared,
Casual fruition, nor in court amours
Mixed dance, or wanton mask, or midnight ball,

743, 750. *mysterious:* Cf. Ephesians 5:32, "This is a great mystery."

747. Cf. Hebrews 13:4, "Marriage is honorable in all."

748. Cf. Genesis 1:28, "Be fruitful, and multiply, and replenish the earth."

751. *sole propriety:* the only exclusive possession.

756. *charities:* feelings of love and affection.

763. Some of Cupid's arrows were tipped with gold to inspire love, some with lead to repel it.

764. *constant:* as opposed to the "casual fruition" of line 767.

768. *mask:* an elaborate form of court entertainment that flourished in the reign of Charles I.

Or serenate, which the starved lover sings
To his proud fair, best quitted with disdain.   770
These lulled by nightingales embracing slept,
And on their naked limbs the flow'ry roof
Show'red roses, which the morn repaired. Sleep on
Blest pair; and O yet happiest if ye seek
No happier state, and know to know no more.
   Now had night measured with her shadowy cone
Half way uphill this vast sublunar vault,
And from their ivory port the Cherubim
Forth issuing at th' accustomed hour stood armed
To their night watches in warlike parade,   780
When Gabriel to his next in power thus spake.
   "Uzziel, half these draw off, and coast the south
With strictest watch; these other wheel the north,
Our circuit meets full west." As flame they part
Half wheeling to the shield, half to the spear.
From these, two strong and subtle spirits he called
That near him stood, and gave them thus in charge.
   "Ithuriel and Zephon, with winged speed
Search through this garden, leave unsearched no nook,
But chiefly where those two fair creatures lodge,   790
Now laid perhaps asleep secure of harm.
This evening from the sun's decline arrived
Who tells of some infernal spirit seen
Hitherward bent (who could have thought?) escaped

769–770. M.'s contemptuous dismissal of the Petrarchan tradition with its fair, disdainful mistresses and dying (*starved*) lovers.
   773. *repaired:* replenished (with fresh roses).
   776. The *cone* of the shadow cast by the earth is half way to
the zenith; i.e., it is 9 P.M. and time for the second angelic watch,
who issue from their ivory gate (*port*).
   782. The name *Uzziel* means "strength of God."
   785. i.e., to the left (*shield*) and right (*spear*).
   788. The names *Ithuriel* and *Zephon* mean "discovery of God"
and "searcher" respectively.
   791. *secure of:* not fearing.
   793. *who:* one who (i.e., Uriel).

The bars of Hell, on errand bad no doubt:
Such where ye find, seize fast, and hither bring."
    So saying, on he led his radiant files,
Dazzling the moon; these to the bow'r direct
In search of whom they sought: him there they found
Squat like a toad, close at the ear of Eve;   800
Assaying by his devilish art to reach
The organs of her fancy, and with them forge
Illusions as he list, phantasms and dreams,
Or if, inspiring venom, he might taint
Th' animal spirits that from pure blood arise
Like gentle breaths from rivers pure, thence raise
At least distempered, discontented thoughts,
Vain hopes, vain aims, inordinate desires
Blown up with high conceits engendering pride.
Him thus intent Ithuriel with his spear   810
Touched lightly; for no falsehood can endure
Touch of celestial temper, but returns
Of force to its own likeness: up he starts
Discovered and surprised. As when a spark
Lights on a heap of nitrous powder, laid
Fit for the tun some magazine to store
Against a rumored war, the smutty grain
With sudden blaze diffused, inflames the air:
So started up in his own shape the Fiend.
Back stepped those two fair angels half amazed   820
So sudden to behold the grisly king;
Yet thus, unmoved with fear, accost him soon.
    "Which of those rebel spirits adjudged to Hell
Com'st thou, escaped thy prison, and transformed,
Why sat'st thou like an enemy in wait

---

805. *animal spirits:* rarefied substances in the body that enabled
the sensible soul to carry out its functions of motion and apprehension.
812. *celestial temper:* weapon tempered in Heaven.
815. *nitrous powder:* gunpowder.
816. *tun:* barrel.
817. *against:* in anticipation of.

Here watching at the head of these that sleep?"
    "Know ye not then," said Satan, filled with scorn,
"Know ye not me? Ye knew me once no mate
For you, there sitting where ye durst not soar;
Not to know me argues yourselves unknown,   830
The lowest of your throng; or if ye know,
Why ask ye, and superfluous begin
Your message, like to end as much in vain?"
To whom thus Zephon, answering scorn with scorn.
"Think not, revolted spirit, thy shape the same,
Or undiminished brightness, to be known
As when thou stood'st in Heav'n upright and pure;
That glory then, when thou no more wast good,
Departed from thee, and thou resemblest now
Thy sin and place of doom obscure and foul.   840
But come, for thou, be sure, shalt give account
To him who sent us, whose charge is to keep
This place inviolable, and these from harm."
    So spake the Cherub, and his grave rebuke
Severe in youthful beauty, added grace
Invincible: abashed the Devil stood,
And felt how awful goodness is, and saw
Virtue in her shape how lovely, saw, and pined
His loss; but chiefly to find here observed
His luster visibly impaired; yet seemed   850
Undaunted. "If I must contend," said he,
"Best with the best, the Sender not the sent,
Or all at once; more glory will be won,
Or less be lost." "Thy fear," said Zephon bold,
"Will save us trial what the least can do
Single against thee wicked, and thence weak."
    The Fiend replied not, overcome with rage;
But like a proud steed reined, went haughty on,
Champing his iron curb: to strive or fly
He held it vain; awe from above had quelled   860
His heart, not else dismayed. Now drew they nigh

_____

    830. *argues:* proves.
    840. *obscure:* dark, gloomy.

The western point, where those half-rounding guards
Just met, and closing stood in squadron joined
Awaiting next command. To whom their chief
Gabriel from the front thus called aloud.
    "O friends, I hear the tread of nimble feet
Hasting this way, and now by glimpse discern
Ithuriel and Zephon through the shade,
And with them comes a third of regal port,
But faded splendor wan; who by his gait   870
And fierce demeanor seems the Prince of Hell,
Not likely to part hence without contest;
Stand firm, for in his look defiance lours."
    He scarce had ended, when those two approached
And brief related whom they brought, where found,
How busied, in what form and posture couched.
    To whom with stern regard thus Gabriel spake.
"Why hast thou, Satan, broke the bounds prescribed
To thy transgressions, and disturbed the charge
Of others, who approve not to trangress   880
By thy example, but have power and right
To question thy bold entrance on this place;
Employed it seems to violate sleep, and those
Whose dwelling God hath planted here in bliss?"
    To whom thus Satan, with contemptuous brow.
"Gabriel, thou hadst in Heav'n th' esteem of wise,
And such I held thee; but this question asked
Puts me in doubt. Lives there who loves his pain?
Who would not, finding way, break loose from Hell,
Though thither doomed? Thou wouldst thyself, no
        doubt,   890
And boldly venture to whatever place
Farthest from pain, where thou mightst hope to change
Torment with ease, and soonest recompense
Dole with delight, which in this place I sought;

862–83. The *guards* who wheeled to the left and to the right
in lines 782–784 are now meeting "full west."
    879. *charge:* i.e., Adam and Eve, whom Gabriel and his fol-
lowers are charged with protecting.
    894. *dole:* pain.

To thee no reason; who know'st only good,
But evil hast not tried: and wilt object
His will who bound us? Let him surer bar
His iron gates, if he intends our stay
In that dark durance: thus much what was asked.
The rest is true, they found me where they say;   900
But that implies not violence or harm."
    Thus he in scorn. The warlike angel moved,
Disdainfully half smiling thus replied.
"O loss of one in Heav'n to judge of wise,
Since Satan fell, whom folly overthrew,
And now returns him from his prison scaped,
Gravely in doubt whether to hold them wise
Or not, who ask what boldness brought him hither
Unlicensed from his bounds in Hell prescribed;
So wise he judges it to fly from pain   910
However, and to scape his punishment.
So judge thou still, presumptuous, till the wrath,
Which thou incurr'st by flying, meet thy flight
Sev'nfold, and scourge that wisdom back to Hell,
Which taught thee yet no better, that no pain
Can equal anger infinite provoked.
But wherefore thou alone? Wherefore with thee
Came not all Hell broke loose? Is pain to them
Less pain, less to be fled, or thou than they
Less hardy to endure? Courageous chief,   920
The first in flight from pain, hadst thou alleged
To thy deserted host this cause of flight,
Thou surely hadst not come sole fugitive."
    To which the Fiend thus answered frowning
        stern.
"Not that I less endure, or shrink from pain,
Insulting angel, well thou know'st I stood
Thy fiercest, when in battle to thy aid
The blasting volleyed thunder made all speed
And seconded thy else not dreaded spear.

---

899. *durance*: prison, imprisonment.
911. *however*: howsoever.

But still thy words at random, as before,   930
Argue thy inexperience what behooves
From hard assays and ill successes past
A faithful leader, not to hazard all
Through ways of danger by himself untried.
I therefore, I alone first undertook
To wing the desolate abyss, and spy
This new created world, whereof in Hell
Fame is not silent, here in hope to find
Better abode, and my afflicted powers
To settle here on earth, or in mid air;   940
Though for possession put to try once more
What thou and thy gay legions dare against;
Whose easier business were to serve their Lord
High up in Heav'n, with songs to hymn his throne,
And practised distances to cringe, not fight."
    To whom the warrior angel soon replied.
"To say and straight unsay, pretending first
Wise to fly pain, professing next the spy,
Argues no leader but a liar traced,
Satan, and couldst thou faithful add? O name,   950
O sacred name of faithfulness profaned!
Faithful to whom? to thy rebellious crew?
Army of fiends, fit body to fit head;
Was this your discipline and faith engaged,
Your military obedience, to dissolve
Allegiance to th' acknowledged Power supreme?
And thou sly hypocrite, who now wouldst seem
Patron of liberty, who more than thou
Once fawned, and cringed, and servilely adored
Heav'n's awful Monarch? Wherefore but in
    hope   960
To dispossess him, and thyself to reign?

931–934. Satan taunts Gabriel with not knowing, because of his lack of experience, that after defeat a faithful leader knows better than to lead all his troops into an unknown danger.

941–942. "Although in order to gain possession (of earth) I am forced to make trial of the power you and your gay legions dare to use against me."

But mark what I arede thee now, avaunt;
Fly thither whence thou fled'st: if from this hour
Within these hallowed limits thou appear,
Back to th' infernal pit I drag thee chained,
And seal thee so, as henceforth not to scorn
The facile gates of Hell too slightly barred."
   So threatened he, but Satan to no threats
Gave heed, but waxing more in rage replied.
   "Then when I am thy captive talk of chains,   97
Proud limitary Cherub, but ere then
Far heavier load thyself expect to feel
From my prevailing arm, though Heaven's King
Ride on thy wings, and thou with thy compeers,
Used to the yoke, draw'st his triumphant wheels
In progress through the road of Heav'n star-paved."
   While thus he spake, th' angelic squadron bright
Turned fiery red, sharp'ning in mooned horns
Their phalanx, and began to hem him round
With ported spears, as thick as when a field   98
Of Ceres ripe for harvest waving bends
Her bearded grove of ears, which way the wind
Sways them; the careful plowman doubting stands
Lest on the threshing floor his hopeful sheaves
Prove chaff. On th' other side Satan alarmed
Collecting all his might dilated stood,
Like Tenerife or Atlas unremoved:
His stature reached the sky, and on his crest

---

962. *arede:* advise.

971. *limitary:* a scournful reference both to Gabriel's office o
protecting "these hallowed limits" (line 964) and to his threat o
placing limits on Satan by dragging him back to Hell.

973–974. Cf. the description of the chariot of God in VI, 770
771.

978–979. *sharp'ning . . ./ Their phalanx:* forming their phalan
in the shape of a crescent moon.

980. *ported:* held at "port arms"; i.e., slanted across the breas
ready for the attack.

981. *Ceres:* goddess of agriculture; used here for the grain itsel

983. *careful:* anxious, full of care.

987. i.e., as unmovable as mountain peaks.

Sat horror plumed; nor wanted in his grasp
What seemed both spear and shield: now dreadful
    deeds   990
Might have ensued, nor only Paradise
In this commotion, but the starry cope
Of heav'n perhaps, or all the elements
At least had gone to rack, disturbed and torn
With violence of this conflict, had not soon
Th' Eternal to prevent such horrid fray
Hung forth in heav'n his golden scales, yet seen
Betwixt Astraea and the Scorpion sign,
Wherein all things created first he weighed,
The pendulous round earth with balanced air   1000
In counterpoise, now ponders all events,
Battles and realms: in these he put two weights
The sequel each of parting and of fight;
The latter quick up flew, and kicked the beam;
Which Gabriel spying, thus bespake the Fiend.

   "Satan, I know thy strength, and thou know'st mine,
Neither our own but giv'n; what folly then
To boast what arms can do, since thine no more
Than Heav'n permits, nor mine, though doubled now
To trample thee as mire: for proof look up,   1010
And read thy lot in yon celestial sign
Where thou art weighed, and shown how light, how
    weak,
If thou resist." The Fiend looked up and knew
His mounted scale aloft: nor more; but fled
Murmuring, and with him fled the shades of night.

997–1004. The reader must imagine a goldsmith's balance such
as is seen in conventional representations of Justice. Since Satan
will be better off parting than fighting, the scale containing the
consequences (to him) of fighting is lighter than the other and
hence rises and hits the beam or crosspiece from which the scales
are suspended. M. heightens the grandeur of this image, which
is found in the *Iliad* (VIII, 69–72) and in the *Aeneid* (XII, 725–
727), by identifying the scales with Libra, the sign of the zodiac
standing between Virgo (*Astraea*) and Scorpio.

1001. *ponders:* weighs.

BOOK V ❧

THE ARGUMENT

Morning approached, Eve relates to Adam her troublesome dream; he likes it not, yet comforts her. They come forth to their day labors: their morning hymn at the door of their bower. God to render man inexcusable sends Raphael to admonish him of his obedience, of his free estate, of his enemy near at hand; who he is, and why his enemy, and whatever else may avail Adam to know. Raphael comes down to Paradise, his appearance described, his coming discerned by Adam afar off sitting at the door of his bower; he goes out to meet him, brings him to his lodge, entertains him with the choicest fruits of Paradise got together by Eve; their discourse at table: Raphael performs his message, minds Adam of his state and of his enemy; relates at Adam's request who that enemy is, and how he came to be so, beginning from his first revolt in Heaven, and the occasion thereof; how he drew his legions after him to the parts of the north, and there incited them to rebel with him, persuading all but only Abdiel, a Seraph, who in argument dissuades and opposes him, then forsakes him.

Now morn her rosy steps in th' eastern clime
Advancing, sowed the earth with orient pearl,
When Adam waked, so customed, for his sleep

Was aery light from pure digestion bred,
And temperate vapors bland, which th' only sound
Of leaves and fuming rills, Aurora's fan,
Lightly dispersed, and the shrill matin song
Of birds on every bough; so much the more
His wonder was to find unwakened Eve
With tresses discomposed, and glowing cheek,　　10
As through unquiet rest: he on his side
Leaning half-raised, with looks of cordial love
Hung over her enamored, and beheld
Beauty, which whether waking or asleep,
Shot forth peculiar graces; then with voice
Mild, as when Zephyrus on Flora breathes,
Her hand soft touching, whispered thus. "Awake
My fairest, my espoused, my latest found,
Heav'n's last best gift, my ever new delight,
Awake, the morning shines, and the fresh field　　20
Calls us, we lose the prime, to mark how spring
Our tended plants, how blows the citron grove,
What drops the myrrh, and what the balmy reed,
How nature paints her colors, how the bee
Sits on the bloom extracting liquid sweet."
　Such whispering waked her, but with startled eye
On Adam, whom embracing, thus she spake.
　"O sole in whom my thoughts find all repose,
My glory, my perfection, glad I see
Thy face, and morn returned, for I this night,　　30
Such night till this I never passed, have dreamed,
If dreamed, not as I oft am wont, of thee,
Works of day past, or morrow's next design,
But of offense and trouble, which my mind
Knew never till this irksome night; methought
Close at mine ear one called me forth to walk

　　5. *th' only sound:* only the sound.
　　6. *fuming:* smoking (with early morning vapor); cf. lines 185–
186, below. *Aurora:* goddess of morning.
　　16. *Zephyrus:* the west wind. *Flora:* goddess of flowers.
　　21. *prime:* the first part of the day.
　　22. *blows:* blooms.

With gentle voice, I thought it thine; it said,
'Why sleep'st thou Eve? Now is the pleasant time,
The cool, the silent, save where silence yields
To the night-warbling bird, that now awake   40
Tunes sweetest his love-labored song; now reigns
Full orbed the moon, and with more pleasing light
Shadowy sets off the face of things; in vain,
If none regard; heav'n wakes with all his eyes,
Whom to behold but thee, nature's desire,
In whose sight all things joy, with ravishment
Attracted by thy beauty still to gaze.'
I rose as at thy call, but found thee not;
To find thee I directed then my walk;
And on, methought, alone I passed through ways   50
That brought me on a sudden to the Tree
Of interdicted knowledge: fair it seemed,
Much fairer to my fancy than by day:
And as I wondering looked, beside it stood
One shaped and winged like one of those from Heav'n
By us oft seen; his dewy locks distilled
Ambrosia; on that Tree he also gazed;
And 'O fair plant,' said he, 'with fruit surcharged,
Deigns none to ease thy load and taste thy sweet,
Nor god, nor man; is knowledge so despised?   60
Or envy, or what reserve forbids to taste?
Forbid who will, none shall from me withhold
Longer thy offered good, why else set here?'
This said he paused not, but with vent'rous arm
He plucked, he tasted; me damp horror chilled
At such bold words vouched with a deed so bold:
But he thus overjoyed, 'O fruit divine,
Sweet of thyself, but much more sweet thus cropped,
Forbidden here, it seems, as only fit

38–43. In lines 17–25, Adam's call to Eve at daybreak is a para-
phrase of the Song of Solomon, 2:10–13. Here Satan inverts the
values of the biblical passage, substituting night for day, the nightingale for the turtle-dove, the moon for the sun, shadow for substance, Eve for God.

60. *god:* angel (as often).

For gods, yet able to make gods of men: 70
And why not gods of men, since good, the more
Communicated, more abundant grows,
The Author not impaired, but honored more?
Here, happy creature, fair angelic Eve,
Partake thou also; happy though thou art,
Happier thou mayst be, worthier canst not be:
Taste this, and be henceforth among the gods
Thyself a goddess, not to earth confined,
But sometimes in the air, as we, sometimes
Ascend to Heav'n, by merit thine, and see   80
What life the gods live there, and such live thou.'
So saying, he drew nigh, and to me held,
Even to my mouth of that same fruit held part
Which he had plucked; the pleasant savory smell
So quickened appetite, that I, methought,
Could not but taste. Forthwith up to the clouds
With him I flew, and underneath beheld
The earth outstretched immense, a prospect wide
And various: wondering at my flight and change
To this high exaltation; suddenly   90
My guide was gone, and I, methought, sunk down,
And fell asleep; but O how glad I waked
To find this but a dream!" Thus Eve her night
Related, and thus Adam answered sad.
    "Best image of myself and dearer half,
The trouble of thy thoughts this night in sleep
Affects me equally; nor can I like
This uncouth dream, of evil sprung I fear;
Yet evil whence? in thee can harbor none,
Created pure. But know that in the soul   100
Are many lesser faculties that serve
Reason as chief; among these fancy next
Her office holds; of all external things,
Which the five watchful senses represent,

---

94. *sad:* seriously.
98. *uncouth:* strange.
102. *fancy:* the imagination or image-faculty of the mind.

She forms imaginations, aery shapes,
Which reason joining or disjoining, frames
All what we affirm or what deny, and call
Our knowledge or opinion; then retires
Into her private cell when nature rests.
Oft in her absence mimic fancy wakes   110
To imitate her; but misjoining shapes,
Wild work produces oft, and most in dreams,
Ill matchings words and deeds long past or late.
Some such resemblances methinks I find
Of our last evening's talk, in this thy dream,
But with addition strange; yet be not sad.
Evil into the mind of god or man
May come and go, so unapproved, and leave
No spot or blame behind: which gives me hope
That what in sleep thou didst abhor to dream,   120
Waking thou never wilt consent to do.
Be not disheartened then, nor cloud those looks
That wont to be more cheerful and serene
Than when fair morning first smiles on the world,
And let us to our fresh employments rise
Among the groves, the fountains, and the flow'rs
That open now their choicest bosomed smells
Reserved from night, and kept for thee in store."
    So cheered he his fair spouse, and she was cheered,
But silently a gentle tear let fall   130
From either eye, and wiped them with her hair;
Two other precious drops that ready stood,
Each in their crystal sluice, he ere they fell
Kissed as the gracious signs of sweet remorse
And pious awe, that feared to have offended.
    So all was cleared, and to the field they haste.

---

110. *mimic fancy:* Adam supposes that in sleep a kind of false imagination operates.

117. *god:* angel (as in line 60 above). There is no need to suppose that Adam refers to God.

118. *so unapproved:* either "not approved, as you have not approved it," or "so long as it is not approved."

But first from under shady arborous roof,
Soon as they forth were come to open sight
Of dayspring, and the sun, who scarce up ris'n
With wheels yet hovering o'er the ocean brim,   140
Shot parallel to the earth his dewy ray,
Discovering in wide landscape all the east
Of Paradise and Eden's happy plains,
Lowly they bowed adoring, and began
Their orisons, each morning duly paid
In various style, for neither various style
Nor holy rapture wanted they to praise
Their Maker, in fit strains pronounced or sung
Unmeditated, such prompt eloquence
Flowed from their lips, in prose or numerous verse,   150
More tuneable than needed lute or harp
To add more sweetness, and they thus began.
   "These are thy glorious works, Parent of good,
Almighty, thine this universal frame,
Thus wondrous fair; thy self how wondrous then!
Unspeakable, who sit'st above these heav'ns
To us invisible or dimly seen
In these thy lowest works, yet these declare
Thy goodness beyond thought, and power divine:
Speak ye who best can tell, ye sons of light,   160
Angels, for ye behold him, and with songs
And choral symphonies, day without night,
Circle his throne rejoicing, ye in Heav'n,
On earth join all ye creatures to extol
Him first, him last, him midst, and without end.
Fairest of stars, last in the train of night,

---

137. *arborous:* arbor-like; cf. IV, 692–695.
145–150. Cf. M.'s reference to his "unpremeditated verse" in
IX, 20–24.
153–208. Cf. Psalm 148.
154. *frame:* fabric, structure.
156–159. God cannot be adequately spoken of and is only dimly
seen in his creatures (cf. VIII, 119–122), yet even these declare his
goodness and power (cf. VIII, 273–279).
166. *fairest of stars:* the planet Venus, called Hesperus when it
is the evening star, Lucifer when it is the morning star.

If better thou belong not to the dawn,
Sure pledge of day, that crown'st the smiling morn
With thy bright circlet, praise him in thy sphere
While day arises, that sweet hour of prime.   170
Thou sun, of this great world both eye and soul,
Acknowledge him thy greater, sound his praise
In thy eternal course, both when thou climb'st,
And when high noon hast gained, and when thou
     fall'st.
Moon, that now meet'st the orient sun, now fli'st
With the fixed stars, fixed in their orb that flies,
And ye five other wandering fires that move
In mystic dance not without song, resound
His praise, who out of darkness called up light.
Air, and ye elements the eldest birth   180
Of nature's womb, that in quaternion run
Perpetual circle, multiform; and mix
And nourish all things, let your ceaseless change
Vary to our great Maker still new praise.
Ye mists and exhalations that now rise
From hill or steaming lake, dusky or gray,
Till the sun paint your fleecy skirts with gold,
In honor to the world's great Author rise,
Whether to deck with clouds th' uncolored sky,
Or wet the thirsty earth with falling show'rs,   190
Rising or falling still advance his praise.
His praise ye winds, that from four quarters blow,
Breathe soft or loud; and wave your tops, ye pines,
With every plant, in sign of worship wave.
Fountains and ye, that warble, as ye flow,
Melodious murmurs, warbling tune his praise.
Join voices all ye living souls, ye birds,

---

176. i.e., the stars are fixed in their sphere, but the sphere moves.

177. *wandering fires:* the planets, which are not fixed.

178. *song:* i.e., the music of the spheres.

181. *quaternion:* fourfold mixture; the four elements constantly change into each other.

189. *uncolored:* i.e., all of one color.

That singing up to Heaven gate ascend,
Bear on your wings and in your notes his praise;
Ye that in waters glide, and ye that walk   200
The earth, and stately tread, or lowly creep;
Witness if I be silent, morn or even,
To hill, or valley, fountain, or fresh shade
Made vocal by my song, and taught his praise.
Hail universal Lord, be bounteous still
To give us only good; and if the night
Have gathered aught of evil or concealed,
Disperse it, as now light dispels the dark."
    So prayed they innocent, and to their thoughts
Firm peace recovered soon and wonted calm.   210
On to their morning's rural work they haste
Among sweet dews and flow'rs; where any row
Of fruit trees overwoody reached too far
Their pampered boughs, and needed hands to check
Fruitless embraces: or they led the vine
To wed her elm; she spoused about him twines
Her marriageable arms, and with her brings
Her dow'r th' adopted clusters, to adorn
His barren leaves. Them thus employed beheld
With pity Heav'n's high King, and to him called   220
Raphael, the social spirit, that deigned
To travel with Tobias, and secured
His marriage with the sev'ntimes-wedded maid.
    "Raphael," said he, "thou hear'st what stir on earth
Satan from Hell scaped through the darksome gulf
Hath raised in Paradise, and how disturbed
This night the human pair, how he designs
In them at once to ruin all mankind.
Go therefore, half this day as friend with friend
Converse with Adam, in what bow'r or shade   230
Thou find'st him from the heat of noon retired,
To respite his day-labor with repast,
Or with repose; and such discourse bring on,

---

221. The name *Raphael* means "health of God." For *Tobias,* cf.
IV, 166–171, and note.

As may advise him of his happy state,
Happiness in his power left free to will,
Left to his own free will, his will though free
Yet mutable; whence warn him to beware
He swerve not too secure: tell him withal
His danger, and from whom, what enemy
Late fall'n himself from Heav'n, is plotting now   240
The fall of others from like state of bliss;
By violence, no, for that shall be withstood,
But by deceit and lies; this let him know,
Lest wilfully transgressing he pretend
Surprisal, unadmonished, unforewarned."
     So spake th' Eternal Father, and fulfilled
All justice: nor delayed the wingéd saint
After his charge received; but from among
Thousand celestial ardors, where he stood
Veiled with his gorgeous wings, up springing light   250
Flew through the midst of Heav'n; th' angelic choirs
On each hand parting, to his speed gave way
Through all th' empyreal road; till at the gate
Of Heav'n arrived, the gate self-opened wide
On golden hinges turning, as by work
Divine the sovran Architect had framed.
From hence, no cloud, or, to obstruct his sight,
Star interposed, however small he sees,
Not unconform to other shining globes,
Earth and the Gard'n of God, with cedars crowned   260
Above all hills. As when by night the glass
Of Galileo, less assured, observes
Imagined lands and regions in the moon:
Or pilot from amidst the Cyclades
Delos or Samos first appearing kens
A cloudy spot. Down thither prone in flight

234. *advise:* inform.
238. *secure:* free from care.
249. *ardors:* angels; cf. Hebrews 1:7, "Who maketh his angels
spirits, and his ministers a flame of fire."
259. *not unconform to:* not unlike.
264. *Cyclades:* a group of islands in the Aegean Sea.

He speeds, and through the vast ethereal sky
Sails between worlds and worlds, with steady wing
Now on the polar winds, then with quick fan
Winnows the buxom air; till within soar   270
Of towering eagles, to all the fowls he seems
A phoenix, gazed by all, as that sole bird
When to enshrine·his relics in the sun's
Bright temple, to Egyptian Thebes he flies.
At once on th' eastern cliff of Paradise
He lights, and to his proper shape returns
A Seraph winged; six wings he wore, to shade
His lineaments divine; the pair that clad
Each shoulder broad, came mantling o'er his breast
With regal ornament; the middle pair   280
Girt like a starry zone his waist, and round
Skirted his loins and thighs with downy gold
And colors dipped in Heav'n; the third his feet
Shadowed from either heel with feathered mail
Sky-tinctured grain. Like Maia's son he stood,
And shook his plumes, that heav'nly fragrance filled
The circuit wide. Straight knew him all the bands
Of angels under watch; and to his state,
And to his message high in honor rise;
For on some message high they guessed him bound.   290
Their glittering tents he passed, and now is come
Into the blissful field, through groves of myrrh,
And flow'ring odors, cassia, nard, and balm;
A wilderness of sweets; for nature here
Wantoned as in her prime, and played at will
Her virgin fancies, pouring forth more sweet,

---

269. *fan:* wing.

270. *buxom:* yielding.

272. *phoenix:* a unique bird which periodically immolated itself
in a nest of spices; a new phoenix rose out of the ashes and carried them to Heliopolis, the City of the Sun in Egypt close to
Thebes.

280. *regal ornament:* probably purple is meant.

285. *sky-tinctured grain:* sky-blue. *Maia's son:* Mercury.

296. *more sweet:* more sweetly (than now).

Wild above rule or art; enormous bliss.
Him through the spicy forest onward come
Adam discerned, as in the door he sat
Of his cool bow'r, while now the mounted sun   300
Shot down direct his fervid rays to warm
Earth's inmost womb, more warmth than Adam needs;
And Eve within, due at her hour prepared
For dinner savory fruits, of taste to please
True appetite, and not disrelish thirst
Of nectarous draughts between, from milky stream,
Berry or grape: to whom thus Adam called.

    "Haste hither Eve, and worth thy sight behold
Eastward among those trees, what glorious shape
Comes this way moving; seems another morn   310
Ris'n on mid-noon; some great behest from Heav'n
To us perhaps he brings, and will vouchsafe
This day to be our guest. But go with speed,
And what thy stores contain, bring forth and pour
Abundance, fit to honor and receive
Our heav'nly stranger; well we may afford
Our givers their own gifts, and large bestow
From large bestowed, where nature multiplies
Her fertile growth, and by disburd'ning grows
More fruitful, which instructs us not to spare."   320

    To whom thus Eve. "Adam, earth's hallowed mold,
Of God inspired, small store will serve, where store,
All seasons, ripe for use hangs on the stalk;
Save what by frugal storing firmness gains
To nourish, and superfluous moist consumes:
But I will haste and from each bough and brake,
Each plant and juiciest gourd will pluck such choice
To entertain our angel guest, as he
Beholding shall confess that here on earth
God hath dispensed his bounties as in Heav'n."   330

    So saying, with dispatchful looks in haste

---

297. *enormous:* out of all rule, beyond the norm.
321–322. *earth's hallowed mold,/ Of God inspired* is in apposi-
tion to *Adam.*

She turns, on hospitable thoughts intent
What choice to choose for delicacy best,
What order, so contrived as not to mix
Tastes, not well joined, inelegant, but bring
Taste after taste upheld with kindliest change,
Bestirs her then, and from each tender stalk
Whatever earth all-bearing mother yields
In India east or west, or middle shore
In Pontus or the Punic coast, or where   340
Alcinous reigned, fruit of all kinds, in coat,
Rough, or smooth-rined, or bearded husk, or shell
She gathers, tribute large, and on the board
Heaps with unsparing hand; for drink the grape
She crushes, inoffensive must, and meaths
From many a berry, and from sweet kernels pressed
She tempers dulcet creams, nor these to hold
Wants her fit vessels pure, then strews the ground
With rose and odors from the shrub unfumed.
Meanwhile our primitive great sire, to meet   350
His godlike guest, walks forth, without more train
Accompanied than with his own complete
Perfections, in himself was all his state,
More solemn than the tedious pomp that waits
On princes, when their rich retínue long
Of horses led, and grooms besmeared with gold
Dazzles the crowd, and sets them all agape.
Nearer his presence Adam though not awed,
Yet with submiss approach and reverence meek,
As to a superior nature, bowing low,   360
    Thus said. "Native of Heav'n, for other place
None can than Heav'n such glorious shape contain;
Since by descending from the thrones above,

---

336. *kindliest:* most natural.
340. *Pontus:* southern shore of the Black Sea. *Punic:* southern
coast of the Mediterranean.
341. *Alcinous:* the king of the Phaeacians, who entertained
Odysseus. Homer describes his gardens in *Odyssey,* VII.
345. *must:* unfermented wine. *meaths:* meads.
349. *unfumed:* not burned (for incense).

Those happy places thou hast deigned a while
To want, and honor these, vouchsafe with us
Two only, who yet by sovran gift possess
This spacious ground, in yonder shady bow'r
To rest, and what the garden choicest bears
To sit and taste, till this meridian heat
Be over, and the sun more cool decline."   370
    Whom thus th' angelic Virtue answered mild.
"Adam, I therefore came, nor art thou such
Created, or such place hast here to dwell,
As may not oft invite, though spirits of Heav'n,
To visit thee; lead on then where thy bow'r
O'ershades; for these mid-hours, till evening rise
I have at will." So to the sylvan lodge
They came, that like Pomona's arbor smiled
With flow'rets decked and fragrant smells; but Eve
Undecked, save with herself, more lovely fair   380
Than wood-nymph, or the fairest goddess feigned
Of three that in Mount Ida naked strove,
Stood to entertain her guest from Heav'n; no veil
She needed, virtue-proof, no thought infirm
Altered her cheek. On whom the angel "Hail"
Bestowed, the holy salutation used
Long after to blest Mary, second Eve.
    "Hail mother of mankind, whose fruitful womb
Shall fill the world more numerous with thy sons

---

365. *want:* do without.
371. *Virtue:* one of the nine angelic ranks. Elsewhere Raphael is
called a Seraph (V, 277) and an Archangel (VII, 41). Apparently
M. wants to avail himself of the traditional names of the angelic
hierarchy without seeming to set as much store by them as the
fallen angels do.
378. *Pomona:* Roman goddess of fruit trees.
382. Juno, Venus, and Minerva contended for a golden apple
inscribed "For the fairest." Paris judged Venus to be the fairest.
384. *virtue-proof:* strong because of her virtue.
385-387. Cf. Luke 1:28. Mary is the *second Eve* as Christ is "the
last Adam" (1 Corinthians 15:45).

Than with these various fruits the trees of God   390
Have heaped this table." Raised of grassy turf
Their table was, and mossy seats had round,
And on her ample square from side to side
All autumn piled, though spring and autumn here
Danced hand in hand. A while discourse they hold;
No fear lest dinner cool; when thus began
Our author. "Heav'nly stranger, please to taste
These bounties which our Nourisher, from whom
All perfect good unmeasured out, descends,
To us for food and for delight hath caused   400
The earth to yield; unsavory food perhaps
To spiritual natures; only this I know,
That one celestial Father gives to all."
　　To whom the angel. "Therefore what he gives
(Whose praise be ever sung) to man in part
Spiritual, may of purest spirits be found
No ingrateful food: and food alike those pure
Intelligential substances require
As doth your rational; and both contain
Within them every lower faculty   410
Of sense, whereby they hear, see, smell, touch, taste,
Tasting concoct, digest, assimilate,
And corporeal to incorporeal turn.
For know, whatever was created, needs
To be sustained and fed; of elements
The grosser feeds the purer, earth the sea,
Earth and the sea feed air, the air those fires
Ethereal, and as lowest first the moon;
Whence in her visage round those spots, unpurged
Vapors not yet into her substance turned.   420
Nor doth the moon no nourishment exhale
From her moist continent to higher orbs.
The sun that light imparts to all, receives
From all his alimental recompense
In humid exhalations, and at even
Sups with the ocean: though in Heav'n the trees
Of life ambrosial fruitage bear, and vines

Yield nectar, though from off the boughs each morn
We brush mellifluous dews, and find the ground
Covered with pearly grain: yet God hath here   43
Varied his bounty so with new delights,
As may compare with Heaven; and to taste
Think not I shall be nice." So down they sat,
And to their viands fell, nor seemingly
The angel, nor in mist, the common gloss
Of theologians, but with keen dispatch
Of real hunger, and concoctive heat
To transubstantiate; what redounds, transpires
Through spirits with ease; nor wonder; if by fire
Of sooty coal th' empiric alchemist   44
Can turn, or holds it possible to turn
Metals of drossiest ore to perfect gold
As from the mine. Meanwhile at table Eve
Ministered naked, and their flowing cups
With pleasant liquors crowned: O innocence
Deserving Paradise! If ever, then,
Then had the sons of God excuse to have been
Enamored at that sight; but in those hearts
Love unlibidinous reigned, nor jealousy
Was understood, the injured lover's hell.   45
    Thus when with meats and drinks they had sufficed,
Not burdened nature, sudden mind arose
In Adam, not to let th' occasion pass
Giv'n him by this great conference to know
Of things above his world, and of their being
Who dwell in Heav'n, whose excellence he saw
Transcend his own so far, whose radiant forms
Divine effulgence, whose high power so far
Exceeded human, and his wary speech

---

429. *mellifluous:* flowing with honey.
433. *nice:* dainty.
435. *gloss:* interpretation.
438. *redounds:* is left over, not assimilated.
447. Cf. Genesis 6:1–4.

Thus to th' empyreal minister he framed.   460
   "Inhabitant with God, now know I well
Thy favor, in this honor done to man,
Under whose lowly roof thou hast vouchsafed
To enter, and these earthly fruits to taste,
Food not of angels, yet accepted so,
As that more willingly thou couldst not seem
At Heav'n's high feasts to have fed: yet what compare?"
   To whom the wingéd hierarch replied.
"O Adam, one Almighty is, from whom
All things proceed, and up to him return,   470
If not depraved from good, created all
Such to perfection, one first matter all,
Indued with various forms, various degrees
Of substance, and in things that live, of life;
But more refined, more spiritous, and pure,
As nearer to him placed or nearer tending,
Each in their several active spheres assigned,
Till body up to spirit work, in bounds
Proportioned to each kind. So from the root   479
Springs lighter the green stalk, from thence the leaves
More aery, last the bright consummate flow'r
Spirits odorous breathes: flow'rs and their fruit
Man's nourishment, by gradual scale sublimed
To vital spirits aspire, to animal,
To intellectual, give both life and sense,
Fancy and understanding, whence the soul
Reason receives, and reason is her being,
Discursive, or intuitive; discourse
Is oftest yours, the latter most is ours,
Differing but in degree, of kind the same.   490
Wonder not then, what God for you saw good
If I refuse not, but convert, as you,

---

   472. *such:* i.e., good.
   487-490. The immediate, *intuitive* apprehension of the angelic
intellect is distinguished from the usual processes of inference,
deduction, etc., that characterize man's *discursive* reason.

To proper substançe; time may come when men
With angels may participate, and find
No inconvenient diet, nor too light fare:
And from these corporal nutriments perhaps
Your bodies may at last turn all to spirit,
Improved by tract of time, and winged ascend
Ethereal, as we, or may at choice
Here or in heav'nly Paradises dwell;   500
If ye be found obedient, and retain
Unalterably firm his love entire
Whose progeny you are. Meanwhile enjoy
Your fill what happiness this happy state
Can comprehend, incapable of more."
    To whom the patriarch of mankind replied.
"O favorable spirit, propitious guest,
Well hast thou taught the way that might direct
Our knowledge, and the scale of nature set
From center to circumference, whereon   510
In contemplation of created things
By steps we may ascend to God. But say,
What meant that caution joined, 'If ye be found
Obedient'? Can we want obedience then
To him, or possibly his love desert
Who formed us from the dust, and placed us here
Full to the utmost measure of what bliss
Human desires can seek or apprehend?"
    To whom the angel. "Son of Heav'n and earth,
Attend: That thou art happy, owe to God;   520
That thou continu'st such, owe to thyself,
That is, to thy obedience; therein stand.
This was that caution giv'n thee; be advised.
God made thee perfect, not immutable;
And good he made thee, but to persevere
He left it in thy power, ordained thy will

---

493. *proper:* i.e., the substance proper to angels.
    493–500. With this hypothetical description of the destiny of
unfallen man, cf. God's statement about the even higher destiny
of fallen and regenerated man in III, 281–317.

By nature free, not overruled by fate
Inextricable, or strict necessity;
Our voluntary service he requires,
Not our necessitated, such with him   530
Finds no acceptance, nor can find, for how
Can hearts, not free, be tried whether they serve
Willing or no, who will but what they must
By destiny, and can no other choose?
Myself and all th' angelic host that stand
In sight of God enthroned, our happy state
Hold, as you yours, while our obedience holds;
On other surety none; freely we serve,
Because we freely love, as in our will
To love or not; in this we stand or fall: 540
And some are fall'n, to disobedience fall'n,
And so from Heav'n to deepest Hell; O fall
From what high state of bliss into what woe!"
　　To whom our great progenitor. "Thy words
Attentive, and with more delighted ear,
Divine instructor, I have heard, than when
Cherubic songs by night from neighboring hills
Aëreal music send: nor knew I not
To be both will and deed created free;
Yet that we never shall forget to love   550
Our Maker, and obey him whose command
Single, is yet so just, my constant thoughts
Assured me, and still assure: though what thou tell'st
Hath passed in Heav'n, some doubt within me move,
But more desire to hear, if thou consent,
The full relation, which must needs be strange,
Worthy of sacred silence to be heard;
And we have yet large day, for scarce the sun
Hath finished half his journey, and scarce begins
His other half in the great zone of heav'n."   560
　　Thus Adam made request, and Raphael
After short pause assenting, thus began.
　　"High matter thou enjoin'st me, O prime of men,
Sad task and hard, for how shall I relate
To human sense th' invisible exploits

Of warring spirits; how without remorse
The ruin of so many glorious once
And perfect while they stood; how last unfold
The secrets of another world, perhaps
Not lawful to reveal? Yet for thy good   570
This is dispensed, and what surmounts the reach
Of human sense, I shall delineate so,
By lik'ning spiritual to corporal forms,
As may express them best, though what if earth
Be but the shadow of Heav'n, and things therein
Each to other like, more than on earth is thought?
    "As yet this world was not, and Chaos wild
Reigned where these heav'ns now roll, where earth now
        rests
Upon her center poised, when on a day
(For time, though in eternity, applied   580
To motion, measures all things durable
By present, past, and future) on such day
As Heav'n's great year brings forth, th' empyreal host
Of angels by imperial summons called,
Innumerable before th' Almighty's throne
Forthwith from all the ends of Heav'n appeared
Under their hierarchs in orders bright
Ten thousand thousand ensigns high advanced,
Standards, and gonfalons 'twixt van and rear
Stream in the air, and for distinction serve   590
Of hierarchies, of order, and degrees;
Or in their glittering tissues bear emblazed
Holy memorials, acts of zeal and love
Recorded eminent. Thus when in orbs
Of circuit inexpressible they stood,

---

566. *remorse:* pity.

575. The word *shadow* here may be taken either in its
Platonic sense of "copy" or "simulacrum," or in its Christian sense
of "foreshadowing" as in Colossians 2:16–17.

583. *great year:* an allusion to the Platonic notion (*Timaeus*,
39) that after some thousands of years all the heavenly bodies
return to their original relative positions.

589. *gonfalons:* flags.

Orb within orb, the Father infinite,
By whom in bliss embosomed sat the Son,
Amidst as from a flaming mount, whose top
Brightness had made invisible, thus spake.
   " 'Hear all ye angels, progeny of light,   600
Thrones, Dominations, Princedoms, Virtues, Powers,
Hear my decree, which unrevoked shall stand.
This day I have begot whom I declare
My only Son, and on this holy hill
Him have anointed, whom ye now behold
At my right hand; your Head I him appoint;
And by my Self have sworn to him shall bow
All knees in Heav'n, and shall confess him Lord:
Under his great vice-gerent reign abide
United as one individual soul   610
Forever happy: him who disobeys
Me disobeys, breaks union, and that day
Cast out from God and blesséd vision, falls
Into utter darkness, deep ingulfed, his place
Ordained without redemption, without end.'
   "So spake th' Omnipotent, and with his words
All seemed well pleased, all seemed, but were not all.
That day, as other solemn days, they spent
In song and dance about the sacred hill,
Mystical dance, which yonder starry sphere   620
Of planets and of fixed in all her wheels
Resembles nearest, mazes intricate,
Eccentric, intervolved, yet regular
Then most, when most irregular they seem,
And in their motions harmony divine

603–615. Like most of God's speeches, these lines are a network
of biblical allusions: Psalm 2:6–7; Psalm 110:1; Ephesians 4:15;
Genesis 22:16; Philippians 2:10–11; Hebrews 1:5–6.

603. The word *begot* (or begotten), which appears in Psalm 2:7
in a verse that is quoted in Acts 13:33 and Hebrews 1:5 and 5:5,
was interpreted by biblical commentators, including M., as meaning "exalted." The word cannot mean "generated" here, since
elsewhere in *PL* it is made clear that the Son created the angels.

605. *anointed:* "Messiah" means "anointed."

So smooths her charming tones, that God's own ear
Listens delighted. Evening now approached
(For we have also our evening and our morn,
We ours for change delectable, not need)
Forthwith from dance to sweet repast they turn   63◦
Desirous; all in circles as they stood,
Tables are set, and on a sudden piled
With angels' food, and rubied nectar flows
In pearl, in diamond, and massy gold,
Fruit of delicious vines, the growth of Heav'n.
On flow'rs reposed, and with fresh flow'rets crowned,
They eat, they drink, and in communion sweet
Quaff immortality and joy, secure
Of surfeit where full measure only bounds
Excess, before th' all-bounteous King, who show'red   640
With copious hand, rejoicing in their joy.
Now when ambrosial night with clouds exhaled
From that high mount of God, whence light and shade
Spring both, the face of brightest Heav'n had changed
To grateful twilight (for night comes not there
In darker veil) and roseate dews disposed
All but th' unsleeping eyes of God to rest,
Wide over all the plain, and wider far
Than all this globous earth in plain outspread,
(Such are the courts of God) th' angelic throng   650
Dispersed in bands and files their camp extend
By living streams among the trees of life,
Pavilions numberless, and sudden reared,
Celestial tabernacles, where they slept
Fanned with cool winds, save those who in their course
Melodious hymns about the sovran throne
Alternate all night long: but not so waked
Satan, so call him now, his former name
Is heard no more in Heav'n; he of the first,
If not the first Archangel, great in power,   660
In favor and preeminence, yet fraught
With envy against the Son of God, that day

653–654. *pavilions, tabernacles:* tents.

Honored by his great Father, and proclaimed
Messiah King anointed, could not bear
Through pride that sight, and thought himself
     impaired.
Deep malice thence conceiving and disdain,
Soon as midnight brought on the dusky hour
Friendliest to sleep and silence, he resolved
With all his legions to dislodge, and leave
Unworshipped, unobeyed the throne supreme   670
Contemptuous, and his next subordinate
Awak'ning, thus to him in secret spake.

   " 'Sleep'st thou companion dear, what sleep can close
Thy eyelids? and rememb'rest what decree
Of yesterday, so late hath passed the lips
Of Heav'n's Almighty. Thou to me thy thoughts
Wast wont, I mine to thee was wont to impart;
Both waking we were one; how then can now
Thy sleep dissent? New laws thou seest imposed;
New laws from him who reigns, new minds may raise   680
In us who serve, new counsels, to debate
What doubtful may ensue, more in this place
To utter is not safe. Assemble thou
Of all those myriads which we lead the chief;
Tell them that by command, ere yet dim night
Her shadowy cloud withdraws, I am to haste,
And all who under me their banners wave,
Homeward with flying march where we possess
The quarters of the north, there to prepare
Fit entertainment to receive our King   690
The great Messiah, and his new commands,
Who speedily through all the hierarchies
Intends to pass triumphant, and give laws.'
   "So spake the false Archangel, and infused

---

665. *impaired:* made inferior (Lat. *impar,* unequal).
671. *his next subordinate:* Beëlzebub.
689. Cf. Isaiah 14:13, "For thou [Lucifer] hast said in thine heart, I will ascend into heaven, I will exalt my throne above the stars of God: I will sit also upon the mount of the congregation, in the sides of the north."

Bad influence into th' unwary breast
Of his associate; he together calls,
Or several one by one, the regent powers,
Under him regent, tells, as he was taught,
That the most High commanding, now ere night,
Now ere dim night had disencumbered Heav'n,   700
The great hierarchal standard was to move;
Tells the suggested cause, and casts between
Ambiguous words and jealousies, to sound
Or taint integrity; but all obeyed
The wonted signal, and superior voice
Of their great potentate; for great indeed
His name, and high was his degree in Heav'n;
His count'nance, as the morning star that guides
The starry flock, allured them, and with lies
Drew after him the third part of Heav'n's host: 710
Meanwhile th' eternal eye, whose sight discerns
Abstrusest thoughts, from forth his holy mount
And from within the golden lamps that burn
Nightly before him, saw without their light
Rebellion rising, saw in whom, how spread
Among the sons of morn, what multitudes
Were banded to oppose his high decree;
And smiling to his only Son thus said.
    " 'Son, thou in whom my glory I behold
In full resplendence, heir of all my might,   720
Nearly it now concerns us to be sure
Of our omnipotence, and with what arms
We mean to hold what anciently we claim
Of deity or empire, such a foe
Is rising, who intends to erect his throne
Equal to ours, throughout the spacious north;
Nor so content, hath in his thought to try
In battle, what our power is, or our right.
Let us advise, and to this hazard draw

---

703. *jealousies:* suspicions.
713. Revelation 4:5 speaks of "seven lamps of fire burning before the throne."

With speed what force is left, and all employ   730
In our defense, lest unawares we lose
This our high place, our sanctuary, our hill.'
    "To whom the Son with calm aspect and clear
Light'ning divine, ineffable, serene,
Made answer. 'Mighty Father, thou thy foes
Justly hast in derision, and secure
Laugh'st at their vain designs and tumults vain,
Matter to me of glory, whom their hate
Illustrates, when they see all regal power
Giv'n me to quell their pride, and in event   740
Know whether I be dextrous to subdue
Thy rebels, or be found the worst in Heav'n.'
    "So spake the Son, but Satan with his powers
Far was advanced on wingéd speed, an host
Innumerable as the stars of night,
Or stars of morning, dewdrops, which the sun
Impearls on every leaf and every flow'r.
Regions they passed, the mighty regencies
Of Seraphim and Potentates and Thrones
In their triple degrees, regions to which   750
All thy dominion, Adam, is no more
Than what this garden is to all the earth,
And all the sea, from one entire globose
Stretched into longitude; which having passed
At length into the limits of the north
They came, and Satan to his royal seat
High on a hill, far blazing, as a mount
Raised on a mount, with pyramids and tow'rs
From diamond quarries hewn, and rocks of gold,
The palace of great Lucifer (so call   760
That structure in the dialect of men
Interpreted) which not long after, he

735–737. Cf. Psalm 2:4, "He that sitteth in the heavens shall
laugh: the Lord shall have them in derision."

739. *illustrates:* makes illustrious.

740. *event:* outcome.

753. *globose:* sphere.

Affecting all equality with God,
In imitation of that mount whereon
Messiah was declared in sight of Heav'n,
The Mountain of the Congregation called;
For thither he assembled all his train,
Pretending so commanded to consult
About the great reception of their King,
Thither to come, and with calumnious art   770
Of counterfeited truth thus held their ears.
  " 'Thrones, Dominations, Princedoms, Virtues, Pow-
        ers,
If these magnific titles yet remain
Not merely titular, since by decree
Another now hath to himself engrossed
All power, and us eclipsed under the name
Of King anointed, for whom all this haste
Of midnight march, and hurried meeting here,
This only to consult how we may best
With what may be devised of honors new   780
Receive him coming to receive from us
Knee-tribute yet unpaid, prostration vile,
Too much to one, but double how endured,
To one and to his image now proclaimed?
But what if better counsels might erect
Our minds and teach us to cast off this yoke?
Will ye submit your necks, and choose to bend
The supple knee? Ye will not, if I trust
To know ye right, or if ye know yourselves
Natives and sons of Heav'n possessed before   790
By none, and if not equal all, yet free,
Equally free; for orders and degrees
Jar not with liberty, but well consist.
Who can in reason then or right assume
Monarchy over such as live by right
His equals, if in power and splendor less,

----

763. *affecting:* striving to attain; laying claim to.
790. *possessed:* modifies "Heav'n." Satan suggests that God and
the Son are now claiming Heaven as their exclusive possession.

In freedom equal? or can introduce
Law and edict on us, who without law
Err not, much less for this to be our Lord,
And look for adoration to th' abuse   800
Of those imperial titles which assert
Our being ordained to govern, not to serve?'
    "Thus far his bold discourse without control
Had audience, when among the Seraphim
Abdiel, than whom none with more zeal adored
The Deity, and divine commands obeyed,
Stood up, and in a flame of zeal severe
The current of his fury thus opposed.
    " 'O argument blasphémous, false and proud!
Words which no ear ever to hear in Heav'n   810
Expected, least of all from thee, ingrate,
In place thyself so high above thy peers.
Canst thou with impious obloquy condemn
The just decree of God, pronounced and sworn,
That to his only Son by right endued
With regal scepter, every soul in Heav'n
Shall bend the knee, and in that honor due
Confess him rightful King? Unjust thou say'st
Flatly unjust, to bind with laws the free,
And equal over equals to let reign,   820
One over all with unsucceeded power.
Shalt thou give law to God, shalt thou dispute
With him the points of liberty, who made
Thee what thou art, and formed the Powers of Heav'n
Such as he pleased, and circumscribed their being?
Yet by experience taught we know how good,

---

799. *for this:* for this reason. The phrase may look back to the
idea that they do not need laws to know what is right, or forward
to the idea that their titles show they are ordained to govern, not
to serve.

805. The name *Abdiel* means "servant of God" (cf. VI, 29). Abdiel provides an example of true rebellion, i.e., rebellion against
evil power, as opposed to Satan's false rebellion. M. himself was
a rebel against what he considered the evil power of the English
monarchy and ecclesiastical hierarchy.

And of our good, and of our dignity
How provident he is, how far from thought
To make us less, bent rather to exalt
Our happy state under one Head more near   830
United. But to grant it thee unjust,
That equal over equals monarch reign:
Thyself though great and glorious dost thou count,
Or all angelic nature joined in one,
Equal to him begotten Son, by whom
As by his Word the mighty Father made
All things, ev'n thee, and all the spirits of Heav'n
By him created in their bright degrees,
Crowned them with glory, and to their glory named
Thrones, Dominations, Princedoms, Virtues, Powers, 840
Essential Powers, nor by his reign obscured,
But more illustrious made, since he the Head
One of our number thus reduced becomes,
His laws our laws, all honor to him done
Returns our own. Cease then this impious rage,
And tempt not these; but hasten to appease
Th' incensèd Father, and th' incensèd Son,
While pardon may be found in time besought.'

    "So spake the fervent angel, but his zeal
None seconded, as out of season judged,   850
Or singular and rash, whereat rejoiced
Th' Apostate, and more haughty thus replied.
'That we were formed then say'st thou? and the work
Of secondary hands, by task transferred
From Father to his Son? Strange point and new!
Doctrine which we would know whence learnt: who saw
When this creation was? Remember'st thou
Thy making, while the Maker gave thee being?
We know no time when we were not as now;

835–842. Cf. Colossians 1:16–18, "For by him were all things
created, that are in heaven, and that are in earth, visible and invisible, whether they be thrones, or dominions, or principalities,
or powers: all things were created by him, and for him:
    And he is before all things, and by him all things consist.
    And he is the head of the body, the church."

Know none before us, self-begot, self-raised   860
By our own quick'ning power, when fatal course
Had circled his full orb, the birth mature
Of this our native Heav'n, ethereal sons.
Our puissance is our own, our own right hand
Shall teach us highest deeds, by proof to try
Who is our equal: then thou shalt behold
Whether by supplication we intend
Address, and to begirt th' Almighty Throne
Beseeching or besieging. This report,
These tidings carry to th' anointed King;   870
And fly, ere evil intercept thy flight.'
   "He said, and as the sound of waters deep
Hoarse murmur echoed to his words applause
Through the infinite host, nor less for that
The flaming Seraph fearless, though alone
Encompassed round with foes, thus answered bold.
   " 'O alienate from God, O spirit accursed,
Forsaken of all good; I see thy fall
Determined, and thy hapless crew involved
In this perfidious fraud, contagion spread   880
Both of thy crime and punishment: henceforth
No more be troubled how to quit the yoke
Of God's Messiah; those indulgent laws
Will not be now vouchsafed, other decrees
Against thee are gone forth without recall;
That golden scepter which thou didst reject
Is now an iron rod to bruise and break
Thy disobedience. Well thou didst advise,
Yet not for thy advice or threats I fly
These wicked tents devoted, lest the wrath   890
Impendent, raging into sudden flame
Distinguish not: for soon expect to feel
His thunder on thy head, devouring fire.
Then who created thee lamenting learn,

---

   861. *fatal:* once again (cf. I, 116) Satan implies that there is an impersonal power above God.
   890. *devoted:* doomed to destruction.

When who can uncreate thee thou shalt know.'
  "So spake the Seraph Abdiel faithful found,
Among the faithless, faithful only he;
Among innumerable false, unmoved,
Unshaken, unseduced, unterrified
His loyalty he kept, his love, his zeal;   900
Nor number, nor example with him wrought
To swerve from truth, or change his constant mind
Though single. From amidst them forth he passed,
Long way through hostile scorn, which he sustained
Superior, nor of violence feared aught;
And with retorted scorn his back he turned
On those proud tow'rs to swift destruction doomed."

---

  906. *retorted:* flung back.

BOOK VI ᥤᔥ

THE ARGUMENT

  Raphael continues to relate how Michael and Gabriel were sent forth to battle against Satan and his angels. The first fight described: Satan and his powers
retire under night. He calls a council, invents devilish
engines, which in the second day's fight put Michael and
his angels to some disorder; but they at length pulling

up mountains overwhelmed both the force and machines
of Satan: yet the tumult not so ending, God on the third
day sends Messiah his Son, for whom he had reserved
the glory of that victory. He in the power of his Father
coming to the place, and causing all his legions to stand
still on either side, with his chariot and thunder driving
into the midst of his enemies, pursues them unable to
resist towards the wall of Heaven; which opening, they
leap down with horror and confusion into the place of
punishment prepared for them in the deep: Messiah returns with triumph to his Father.

"All night the dreadless angel unpursued
Through Heav'n's wide champaign held his way, till
　　morn,
Waked by the circling hours, with rosy hand
Unbarred the gates of light. There is a cave
Within the mount of God, fast by his throne,
Where light and darkness in perpetual round
Lodge and dislodge by turns, which makes through
　　Heav'n
Grateful vicissitude, like day and night;
Light issues forth, and at the other door
Obsequious darkness enters, till her hour　　　　　　10
To veil the Heav'n, though darkness there might well
Seem twilight here; and now went forth the morn
Such as in highest Heav'n, arrayed in gold
Empyreal: from before her vanished night,
Shot through with orient beams: when all the plain
Covered with thick embattled squadrons bright,
Chariots and flaming arms, and fiery steeds
Reflecting blaze on blaze, first met his view:
War he perceived, war in procinct, and found

---

8. *vicissitude:* alternation.

10. *obsequious:* obedient; or perhaps simply "following."

14. *Empyreal,* like "empyrean," is derived from the Greek word
for "fire."

19. *in procinct:* in readiness.

Already known what he for news had thought
To have reported: gladly then he mixed
Among those friendly powers who him received
With joy and acclamations loud, that one
That of so many myriads fall'n, yet one
Returned not lost: on to the sacred hill
They led him high applauded, and present
Before the seat supreme; from whence a voice
From midst a golden cloud thus mild was heard.
    " 'Servant of God, well done, well hast thou fought
The better fight, who single hast maintained
Against revolted multitudes the cause
Of truth, in word mightier than they in arms;
And for the testimony of truth hast borne
Universal reproach, far worse to bear
Than violence: for this was all thy care,
To stand approved in sight of God, though worlds
Judged thee perverse: the easier conquest now
Remains thee, aided by this host of friends,
Back on thy foes more glorious to return
Than scorned thou didst depart, and to subdue
By force, who reason for their law refuse,
Right reason for their law, and for their king
Messiah, who by right of merit reigns.
Go Michael of celestial armies prince,
And thou in military prowess next,
Gabriel, lead forth to battle these my sons
Invincible, lead forth my arméd saints
By thousands and by millions ranged for fight;
Equal in number to that godless crew
Rebellious, them with fire and hostile arms
Fearless assault, and to the brow of Heav'n
Pursuing drive them out from God and bliss,
Into their place of punishment, the gulf
Of Tartarus, which ready opens wide
His fiery chaos to receive their fall.'

---

44. Cf. Revelation 12:7, "And there was war in heaven: Michae
and his angels fought against the dragon."

"So spake the sovran voice, and clouds began
To darken all the hill, and smoke to roll
In dusky wreaths, reluctant flames, the sign
Of wrath awaked: nor with less dread the loud
Ethereal trumpet from on high gan blow: 60
At which command the powers militant,
That stood for Heav'n, in mighty quadrate joined
Of union irresistible, moved on
In silence their bright legions, to the sound
Of instrumental harmony that breathed
Heroic ardor to advent'rous deeds
Under their godlike leaders, in the cause
Of God and his Messiah. On they move
Indissolubly firm; nor obvious hill,
Nor strait'ning vale, nor wood, nor stream divides   70
Their perfect ranks; for high above the ground
Their march was, and the passive air upbore
Their nimble tread; as when the total kind
Of birds in orderly array on wing
Came summoned over Eden to receive
Their names of thee; so over many a tract
Of Heav'n they marched, and many a province wide
Tenfold the length of this terrene: at last
Far in th' horizon to the north appeared
From skirt to skirt a fiery region, stretched   80
In battailous aspect, and nearer view
Bristled with upright beams innumerable
Of rigid spears, and helmets thronged, and shields
Various, with boastful argument portrayed,
The banded powers of Satan hasting on
With furious expedition; for they weened
That selfsame day by fight, or by surprise
To win the mount of God, and on his throne
To set the envier of his state, the proud
Aspirer, but their thoughts proved fond and vain   90

---

58. *reluctant:* struggling (through the smoke).
69. *obvious:* in the way.
84. *argument:* designs or emblems (on the shields).

In the midway: though strange to us it seemed
At first, that angel should with angel war,
And in fierce hosting meet, who wont to meet
So oft in festivals of joy and love
Unanimous, as sons of one great sire
Hymning th' eternal Father: but the shout
Of battle now began, and rushing sound
Of onset ended soon each milder thought.
High in the midst exalted as a god
Th' Apostate in his sun-bright chariot sat   100
Idol of majesty divine, enclosed
With flaming Cherubim, and golden shields;
Then lighted from his gorgeous throne, for now
'Twixt host and host but narrow space was left,
A dreadful interval, and front to front
Presented stood in terrible array
Of hideous length: before the cloudy van,
On the rough edge of battle ere it joined,
Satan with vast and haughty strides advanced,
Came towering, armed in adamant and gold;   110
Abdiel that sight endured not, where he stood
Among the mightiest, bent on highest deeds,
And thus his own undaunted heart explores.
    " 'O Heav'n! that such resemblance of the Highest
Should yet remain, where faith and realty
Remain not; wherefore should not strength and might
There fail where virtue fails, or weakest prove
Where boldest; though to sight unconquerable?
His puissance, trusting in th' Almighty's aid,
I mean to try, whose reason I have tried   120
Unsound and false; nor is it aught but just,
That he who in debate of truth hath won,
Should win in arms, in both disputes alike

---

93. *hosting:* encounter (of a host of troops).

101. Satan is the false *idol* of God's majesty; the Son is God's
image (III, 63).

115. *realty:* reality.

120. *tried:* tested (and found to be unsound).

Victor; though brutish that contést and foul,
When reason hath to deal with force, yet so
Most reason is that reason overcome.'
  "So pondering, and from his arméd peers
Forth stepping opposite, half way he met
His daring foe, at this prevention more
Incensed, and thus securely him defied.   130
  " 'Proud, art thou met? Thy hope was to have reached
The highth of thy aspiring unopposed,
The throne of God unguarded, and his side
Abandoned at the terror of thy power
Or potent tongue; fool, not to think how vain
Against th' Omnipotent to rise in arms;
Who out of smallest things could without end
Have raised incessant armies to defeat
Thy folly; or with solitary hand
Reaching beyond all limit at one blow   140
Unaided could have finished thee, and whelmed
Thy legions under darkness; but thou seest
All are not of thy train; there be who faith
Prefer, and piety to God, though then
To thee not visible, when I alone
Seemed in thy world erroneous to dissent
From all: my sect thou seest, now learn too late
How few sometimes may know, when thousands err.'
  "Whom the grand Foe with scornful eye askance
Thus answered. 'Ill for thee, but in wished hour   150
Of my revenge, first sought for thou return'st
From flight, seditious angel, to receive
Thy merited reward, the first assay
Of this right hand provoked, since first that tongue
Inspired with contradiction durst oppose
A third part of the gods, in synod met
Their deities to assert, who while they feel

---

129. *prevention:* coming before, confrontation.
143. *there be who:* there are some who.
147. *sect:* Abdiel casts back at Satan the word with which
Royalists and Anglicans taunted the Protestant "sectaries."

Vigor divine within them, can allow
Omnipotence to none. But well thou com'st
Before thy fellows, ambitious to win   160
From me some plume, that thy success may show
Destruction to the rest: this pause between
(Unanswered lest thou boast) to let thee know
At first I thought that liberty and Heav'n
To heav'nly souls had been all one; but now
I see that most through sloth had rather serve,
Ministering spirits, trained up in feast and song;
Such hast thou armed, the minstrelsy of Heav'n,
Servility with freedom to contend,
As both their deeds compared this day shall prove.'   170
   "To whom in brief thus Abdiel stern replied.
'Apostate, still thou err'st, nor end wilt find
Of erring, from the path of truth remote:
Unjustly thou deprav'st it with the name
Of servitude to serve whom God ordains,
Or nature; God and nature bid the same,
When he who rules is worthiest, and excels
Them whom he governs. This is servitude,
To serve th' unwise, or him who hath rebelled
Against his worthier, as thine now serve thee,   180
Thyself not free, but to thyself enthralled;
Yet lewdly dar'st our minist'ring upbraid.
Reign thou in Hell thy kingdom, let me serve
In Heav'n God ever blest, and his divine
Behests obey, worthiest to be obeyed,
Yet chains in Hell, not realms expect: meanwhile
From me returned, as erst thou said'st, from flight,
This greeting on thy impious crest receive.'
   "So saying, a noble stroke he lifted high,
Which hung not, but so swift with tempest fell   190

---

161. *success:* outcome, fortune (whether good or bad).

162–163. i.e., "this pause before the combat is to reply to your arguments, lest you boast that I couldn't answer them."

168. *minstrelsy:* Satan contemptuously dismisses the angels who minister to God by chanting hymns of praise as minstrels. ⌐

174. *deprav'st:* depreciate.

On the proud crest of Satan, that no sight,
Nor motion of swift thought, less could his shield
Such ruin intercept: ten paces huge
He back recoiled; the tenth on bended knee
His massy spear upstayed; as if on earth
Winds under ground or waters forcing way
Sidelong, had pushed a mountain from his seat
Half sunk with all his pines. Amazement seized
The rebel Thrones, but greater rage to see
Thus foiled their mightiest, ours joy filled, and shout, 200
Presage of victory and fierce desire
Of battle: whereat Michael bid sound
Th' archangel trumpet; through the vast of Heav'n
It sounded, and the faithful armies rung
Hosanna to the Highest: nor stood at gaze
The adverse legions, nor less hideous joined
The horrid shock: now storming fury rose,
And clamor such as heard in Heav'n till now
Was never, arms on armor clashing brayed
Horrible discord, and the madding wheels 210
Of brazen chariots raged; dire was the noise
Of conflict; overhead the dismal hiss
Of fiery darts in flaming volleys flew,
And flying vaulted either host with fire.
So under fiery cope together rushed
Both battles main, with ruinous assault
And inextinguishable rage; all Heav'n
Resounded, and had earth been then, all earth
Had to her center shook. What wonder? when
Millions of fierce encountering angels fought 220
On either side, the least of whom could wield
These elements, and arm him with the force
Of all their regions: how much more of power
Army against army numberless to raise
Dreadful combustion warring, and disturb,
Though not destroy, their happy native seat;

---

216. *battles:* armies.
222. *these elements:* i.e., the four elements.

Had not th' eternal King omnipotent
From his stronghold of Heav'n high overruled
And limited their might; though numbered such
As each divided legion might have seemed   230
A numerous host, in strength each arméd hand
A legion; led in fight, yet leader seemed
Each warrior single as in chief, expert
When to advance, or stand, or turn the sway
Of battle, open when, and when to close
The ridges of grim war; no thought of flight,
None of retreat, no unbecoming deed
That argued fear; each on himself relied,
As only in his arm the moment lay
Of victory; deeds of eternal fame   240
Were done, but infinite: for wide was spread
That war and various; sometimes on firm ground
A standing fight, then soaring on main wing
Tormented all the air; all air seemed then
Conflicting fire: long time in even scale
The battle hung; till Satan, who that day
Prodigious power had shown, and met in arms
No equal, ranging through the dire attack
Of fighting Seraphim confused, at length
Saw where the sword of Michael smote, and felled   250
Squadrons at once, with huge two-handed sway
Brandished aloft the horrid edge came down
Wide wasting; such destruction to withstand
He hasted, and opposed the rocky orb
Of tenfold adamant, his ample shield
A vast circumference. At his approach
The great Archangel from his warlike toil
Surceased, and glad as hoping here to end

---

229. *numbered such:* so numerous.

232–233. "though they were led, each individual warrior was as
competent as a commander."

236. *ridges:* ranks.

239. *moment:* balance (i.e., the weight that would tip the balance).

Intestine war in Heav'n, th' Arch-Foe subdued
Or captive dragged in chains, with hostile frown   260
And visage all enflamed first thus began.
  " 'Author of evil, unknown till thy revolt,
Unnamed in Heav'n, now plenteous, as thou seest
These acts of hateful strife, hateful to all,
Though heaviest by just measure on thyself
And thy adherents: how hast thou disturbed
Heav'n's blessèd peace, and into nature brought
Misery, uncreated till the crime
Of thy rebellion? How hast thou instilled
Thy malice into thousands, once upright   270
And faithful, now proved false. But think not here
To trouble holy rest; Heav'n casts thee out
From all her confines. Heav'n the seat of bliss
Brooks not the works of violence and war.
Hence then, and evil go with thee along
Thy offspring, to the place of evil, Hell,
Thou and thy wicked crew; there mingle broils,
Ere this avenging sword begin thy doom,
Or some more sudden vengeance winged from God
Precipitate thee with augmented pain.'   280
  "So spake the prince of angels; to whom thus
The Adversary. 'Nor think thou with wind
Of airy threats to awe whom yet with deeds
Thou canst not. Hast thou turned the least of these
To flight, or if to fall, but that they rise
Unvanquished, easier to transact with me
That thou shouldst hope, imperious, and with threats
To chase me hence? Err not that so shall end
The strife which thou call'st evil, but we style
The strife of glory: which we mean to win,   290
Or turn this Heav'n itself into the Hell

259–260. *Arch-Foe . . . chains:* "when the Arch-Foe should be
subdued or dragged in chains as a captive" (an absolute con-
struction).
  277. *broils:* turmoils.
  288. *err not:* do not make the mistake of thinking.

Thou fablest, here however to dwell free,
If not to reign: meanwhile thy utmost force,
And join him named Almighty to thy aid,
I fly not, but have sought thee far and nigh.'
   "They ended parle, and both addressed for fight
Unspeakable; for who, though with the tongue
Of angels, can relate, or to what things
Liken on earth conspicuous, that may lift
Human imagination to such highth   300
Of godlike power: for likest gods they seemed,
Stood they or moved, in stature, motion, arms,
Fit to decide the empire of great Heav'n.
Now waved their fiery swords, and in the air
Made horrid circles; two broad suns their shields
Blazed opposite, while expectation stood
In horror; from each hand with speed retired
Where erst was thickest fight, th' angelic throng,
And left large field, unsafe within the wind
Of such commotion: such as, to set forth   310
Great things by small, if nature's concord broke,
Among the constellations war were sprung,
Two planets rushing from aspect malign
Of fiercest opposition in mid sky,
Should combat, and their jarring spheres confound.
Together both with next to almighty arm
Uplifted imminent, one stroke they aimed
That might determine, and not need repeat,
As not of power, at once; nor odds appeared
In might or swift prevention; but the sword   320
Of Michael from the armory of God
Was giv'n him tempered so, that neither keen
Nor solid might resist that edge: it met
The sword of Satan with steep force to smite

---

296. *parle:* parley.
313. *aspect:* position. Two planets were said to be in "malign aspect" when they were diametrically opposite each other in the heavens.
318. *determine:* bring to an end.
320. *prevention:* anticipation.

Descending, and in half cut sheer, nor stayed,
But with swift wheel reverse, deep entering sheared
All his right side; then Satan first knew pain,
And writhed him to and fro convolved; so sore
The griding sword with discontinuous wound
Passed through him, but the ethereal substance closed   330
Not long divisible, and from the gash
A stream of nectarous humor issuing flowed
Sanguine, such as celestial spirits may bleed,
And all his armor stained, erewhile so bright.
Forthwith on all sides to his aid was run
By angels many and strong, who interposed
Defense, while others bore him on their shields
Back to his chariot, where it stood retired
From off the files of war; there they him laid
Gnashing for anguish and despite and shame   340
To find himself not matchless, and his pride
Humbled by such rebuke, so far beneath
His confidence to equal God in power.
Yet soon he healed; for spirits that live throughout
Vital in every part, not as frail man
In entrails, heart or head, liver or reins,
Cannot but by annihilating die;
Nor in their liquid texture mortal wound
Receive, no more than can the fluid air:
All heart they live, all head, all eye, all ear,   350
All intellect, all sense, and as they please,
They limb themselves, and color, shape or size
Assume, as likes them best, condense or rare.
   "Meanwhile in other parts like deeds deserved
Memorial, where the might of Gabriel fought,
And with fierce ensigns pierced the deep array
Of Moloch furious king, who him defied,

---

329. *griding:* piercing. *discontinuous:* severing the continuity of
the body (a medical term).

355. *the might of Gabriel:* the mighty Gabriel.

357–372. *Moloch, Adramelech, Asmadai, Ariel, Arioch,* and
Ramiel are the "new names" fallen angels got "among the sons
of Eve" (I, 364–365).

And at his chariot wheels to drag him bound
Threatened, nor from the Holy One of Heav'n
Refrained his tongue blasphémous; but anon   360
Down cloven to the waist, with shattered arms
And uncouth pain fled bellowing. On each wing
Uriel and Raphael his vaunting foe,
Though huge, and in a rock of diamond armed,
Vanquished Adramelech, and Asmadai,
Two potent Thrones, that to be less than gods
Disdained, but meaner thoughts learned in their flight,
Mangled with ghastly wounds through plate and mail.
Nor stood unmindful Abdiel to annoy
The atheist crew, but with redoubled blow   370
Ariel and Arioch, and the violence
Of Ramiel, scorched and blasted, overthrew.
I might relate of thousands, and their names
Eternize here on earth; but those elect
Angels contented with their fame in Heav'n
Seek not the praise of men: the other sort
In might though wondrous and in acts of war,
Nor of renown less eager, yet by doom
Canceled from Heav'n and sacred memory,
Nameless in dark oblivion let them dwell.   380
For strength from truth divided and from just,
Illaudable, naught merits but dispraise
And ignominy, yet to glory aspires
Vainglorious, and through infamy seeks fame:
Therefore eternal silence be their doom.
    "And now their mightiest quelled, the battle swerved,
With many an inroad gored; deforméd rout
Entered, and foul disorder; all the ground
With shivered armor strewn, and on a heap
Chariot and charioteer lay overturned   390
And fiery foaming steeds; what stood, recoiled
O'erwearied, through the faint Satanic host
Defensive scarce, or with pale fear surprised,

---

391. *what stood:* those who stood.
393. *defensive scarce:* scarcely offering any defense.

Then first with fear surprised and sense of pain
Fled ignominious, to such evil brought
By sin of disobedience, till that hour
Not liable to fear or flight or pain.
Far otherwise th' inviolable saints
In cubic phalanx firm advanced entire,
Invulnerable, impenetrably armed: 400
Such high advantages their innocence
Gave them above their foes, not to have sinned,
Not to have disobeyed; in fight they stood
Unwearied, unobnoxious to be pained
By wound, though from their place by violence moved.
    "Now night her course began, and over Heav'n
Inducing darkness, grateful truce imposed,
And silence on the odious din of war:
Under her cloudy covert both retired,
Victor and vanquished: on the foughten field   410
Michael and his angels prevalent
Encamping, placed in guard their watches round,
Cherubic waving fires: on th' other part
Satan with his rebellious disappeared,
Far in the dark dislodged, and void of rest,
His potentates to council called by night;
And in the midst thus undismayed began.
    " 'O now in danger tried, now known in arms
Not to be overpowered, companions dear,
Found worthy not of liberty alone   420
Too mean pretense, but what we more affect,
Honor, dominion, glory, and renown,
Who have sustained one day in doubtful fight
(And if one day, why not eternal days?)
What Heaven's Lord had powerfullest to send
Against us from about his throne, and judged
Sufficient to subdue us to his will,
But proves not so: then fallible, it seems,

---

404. *unobnoxious:* not liable.
411. *prevalent:* prevailing, victorious.
421. *too mean pretense:* too low an ambition.

Of future we may deem him, though till now
Omniscient thought. True is, less firmly armed,   430
Some disadvantage we endured and pain,
Till now not known, but known as soon contemned,
Since now we find this our empyreal form
Incapable of mortal injury
Imperishable, and though pierced with wound,
Soon closing, and by native vigor healed.
Of evil then so small as easy think
The remedy; perhaps more valid arms,
Weapons more violent, when next we meet,
May serve to better us, and worse our foes,   440
Or equal what between us made the odds,
In nature none: if other hidden cause
Left them superior, while we can preserve
Unhurt our minds, and understanding sound,
Due search and consultation will disclose.'
   "He sat; and in th' assembly next upstood
Nisroch, of Principalities the prime;
As one he stood escaped from cruel fight,
Sore toiled, his riven arms to havoc hewn,
And cloudy in aspect thus answering spake.   450
'Deliverer from new lords, leader to free
Enjoyment of our right as gods; yet hard
For gods, and too unequal work we find
Against unequal arms to fight in pain,
Against unpained, impassive; from which evil
Ruin must needs ensue; for what avails
Valor or strength, though matchless, quelled with pain
Which all subdues, and makes remiss the hands
Of mightiest. Sense of pleasure we may well
Spare out of life perhaps, and not repine,   460
But live content, which is the calmest life:
But pain is perfect misery, the worst

---

   429. *of future:* in future.
   432. *known as soon contemned:* despised as soon as it is known.
   455. *unpained, impassive:* those unable to feel pain or to suffer (i.e., the loyal angels).

Of evils, and excessive, overturns
All patience. He who therefore can invent
With what more forcible we may offend
Our yet unwounded enemies, or arm
Ourselves with like defense, to me deserves
No less than for deliverance what we owe.'
   "Whereto with look composed Satan replied.
'Not uninvented that, which thou aright   470
Believ'st so main to our success, I bring;
Which of us who beholds the bright surface
Of this ethereous mold whereon we stand,
This continent of spacious Heav'n, adorned
With plant, fruit, flow'r ambrosial, gems and gold,
Whose eye so superficially surveys
These things, as not to mind from whence they grow
Deep under ground, materials dark and crude,
Of spiritous and fiery spume, till touched
With Heaven's ray, and tempered they shoot forth   480
So beauteous, opening to the ambient light.
These in their dark nativity the deep
Shall yield us, pregnant with infernal flame,
Which into hollow engines long and round
Thick-rammed, at th' other bore with touch of fire
Dilated and infuriate shall send forth
From far with thundering noise among our foes
Such implements of mischief as shall dash
To pieces, and o'erwhelm whatever stands
Adverse, that they shall fear we have disarmed   490
The Thunderer of his only dreaded bolt.
Nor long shall be our labor, yet ere dawn,
Effect shall end our wish. Meanwhile revive;
Abandon fear; to strength and counsel joined
Think nothing hard, much less to be despaired.'

---

465. *offend:* strike.
467–468. *to me . . . owe:* "in my opinion deserves no less than
we owe to Satan for our deliverance."
478. *crude:* raw.
479. *spume:* foam, froth.

He ended, and his words their drooping cheer
Enlightened, and their languished hope revived.
Th' invention all admired, and each, how he
To be th' inventor missed, so easy it seemed
Once found, which yet unfound most would have
      thought   500
Impossible: yet haply of thy race
In future days, if malice should abound,
Someone intent on mischief, or inspired
With devilish machination might devise
Like instrument to plague the sons of men
For sin, on war and mutual slaughter bent.
Forthwith from council to the work they flew,
None arguing stood, innumerable hands
Were ready, in a moment up they turned
Wide the celestial soil, and saw beneath   510
Th' originals of nature in their crude
Conception; sulphurous and nitrous foam
They found, they mingled, and with subtle art,
Concocted and adusted they reduced
To blackest grain, and into store conveyed:
Part hidden veins digged up (nor hath this earth
Entrails unlike) of mineral and stone,
Whereof to found their engines and their balls
Of missive ruin; part incentive reed
Provide, pernicious with one touch to fire.   520
So all ere day-spring, under conscious night
Secret they finished, and in order set,
With silent circumspection unespied.
Now when fair morn orient in Heav'n appeared
Up rose the victor angels, and to arms
The matin trumpet sung: in arms they stood

---

496. *cheer:* literally, "face"; by extension, "aspect," "frame of
mind."

514. *concocted and adusted:* heated and reduced to ashes.

519. *incentive reed:* i.e., the gunner's match.

520. *pernicious:* quick to destroy.

521. *conscious night:* i.e., night was aware of their deeds.

Of golden panoply, refulgent host,
Soon banded; others from the dawning hills
Looked round, and scouts each coast light-arméd scour,
Each quarter, to descry the distant foe,　　　　530
Where lodged, or whither fled, or if for fight,
In motion or in alt: him soon they met
Under spread ensigns moving nigh, in slow
But firm battalion; back with speediest sail
Zophiel, of Cherubim the swiftest wing,
Came flying, and in mid air aloud thus cried.

　　" 'Arm, warriors, arm for fight, the foe at hand,
Whom fled we thought, will save us long pursuit
This day, fear not his flight; so thick a cloud
He comes, and settled in his face I see　　　　540
Sad resolution and secure: let each
His adamantine coat gird well; and each
Fit well his helm, grip fast his orbéd shield,
Borne ev'n or high, for this day will pour down,
If I conjecture aught, no drizzling show'r,
But rattling storm of arrows barbed with fire.'
So warned he them aware themselves, and soon
In order, quit of all impediment;
Instant without disturb they took alarm,
And onward move embattled; when behold　　　　550
Not distant far with heavy pace the foe
Approaching gross and huge; in hollow cube
Training his devilish enginry, impaled
On every side with shadowing squadrons deep,
To hide the fraud. At interview both stood
Awhile, but suddenly at head appeared
Satan: and thus was heard commanding loud.

　　" 'Vanguard, to right and left the front unfold;

---

541. *sad:* steadfast. *secure:* free from care (implying, as often,
a false sense of security).
548. *impediment:* baggage (of an army); i.e., they have no artillery.
549. *took alarm:* sprang to arms.
553. *training:* dragging. *impaled:* fenced round.

That all may see who hate us, how we seek
Peace and composure, and with open breast   56
Stand ready to receive them, if they like
Our overture, and turn not back perverse;
But that I doubt; however witness Heav'n,
Heav'n witness thou anon, while we discharge
Freely our part; ye who appointed stand
Do as you have in charge, and briefly touch
What we propound, and loud that all may hear.'
    "So scoffing in ambiguous words, he scarce
Had ended; when to right and left the front
Divided, and to either flank retired.   57
Which to our eyes discovered new and strange,
A triple-mounted row of pillars laid
On wheels (for like to pillars most they seemed
Or hollowed bodies made of oak or fir
With branches lopped, in wood or mountain felled)
Brass, iron, stony mold, had not their mouths
With hideous orifice gaped on us wide,
Portending hollow truce; at each behind
A Seraph stood, and in his hand a reed
Stood waving tipped with fire; while we suspense, 58
Collected stood within our thoughts amused,
Not long, for sudden all at once their reeds
Put forth, and to a narrow vent applied
With nicest touch. Immediate in a flame,
But soon obscured with smoke, all Heav'n appeared,
From those deep-throated engines belched, whose roar
Emboweled with outrageous noise the air,

564–566. The wordplay in *discharge, charge,* and *touch* has bee
regarded as a deplorable attempt at humor on M.'s part. Th
point is rather that these puns, like those of Belial in lines 621
627, are characteristically Satanic reductions from the metaphori
cal to the literal. Raphael's pun in "hollow truce" (line 578) work
the other way: it moves from the literal to the metaphorical.

576. *mold:* substance.

580. *suspense:* in suspense.

581. *amused:* in a muse, wondering.

584. *nicest:* most exact.

587. *emboweled:* filled.

And all her entrails tore, disgorging foul
Their devilish glut, chained thunderbolts and hail
Of iron globes, which on the victor host   590
Leveled, with such impetuous fury smote,
That whom they hit, none on their feet might stand,
Though standing else as rocks, but down thcy fell
By thousands, angel on archangel rolled;
The sooner for their arms, unarmed they might
Have easily as spirits evaded swift
By quick contraction or remove; but now
Foul dissipation followed and forced rout;
Nor served it to relax their serried files.
What should they do? If on they rushed, repulse   600
Repeated, and indecent overthrow
Doubled, would render them yet more despised,
And to their foes a laughter; for in view
Stood ranked of Seraphim another row
In posture to displode their second tire
Of thunder: back defeated to return
They worse abhorred. Satan beheld their plight,
And to his mates thus in derision called.

" 'O friends, why come not on these victors proud?
Erewhile they fierce were coming, and when we,   610
To entertain them fair with open front
And breast (what could we more?), propounded terms
Of composition, straight they changed their minds,
Flew off, and into strange vagaries fell,
As they would dance, yet for a dance they seemed
Somewhat extravagant and wild, perhaps
For joy of offered peace: but I suppose
If our proposals once again were heard
We should compel them to a quick result.'

"To whom thus Belial in like gamesome mood.   620
'Leader, the terms we sent were terms of weight,
Of hard contents, and full of force urged home,

---

598. *dissipation:* dispersal.
601. *indecent:* disgraceful.
605. *displode:* explode. *tire:* volley.

Such as we might perceive amused them all,
And stumbled many; who receives them right,
Had need from head to foot well understand;
Not understood, this gift they have besides,
They show us when our foes walk not upright.'
  "So they among themselves in pleasant vein
Stood scoffing, highthened in their thoughts beyond
All doubt of victory, eternal might   630
To match with their inventions they presumed
So easy, and of his thunder made a scorn,
And all his host derided, while they stood
Awhile in trouble; but they stood not long,
Rage prompted them at length, and found them arms
Against such hellish mischief fit to oppose.
Forthwith (behold the excellence, the power
Which God hath in his mighty angels placed)
Their arms away they threw, and to the hills
(For earth hath this variety from Heav'n   640
Of pleasure situate in hill and dale)
Light as the lightning glimpse they ran, they flew,
From their foundations loos'ning to and fro
They plucked the seated hills with all their load,
Rocks, waters, woods, and by the shaggy tops
Up lifting bore them in their hands. Amaze,
Be sure, and terror seized the rebel host,
When coming towards them so dread they saw
The bottom of the mountains upward turned,
Till on those cursed engines triple-row   650
They saw them whelmed, and all their confidence
Under the weight of mountains buried deep,
Themselves invaded next, and on their heads
Main promontories flung, which in the air
Came shadowing, and oppressed whole legions armed.
Their armor helped their harm, crushed in and bruised
Into their substance pent, which wrought them pain

---

633. *they:* i.e., God's host of angels.
651. *whelmed:* thrown violently.

Implacable, and many a dolorous groan,
Long struggling underneath, ere they could wind
Out of such prison, though spirits of purest light,   660
Purest at first, now gross by sinning grown.
The rest in imitation to like arms
Betook them, and the neighboring hills uptore;
So hills amid the air encountered hills
Hurled to and fro with jaculation dire,
That under ground they fought in dismal shade;
Infernal noise; war seemed a civil game
To this uproar; horrid confusion heaped
Upon confusion rose: and now all Heav'n
Had gone to wrack, with ruin overspread,   670
Had not th' Almighty Father where he sits
Shrined in his sanctuary of Heav'n secure,
Consulting on the sum of things, foreseen
This tumult, and permitted all, advised:
That his great purpose he might so fulfill,
To honor his anointed Son avenged
Upon his enemies, and to declare
All power on him transferred: whence to his Son
Th' assessor of his throne he thus began.

    " 'Effulgence of my glory, Son beloved,   680
Son in whose face invisible is beheld
Visibly, what by Deity I am,
And in whose hand what by decree I do,
Second omnipotence, two days are passed,
Two days, as we compute the days of Heav'n,
Since Michael and his powers went forth to tame
These disobedient; sore hath been their fight,
As likeliest was, when two such foes met armed;
For to themselves I left them, and thou know'st,

---

665. *jaculation:* hurling.

674. *advised:* having taken counsel with himself (a past part. modifying "Almighty Father").

679. *assessor:* literally, "one who sits by"; still used in England of associate judges.

Equal in their creation they were formed,   690
Save what sin hath impaíred, which yet hath wrought
Insensibly, for I suspend their doom;
Whence in perpetual fight they needs must last
Endless, and no solution will be found:
War wearied hath performed what war can do,
And to disordered rage let loose the reins,
With mountains as with weapons armed, which makes
Wild work in Heav'n, and dangerous to the main.
Two days are therefore passed, the third is thine;
For thee I have ordained it, and thus far   700
Have suffered, that the glory may be thine
Of ending this great war, since none but thou
Can end it. Into thee such virtue and grace
Immense I have transfused, that all may know
In Heav'n and Hell thy power above compare,
And this perverse commotion governed thus,
To manifest thee worthiest to be heir
Of all things, to be heir and to be king
By sacred unction, thy deservéd right.
Go then thou mightiest in thy Father's might,   710
Ascend my chariot, guide the rapid wheels
That shake Heav'n's basis, bring forth all my war,
My bow and thunder, my almighty arms
Gird on, and sword upon thy puissant thigh;
Pursue these sons of darkness, drive them out
From all Heav'n's bounds into the utter deep:
There let them learn, as likes them, to despise
God and Messiah his anointed King.'
    "He said, and on his Son with rays direct
Shone full, he all his Father full expressed   720
Ineffably into his face received,
And thus the Filial Godhead answering spake.

---

692. *insensibly:* imperceptibly.
698. *main:* the whole "land" of Heaven.
701. *suffered:* permitted.
709. *unction:* anointing.
712. *war:* army.
716. *utter:* outer.

" 'O Father, O Supreme of heav'nly Thrones,
First, highest, holiest, best, thou always seek'st
To glorify thy Son, I always thee,
As is most just; this I my glory account,
My exaltation, and my whole delight,
That thou in me well pleased, declar'st thy will
Fulfilled, which to fulfill is all my bliss.
Scepter and power, thy giving, I assume,   730
And gladlier shall resign, when in the end
Thou shalt be all in all, and I in thee
Forever, and in me all whom thou lov'st:
But whom thou hat'st, I hate, and can put on
Thy terrors, as I put thy mildness on,
Image of thee in all things; and shall soon,
Armed with thy might, rid Heav'n of these rebelled,
To their prepared ill mansion driven down
To chains of darkness, and th' undying worm,
That from thy just obedience could revolt,   740
Whom to obey is happiness entire.
Then shall thy saints unmixed, and from th' impure
Far separate, circling thy holy mount
Unfeignéd halleluiahs to thee sing,
Hymns of high praise, and I among them chief.'
So said, he o'er his scepter bowing, rose
From the right hand of glory where he sat,
And the third sacred morn began to shine
Dawning through Heav'n: forth rushed with whirlwind
    sound
The chariot of paternal Deity,   750
Flashing thick flames, wheel within wheel undrawn,
Itself instinct with spirit, but convoyed
By four cherubic shapes, four faces each
Had wondrous, as with stars their bodies all

723–745. Among the New Testament passages of which this speech is woven are John 17:1, Matthew 3:17, 1 Corinthians 15:28, Revelation 20:1–2, and Mark 9:44.

749–759. The chariot comes from the vision in the first chapter of Ezekiel. Jewish commentators interpreted this vision as a prophecy of the Last Day.

And wings were set with eyes, with eyes the wheels
Of beryl, and careering fires between;
Over their heads a crystal firmament,
Whereon a sapphire throne, inlaid with pure
Amber, and colors of the show'ry arch.
He in celestial panoply all armed   760
Of radiant Urim, work divinely wrought,
Ascended, at his right hand victory
Sat eagle-winged, beside him hung his bow
And quiver with three-bolted thunder stored,
And from about him fierce effusion rolled
Of smoke and bickering flame, and sparkles dire;
Attended with ten thousand thousand saints,
He onward came, far off his coming shone,
And twenty thousand (I their number heard)
Chariots of God, half on each hand were seen: 770
He on the wings of Cherub rode sublime
On the crystálline sky, in sapphire throned.
Illustrious far and wide, but by his own
First seen, them unexpected joy surprised,
When the great ensign of Messiah blazed
Aloft by angels borne, his sign in Heav'n:
Under whose conduct Michael soon reduced
His army, circumfused on either wing,
Under their Head embodied all in one.
Before him Power Divine his way prepared;   780
At his command th' uprooted hills retired
Each to his place, they heard his voice and went
Obsequious, Heav'n his wonted face renewed,
And with fresh flow'rets hill and valley smiled.
This saw his hapless foes, but stood obdured,
And to rebellious fight rallied their powers

---

761. *Urim:* objects (perhaps precious stones, since *urim* appears
to mean "lights") worn on the "breastplate of judgment" by the
high-priest Aaron (Exodus 28:30).

766. *bickering:* quivering.

771. *sublime:* uplifted.

777. *reduced:* led back.

785. *obdured:* hardened.

Insensate, hope conceiving from despair.
In heav'nly spirits could such perverseness dwell?
But to convince the proud what signs avail,
Or wonders move th' obdurate to relent?   790
They hardened more by what might most reclaim,
Grieving to see his glory, at the sight
Took envy, and aspiring to his highth,
Stood reimbattled fierce, by force or fraud
Weening to prosper, and at length prevail
Against God and Messiah, or to fall
In universal ruin last, and now
To final battle drew, disdaining flight,
Or faint retreat; when the great Son of God
To all his host on either hand thus spake.   800
    " 'Stand still in bright array ye saints, here stand
Ye angels armed, this day from battle rest;
Faithful hath been your warfare, and of God
Accepted, fearless in his righteous cause,
And as ye have received, so have ye done
Invincibly; but of this curséd crew
The punishment to other hand belongs,
Vengeance is his, or whose he sole appoints;
Number to this day's work is not ordained
Nor multitude, stand only and behold   810
God's indignation on these godless poured
By me, not you but me they have despised,
Yet envied; against me is all their rage,
Because the Father, t' whom in Heav'n supreme
Kingdom and power and glory appertains,
Hath honored me according to his will.
Therefore to me their doom he hath assigned;
That they may have their wish, to try with me
In battle which the stronger proves, they all,
Or I alone against them since by strength   820
They measure all, of other excellence
Not emulous, nor care who them excels;
Nor other strife with them do I vouchsafe.'
    "So spake the Son, and into terror changed
His count'nance too severe to be beheld

And full of wrath bent on his enemies.
At once the four spread out their starry wings
With dreadful shade contiguous, and the orbs
Of his fierce chariot rolled, as with the sound
Of torrent floods, or of a numerous host.   830
He on his impious foes right onward drove,
Gloomy as night; under his burning wheels
The steadfast empyrean shook throughout,
All but the throne itself of God. Full soon
Among them he arrived; in his right hand
Grasping ten thousand thunders, which he sent
Before him, such as in their souls infixed
Plagues; they astonished all resistance lost,
All courage; down their idle weapons dropped;
O'er shields and helms, and helméd heads he rode   840
Of Thrones and mighty Seraphim prostrate,
That wished the mountains now might be again
Thrown on them as a shelter from his ire.
Nor less on either side tempestuous fell
His arrows, from the fourfold-visaged four,
Distinct with eyes, and from the living wheels,
Distinct alike with multitude of eyes,
One spirit in them rules, and every eye
Glared lightning, and shot forth pernicious fire
Among th' accurst, that withered all their strength,   850
And of their wonted vigor left them drained,
Exhausted, spiritless, afflicted, fall'n.
Yet half his strength he put not forth, but checked
His thunder in mid volley, for he meant
Not to destroy, but root them out of Heav'n.
The overthrown he raised, and as a herd
Of goats or timorous flock together thronged
Drove them before him thunder-struck, pursued
With terrors and with furies to the bounds
And crystal wall of Heav'n, which opening wide,   860

838. *astonished:* stupefied.
842. Cf. Revelation 6:16. This is another allusion to the Last Judgment.

Rolled inward, and a spacious gap disclosed
Into the wasteful deep; the monstrous sight
Struck them with horror backward, but far worse
Urged them behind; headlong themselves they threw
Down from the verge of Heav'n, eternal wrath
Burnt after them to the bottomless pit.

    "Hell heard th' unsufferable noise, Hell saw
Heav'n ruining from Heav'n and would have fled
Affrighted; but strict fate had cast too deep
Her dark foundations, and too fast had bound.   870
Nine days they fell; confounded Chaos roared,
And felt tenfold confusion in their fall
Through his wild anarchy, so huge a rout
Encumbered him with ruin: Hell at last
Yawning received them whole, and on them closed,
Hell their fit habitation fraught with fire
Unquenchable, the house of woe and pain.
Disburdened Heav'n rejoiced, and soon repaired
Her mural breach, returning whence it rolled.
Sole victor from th' expulsion of his foes   880
Messiah his triumphal chariot turned:
To meet him all his saints, who silent stood
Eyewitnesses of his almighty acts,
With jubilee advanced; and as they went,
Shaded with branching palm, each order bright,
Sung triumph, and him sung victorious King,
Son, Heir, and Lord, to him dominion giv'n,
Worthiest to reign: he celebrated rode
Triumphant through mid Heav'n, into the courts
And temple of his mighty Father throned   890
On high: who into glory him received,
Where now he sits at the right hand of bliss.

---

  868. *ruining:* falling.

  879. *mural breach:* breach in the walls.

  880–892. These lines contain allusions to biblical passages (e.g.,
1 Timothy 3:16, Hebrews 1:3) which refer to Christ's return to
glory after his Crucifixion and Resurrection. Christ's defeat of the
rebel angels is thus linked to his redemption of man as well as to
the Last Judgment (cf. line 794*n*, and line 842*n* above).

   "Thus measuring things in Heav'n by things on earth
At thy request, and that thou may'st beware
By what is past, to thee I have revealed
What might have else to human race been hid;
The discord which befell, and war in Heav'n
Among th' angelic powers, and the deep fall
Of those too high aspiring, who rebelled
With Satan, he who envies now thy state,   900
Who now is plotting how he may seduce
Thee also from obedience, that with him
Bereaved of happiness thou may'st partake
His punishment, eternal misery;
Which would be all his solace and revenge,
As a despite done against the Most High,
Thee once to gain companion of his woe.
But listen not to his temptations, warn
Thy weaker; let it profit thee to have heard
By terrible example the reward   910
Of disobedience; firm they might have stood,
Yet fell; remember, and fear to transgress."

------

  909. *thy weaker:* i.e., Eve.

BOOK VII

THE ARGUMENT

Raphael at the request of Adam relates how and
wherefore this world was first created; that God, after
the expelling of Satan and his angels out of Heaven,
declared his pleasure to create another world and other
creatures to dwell therein; sends his Son with glory and
attendance of angels to perform the work of creation in
six days: the angels celebrate with hymns the performance thereof, and his reascension into Heaven.

Descend from Heav'n Urania, by that name
If rightly thou art called, whose voice divine
Following, above th' Olympian hill I soar,
Above the flight of Pegasean wing.
The meaning, not the name I call: for thou
Nor of the Muses nine, nor on the top
Of old Olympus dwell'st, but heav'nly born,

---

1. Cf. I, 6–17, and note.
4. *Pegasean:* Pegasus, the winged horse of Greek mythology,
traditionally symbolized poetic inspiration.

Before the hills appeared, or fountain flowed,
Thou with eternal Wisdom didst converse,
Wisdom thy sister, and with her didst play   10
In presence of th' Almighty Father, pleased
With thy celestial song. Up led by thee
Into the Heav'n of Heav'ns I have presumed,
An earthly guest, and drawn empyreal air,
Thy tempering; with like safety guided down
Return me to my native element:
Lest from this flying steed unreined (as once
Bellerophon, though from a lower clime)
Dismounted, on th' Aleian field I fall
Erroneous there to wander and forlorn.   20
Half yet remains unsung, but narrower bound
Within the visible diurnal sphere;
Standing on earth, not rapt above the pole,
More safe I sing with mortal voice, unchanged
To hoarse or mute, though fall'n on evil days,
On evil days though fall'n, and evil tongues;
In darkness, and with dangers compassed round,
And solitude; yet not alone, while thou

8–10. Cf. Proverbs 8:23–24, 30,

  I [Wisdom] was set up from everlasting, from the beginning,
or ever the earth was.
  When there were no depths, I was brought forth; when there
were no fountains abounding with water. . . .
  Then I was by him [God], as one brought up with him: and
I was daily his delight, rejoicing [Vulgate *ludens,* "playing"]
always before him.

M.'s invocations of the Muse combine secular and religious allegory and symbolism, and there is little point in trying to extract
theological dogma from them. In literal terms, M. is praying to
God for inspiration.

15. *thy tempering:* tempered (to my mortal lungs) by thee.

18. *Bellerophon* was thrown to earth by Zeus when he tried to
mount to heaven on Pegasus. Horace alludes to him in *Odes,* IV,
xi, as an example of presumption.

22. *diurnal sphere:* the sphere of the sun, which makes a daily
(diurnal) revolution around the earth.

23. *rapt above the pole:* caught up to the region beyond the
zenith of the created universe.

Visit'st my slumbers nightly, or when morn
Purples the east: still govern thou my song,   30
Urania, and fit audience find, though few.
But drive far off the barbarous dissonance
Of Bacchus and his revelers, the race
Of that wild rout that tore the Thracian bard
In Rhodope, where woods and rocks had ears
To rapture, till the savage clamor drowned
Both harp and voice; nor could the Muse defend
Her son. So fail not thou, who thee implores:
For thou art heav'nly, she an empty dream.
    Say goddess, what ensued when Raphael,   40
The affable Archangel, had forewarned
Adam by dire example to beware
Apostasy, by what befell in Heav'n
To those apostates, lest the like befall
In Paradise to Adam or his race,
Charged not to touch the interdicted tree,
If they transgress, and slight that sole command
So easily obeyed amid the choice
Of all tastes else to please their appetite,
Though wandering. He with his consorted Eve   50
The story heard attentive, and was filled
With admiration, and deep muse to hear
Of things so high and strange, things to their thought
So unimaginable as hate in Heav'n,
And war so near the peace of God in bliss
With such confusion: but the evil soon
Driv'n back redounded as a flood on those
From whom it sprung, impossible to mix
With blessedness. Whence Adam soon repealed
The doubts that in his heart arose: and now   60

32–38. The *Thracian bard* is Orpheus, whose death at the hands
of the worshipers of *Bacchus* (whose spiritual descendants M. saw
all around him in Restoration England) is told in Ovid's *Metamorphoses* XI, 1–43. There was a shrine of Bacchus in the mountain range *Rhodope*.

  50. *consorted:* associated.

  59. *repealed:* recalled.

Led on, yet sinless, with desire to know
What nearer might concern him, how this world
Of heav'n and earth conspicuous first began,
When, and whereof created, for what cause,
What within Eden or without was done
Before his memory, as one whose drouth
Yet scarce allayed still eyes the current stream,
Whose liquid murmur heard new thirst excites,
Proceeded thus to ask his heav'nly guest.
　　"Great things, and full of wonder in our ears,　　70
Far differing from this world, thou hast revealed
Divine interpreter, by favor sent
Down from the empyrean to forewarn
Us timely of what might else have been our loss,
Unknown, which human knowledge could not reach:
For which to the infinitely Good we owe
Immortal thanks, and his admonishment
Receive with solemn purpose to observe
Immutably his sovran will, the end
Of what we are. But since thou hast vouchsafed　　80
Gently for our instruction to impart
Things above earthly thought, which yet concerned
Our knowing, as to highest wisdom seemed,
Deign to descend now lower, and relate
What may no less perhaps avail us known,
How first began this heav'n which we behold
Distant so high, with moving fires adorned
Innumerable, and this which yields or fills
All space, the ambient air wide interfused
Embracing round this florid earth, what cause　　90
Moved the Creator in his holy rest
Through all eternity so late to build
In Chaos, and the work begun, how soon
Absolved, if unforbid thou may'st unfold

---

66. *drouth:* thirst.
79. *end:* purpose.
88. *yields:* i.e., to bodies.
94. *absolved:* finished.

What we, not to explore the secrets ask
Of his eternal empire, but the more
To magnify his works, the more we know.
And the great light of day yet wants to run
Much of his race though steep, suspense in heav'n
Held by thy voice, thy potent voice he hears,   100
And longer will delay to hear thee tell
His generation, and the rising birth
Of nature from the unapparent deep:
Or if the star of evening and the moon
Haste to thy audience, night with her will bring
Silence, and sleep listening to thee will watch,
Or we can bid his absence, till thy song
End, and dismiss thee ere the morning shine."
    Thus Adam his illustrious guest besought:
    And thus the godlike angel answered mild.   110
"This also thy request with caution asked
Obtain: though to recount almighty works
What words or tongue of Seraph can suffice,
Or heart of man suffice to comprehend?
Yet what thou canst attain, which best may serve
To glorify the Maker, and infer
Thee also happier, shall not be withheld
Thy hearing, such commission from above
I have received, to answer thy desire
Of knowledge within bounds; beyond abstain   120
To ask, nor let thine own inventions hope
Things not revealed, which th' invisible King,
Only omniscient, hath suppressed in night,
To none communicable in earth or Heav'n:
Enough is left besides to search and know.
But knowledge is as food, and needs no less
Her temperance over appetite, to know
In measure what the mind may well contain,

---

98. *yet wants:* has yet.
99. *suspense:* suspended.
103. *unapparent deep:* invisible Chaos.
106. *watch:* stay awake.
116. *infer:* show, prove.

Oppresses else with surfeit, and soon turns
Wisdom to folly, as nourishment to wind.
   "Know then, that after Lucifer from Heav'n
(So call him, brighter once amidst the host
Of angels, than that star the stars among)
Fell with his flaming legions through the deep
Into his place, and the great Son returned
Victorious with his saints, th' omnipotent
Eternal Father from his throne beheld
Their multitude, and to his Son thus spake.
   " 'At least our envious foe hath failed, who thought
All like himself rebellious, by whose aid   1
This inaccessible high strength, the seat
Of Deity supreme, us dispossessed,
He trusted to have seized, and into fraud
Drew many, whom their place knows here no more;
Yet far the greater part have kept, I see,
Their station, Heav'n yet populous retains
Number sufficient to possess her realms
Though wide, and this high temple to frequent
With ministeries due and solemn rites:
But lest his heart exalt him in the harm   1
Already done, to have dispeopled Heav'n,
My damage fondly deemed, I can repair
That detriment, if such it be to lose
Self-lost, and in a moment will create
Another world, out of one man a race
Of men innumerable, there to dwell,
Not here, till by degrees of merit raised
They open to themselves at length the way

---

131. *Lucifer:* The famous passage in Isaiah 14:12, "How a
thou fallen from heaven, O Lucifer, son of the morning," is
figurative reference to the king of Babylon. Christian comment
tors regarded it as referring "mystically" to Satan.

142. *us dispossessed:* having dispossessed us.

143. *fraud:* crime.

152. *my damage fondly deemed:* which he foolishly thinks is
damage to me.

153–154. *if . . . Self-lost:* "If it can be called a detriment
lose those who in reality caused themselves to be lost."

Up hither, under long obedience tried,   159
And earth be changed to Heav'n, and Heav'n to earth,
One kingdom, joy and union without end.
Meanwhile inhabit lax, ye powers of Heav'n,
And thou my Word, begotten Son, by thee
This I perform, speak thou, and be it done:
My overshadowing spirit and might with thee
I send along, ride forth, and bid the deep
Within appointed bounds be heav'n and earth;
Boundless the deep, because I am who fill
Infinitude, nor vacuous the space.
Though I uncircumscribed myself retire,   170
And put not forth my goodness, which is free
To act or not, necessity and chance
Approach not me, and what I will is fate.'
　"So spake th' Almighty, and to what he spake
His Word, the Filial Godhead, gave effect.
Immediate are the acts of God, more swift
Than time or motion, but to human ears
Cannot without process of speech be told,
So told as earthly notion can receive.
Great triumph and rejoicing was in Heav'n   180
When such was heard declared th' Almighty's will;

---

162. *inhabit lax*: spread out.

168–173. This knotty philosophical passage is an attack on
mechanistic and fatalistic theories of the universe like those of
Lucretius or M.'s contemporary, Hobbes. God says that Chaos
(*the deep*) is boundless because God, who fills it, is infinite; on
the other hand, God may be present in different ways: though
uncircumscribed, he may freely choose not to put forth his goodness, but this does not mean that the space from which he has
"retired" is empty. The creation of the universe may be viewed
as the "putting forth" of God's goodness into Chaos.

175. For his belief that the creation was effected by the Son, M.
had the authority of John 1:1–3 and Colossians 1:16.

176–179. The belief that creation was instantaneous and that
the biblical account was an "accommodation" to human understanding (*earthly notion*) was thoroughly orthodox. It is char-
acteristic of Satan's mind that he takes the six days literally (IX,
137–138).

Glory they sung to the Most High, good will
To future men, and in their dwellings peace:
Glory to him whose just avenging ire
Had driven out th' ungodly from his sight
And th' habitations of the just; to him
Glory and praise, whose wisdom had ordained
Good out of evil to create, instead
Of spirits malign a better race to bring
Into their vacant room, and thence diffuse   190
His good to worlds and ages infinite.
So sang the hierarchies: meanwhile the Son
On his great expedition now appeared,
Girt with omnipotence, with radiance crowned
Of majesty divine, sapience and love
Immense, and all his Father in him shone.
About his chariot numberless were poured
Cherub and Seraph, Potentates and Thrones,
And Virtues, wingéd spirits, and chariots winged,
From the armory of God, where stand of old   200
Myriads between two brazen mountains lodged
Against a solemn day, harnessed at hand,
Celestial equipage; and now came forth
Spontaneous, for within them spirit lived,
Attendant on their Lord: Heav'n opened wide
Her ever-during gates, harmonious sound
On golden hinges moving, to let forth
The King of glory in his powerful Word
And spirit coming to create new worlds.
On heav'nly ground they stood, and from the shore   210
They viewed the vast immeasurable abyss
Outrageous as a sea, dark, wasteful, wild,
Up from the bottom turned by furious winds
And surging waves, as mountains to assault
Heav'n's highth, and with the center mix the pole.
    " 'Silence, ye troubled waves, and thou deep, peace,'
Said then th' omnific Word, 'your discord end.'

---

202. *against:* in readiness for.
205–206. Cf. Psalm 24:9, and line 565 below.

"Nor stayed, but on the wings of Cherubim
Uplifted, in paternal glory rode
Far into Chaos, and the world unborn;   220
For Chaos heard his voice: him all his train,
Followed in bright procession to behold
Creation, and the wonders of his might.
Then stayed the fervid wheels, and in his hand
He took the golden compasses, prepared
In God's eternal store, to circumscribe
This universe, and all created things:
One foot he centered, and the other turned
Round through the vast profundity obscure,
And said, 'Thus far extend, thus far thy bounds,   230
This be thy just circumference, O world.'
Thus God the heav'n created, thus the earth,
Matter unformed and void: darkness profound
Covered th' abyss: but on the wat'ry calm
His brooding wings the Spirit of God outspread,
And vital virtue infused, and vital warmth
Throughout the fluid mass, but downward purged
The black tartareous cold infernal dregs
Adverse to life: then founded, then conglobed
Like things to like, the rest to several place   240
Disparted, and between spun out the air,
And earth self-balanced on her center hung.

232–242. This passage has been variously interpreted. Lines
232–235 follow closely Genesis 1:1–2. The *cold infernal dregs*
of line 238 would seem to be not the lower elements of earth and
water, but those "dark materials" (II, 916) that are relegated to
Chaos. Two interpretations of lines 239–241 seem possible: (1)
God then established (*founded*) and caused to form into a globe
(*conglobed*) like things; what remained after the earth was thus
formed (*the rest*) he caused to separate in different directions
(*disparted*), each in its own place, and between the earth and
these other elements he spun out the air. (2) What remained after
the dregs had been purged (*the rest*), this remainder having been
established and formed into a globe, like things to like, God caused
to separate in different directions, each in its own place, and between the lower elements and the higher elements he spun out
the air. Line 243 refers back to Genesis 1:3.

" 'Let there be light,' said God, and forthwith light
Ethereal, first of things, quintessence pure
Sprung from the deep, and from her native east
To journey through the airy gloom began,
Sphered in a radiant cloud, for yet the sun
Was not; she in a cloudy tabernacle
Sojourned the while. God saw the light was good;
And light from darkness by the hemisphere   250
Divided: light the day, and darkness night
He named. Thus was the first day ev'n and morn:
Nor passed uncelebrated, nor unsung
By the celestial choirs, when orient light
Exhaling first from darkness they beheld;
Birthday of heav'n and earth; with joy and shout
The hollow universal orb they filled,
And touched their golden harps, and hymning praised
God and his works, Creator him they sung,
Both when first evening was, and when first morn.   260
    "Again, God said, 'Let there be firmament
Amid the waters, and let it divide
The waters from the waters.' And God made
The firmament, expanse of liquid, pure,
Transparent, elemental air, diffused
In circuit to the uttermost convex
Of this great round: partition firm and sure,
The waters underneath from those above
Dividing: for as earth, so he the world
Built on circumfluous waters calm, in wide   270
Crystalline ocean, and the loud misrule
Of Chaos far removed, lest fierce extremes
Contiguous might distemper the whole frame:
And heav'n he named the firmament: so ev'n
And morning chorus sung the second day.
    "The earth was formed, but in the womb as yet

---

257. *universal orb:* the universe.
267–269. *round* and *world* both refer to the universe.
271. The *crystalline ocean* that surrounds the universe is not to
be confused with the ninth or "crystalline sphere" of III, 482.

Of waters, embryon immature involved,
Appeared not: over all the face of earth
Main ocean flowed, not idle, but with warm
Prolific humor softening all her globe,　　　　　280
Fermented the great mother to conceive,
Satiate with genial moisture, when God said
'Be gathered now ye waters under heav'n
Into one place, and let dry land appear.'
Immediately the mountains huge appear
Emergent, and their broad bare backs upheave
Into the clouds, their tops ascend the sky:
So high as heaved the tumid hills, so low
Down sunk a hollow bottom broad and deep,
Capacious bed of waters: thither they　　　　　290
Hasted with glad precipitance, uprolled
As drops on dust conglobing from the dry;
Part rise in crystal wall, or ridge direct,
For haste; such flight the great command impressed
On the swift floods: as armies at the call
Of trumpet (for of armies thou hast heard)
Troop to their standard, so the wat'ry throng,
Wave rolling after wave, where way they found,
If steep, with torrent rapture, if through plain,
Soft-ebbing; nor withstood them rock or hill,　　　　　300
But they, or under ground, or circuit wide
With serpent error wandering, found their way,
And on the washy ooze deep channels wore;
Easy, ere God had bid the ground be dry,
All but within those banks, where rivers now
Stream, and perpetual draw their humid train.
The dry land, earth, and the great receptacle
Of congregated waters he called seas:
And saw that it was good, and said, 'Let th' earth

---

277. *involved:* wrapped.
280. *humor:* moistness.
282. *genial:* creative.
299. *torrent rapture:* torrential movement.
302. *error:* meandering; cf. "mazy error" in IV, 239.
306. *humid train:* liquid flow.

Put forth the verdant grass, herb yielding seed,   310
And fruit tree yielding fruit after her kind;
Whose seed is in herself upon the earth.'
He scarce had said, when the bare earth, till then
Desert and bare, unsightly, unadorned,
Brought forth the tender grass, whose verdure clad
Her universal face with pleasant green,
Then herbs of every leaf, that sudden flow'red
Opening their various colors, and made gay
Her bosom smelling sweet: and these scarce blown,
Forth flourished thick the clustering vine, forth crept   320
The swelling gourd, up stood the corny reed
Embattled in her field: and th' humble shrub,
And bush with frizzled hair implicit: last
Rose as in dance the stately trees, and spread
Their branches hung with copious fruit; or gemmed
Their blossoms: with high woods the hills were
         crowned,
With tufts the valleys and each fountain side,
With borders long the rivers. That earth now
Seemed like to Heav'n, a seat where gods might dwell,
Or wander with delight, and love to haunt   330
Her sacred shades: though God had yet not rained
Upon the earth, and man to till the ground
None was, but from the earth a dewy mist
Went up and watered all the ground, and each
Plant of the field, which ere it was in the earth
God made, and every herb, before it grew
On the green stem; God saw that it was good.
So ev'n and morn recorded the third day.
    "Again th' Almighty spake: 'Let there be lights
High in th' expanse of heaven to divide   340
The day from night; and let them be for signs,
For seasons, and for days, and circling years,

---

321. *swelling:* Bentley's emendation for the "smelling" of the
original edition. *corny:* corn- (i.e., grain) bearing.
323. *implicit:* tangled.
325. *gemmed:* budded.

And let them be for lights as I ordain
Their office in the firmament of heav'n
To give light on the earth'; and it was so.
And God made two great lights, great for their use
To man, the greater to have rule by day,
The less by night altern: and made the stars,
And set them in the firmament of heav'n
To illuminate the earth, and rule the day　　　　　350
In their vicissitude, and rule the night,
And light from darkness to divide. God saw,
Surveying his great work, that it was good:
For of celestial bodies first the sun
A mighty sphere he framed, unlightsome first,
Though of ethereal mold: then formed the moon
Globose, and every magnitude of stars,
And sowed with stars the heav'n thick as a field:
Of light by far the greater part he took,
Transplanted from her cloudy shrine, and placed　　360
In the sun's orb, made porous to receive
And drink the liquid light, firm to retain
Her gathered beams, great palace now of light.
Hither as to their fountain other stars
Repairing, in their golden urns draw light,
And hence the morning planet gilds her horns;
By tincture or reflection they augment
Their small peculiar, though from human sight
So far remote, with diminution seen.
First in his east the glorious lamp was seen,　　　370
Regent of day, and all th' horizon round
Invested with bright rays, jocund to run
His longitude through heav'n's high road: the gray
Dawn, and the Pleiades before him danced
Shedding sweet influence: less bright the moon,

---

351. *vicissitude:* alternation.
356. *mold:* substance.
366. *horns:* a reference to the phases of Venus, discovered by
Galileo.
367. *tincture:* absorption.
368. *their small peculiar:* their own small possession (of light).

But opposite in leveled west was set
His mirror, with full face borrowing her light
From him, for other light she needed none
In that aspect, and still that distance keeps
Till night, then in the east her turn she shines,   380
Revolved on heav'n's great axle, and her reign
With thousand lesser lights dividual holds,
With thousand thousand stars, that then appeared
Spangling the hemisphere: then first adorned
With their bright luminaries that set and rose,
Glad evening and glad morn crowned the fourth day.
   "And God said, 'Let the waters generate
Reptile with spawn abundant, living soul:
And let fowl fly above the earth, with wings
Displayed on the op'n firmament of heav'n.'   390
And God created the great whales, and each
Soul living, each that crept, which plenteously
The waters generated by their kinds,
And every bird of wing after his kind;
And saw that it was good, and blessed them, saying,
'Be fruitful, multiply, and in the seas
And lakes and running streams the waters fill;
And let the fowl be multiplied on th' earth.'
Forthwith the sounds and seas, each creek and bay
With fry innumerable swarm, and shoals   400
Of fish that with their fins and shining scales
Glide under the green wave, in sculls that oft
Bank the mid sea: part single or with mate
Graze the seaweed their pasture, and through groves
Of coral stray, or sporting with quick glance
Show to the sun their waved coats dropped with gold,
Or in their pearly shells at ease, attend

---

382. *dividual:* divided (modifies "reign").
388. *reptile:* any creeping thing, including fish. *living soul:*
combines the "life" of Genesis 1:20 with the marginal note "Hebrew *soul.*"
390. *displayed:* spread out.
402. *sculls:* schools.
403. *bank the mid sea:* make a bank in mid-ocean.
407. *attend:* watch for.

Moist nutriment, or under rocks their food
In jointed armor watch: on smooth the seal,
And bended dolphins play: part huge of bulk   410
Wallowing unwieldy, enormous in their gait
Tempest the ocean: there Leviathan
Hugest of living creatures, on the deep
Stretched like a promontory sleeps or swims,
And seems a moving land, and at his gills
Draws in, and at his trunk spouts out a sea.
Meanwhile the tepid caves, and fens and shores
Their brood as numerous hatch, from th' egg that soon
Bursting with kindly rupture forth disclosed
Their callow young, but feathered soon and fledge   420
They summed their pens, and soaring th' air sublime
With clang despised the ground, under a cloud
In prospect; there the eagle and the stork
On cliffs and cedar tops their eyries build:
Part loosely wing the region, part more wise
In common, ranged in figure wedge their way,
Intelligent of seasons, and set forth
Their aery caravan high over seas
Flying, and over lands with mutual wing
Easing their flight; so steers the prudent crane   430
Her annual voyage, borne on winds; the air
Floats, as they pass, fanned with unnumbered plumes:
From branch to branch the smaller birds with song
Solaced the woods, and spread their painted wings
Till ev'n, nor then the solemn nightingale
Ceased warbling, but all night tuned her soft lays:

---

409. *on smooth:* on the smooth water.
419. *kindly:* natural.
420. *fledge:* fledged.
421. *summed their pens:* developed all their feathers.
422-423. *under a cloud/ In prospect:* viewed from a distance, the numerous birds seemed like a cloud.
425. *loosely:* singly, as opposed to "in common" (line 426).
429-430. *with . . . flight:* In *Natural History,* X, xxxii, Pliny tells how geese and swans "place their necks on the birds in front of them, and when the leaders are tired they receive them in the rear" (Loeb trans.).

Others on silver lakes and rivers bathed
Their downy breast; the swan with archéd neck
Between her white wings mantling proudly, rows
Her state with oary feet: yet oft they quit   440
The dank, and rising on stiff pennons, tow'r
The mid aereal sky: others on ground
Walked firm; the crested cock whose clarion sounds
The silent hours, and th' other whose gay train
Adorns him, colored with the florid hue
Of rainbows and starry eyes. The waters thus
With fish replenished, and the air with fowl,
Evening and morn solemnized the fifth day.
    "The sixth, and of creation last arose
With evening harps and matin, when God said,   450
'Let th' earth bring forth soul living in her kind,
Cattle and creeping things, and beast of th' earth,
Each in their kind.' The earth obeyed, and straight
Opening her fertile womb teemed at a birth
Innumerous living creatures, perfect forms,
Limbed and full grown: out of the ground up rose
As from his lair the wild beast where he wons
In forest wild, in thicket, brake, or den;
Among the trees in pairs they rose, they walked:
The cattle in the fields and meadows green: 460
Those rare and solitary, these in flocks
Pasturing at once, and in broad herds upsprung.
The grassy clods now calved, now half appeared
The tawny lion, pawing to get free
His hinder parts, then springs as broke from bonds,
And rampant shakes his brinded mane; the ounce,
The libbard, and the tiger, as the mole

---

439. *mantling:* making a mantle by raising her wings.
441. *dank:* water.
451. *soul:* Bentley's emendation of "Fowle."
454. *teemed:* brought forth.
457. *wons:* dwells.
461. *rare:* i.e., not "in flocks."
462. *broad:* extensive.
466. *brinded:* brindled. *ounce:* lynx.

Rising, the crumbled earth above them threw
In hillocks; the swift stag from under ground
Bore up his branching head: scarce from his mold   470
Behemoth biggest born of earth upheaved
His vastness: fleeced the flocks and bleating rose,
As plants: ambiguous between sea and land
The river horse and scaly crocodile.
At once came forth whatever creeps the ground,
Insect or worm; those waved their limber fans
For wings, and smallest lineaments exact
In all the liveries decked of summer's pride
With spots of gold and purple, azure and green:
These as a line their long dimension drew,   480
Streaking the ground with sinuous trace; not all
Minims of nature; some of serpent kind
Wondrous in length and corpulence involved
Their snaky folds, and added wings. First crept
The parsimonious emmet, provident
Of future, in small room large heart enclosed,
Pattern of just equality perhaps
Hereafter, joined in her popular tribes
Of commonalty: swarming next appeared
The female bee that feeds her husband drone   490
Deliciously, and builds her waxen cells
With honey stored: the rest are numberless,
And thou their natures know'st, and gav'st them names,
Needless to thee repeated; nor unknown
The serpent subtlest beast of all the field,
Of huge extent sometimes, with brazen eyes
And hairy mane terrific, though to thee

---

471. *Behemoth:* the elephant.
476. *worm:* creeping animals, including serpents.
480. *these:* i.e., the "worm" category.
482. *minims:* smallest creatures.
483. *involved:* coiled.
484. *added wings:* i.e., some serpents had wings, like the "fiery flying serpent" of Isaiah 30:6.
485–489. In *Georgics*, IV, 83, Virgil attributes largeness of heart to bees. M. transfers this quality from the monarchical bee to the republican ant.

Not noxious, but obedient at thy call.
Now heav'n in all her glory shone, and rolled
Her motions, as the great First-mover's hand   500
First wheeled their course; earth in her rich attire
Consummate lovely smiled; air, water, earth,
By fowl, fish, beast, was flown, was swum, was walked
Frequent; and of the sixth day yet remained;
There wanted yet the master work, the end
Of all yet done; a creature who not prone
And brute as other creatures, but endued
With sanctity of reason, might erect
His stature, and upright with front serene
Govern the rest, self-knowing, and from thence   510
Magnanimous to correspond with Heav'n,
But grateful to acknowledge whence his good
Descends, thither with heart and voice and eyes
Directed in devotion, to adore
And worship God supreme, who made him chief
Of all his works: therefore th' omnipotent
Eternal Father (for where is not he
Present) thus to his Son audibly spake.
   " 'Let us make now man in our image, man
In our similitude, and let them rule   520
Over the fish and fowl of sea and air,
Beast of the field, and over all the earth,
And every creeping thing that creeps the ground.'
This said, he formed thee, Adam, thee O man
Dust of the ground, and in thy nostrils breathed
The breath of life; in his own image he
Created thee, in the image of God
Express, and thou becam'st a living soul.
Male he created thee, but thy consort

---

504. *frequent:* in throngs.

510–511. *from . . . Heav'n:* from the possession of these qualities, lofty-minded enough to hold intercourse with Heaven.

528. *express:* exact; cf. Hebrews 1:3, "the express image of his
person."

Female for race; then blessed mankind, and said,　530
'Be fruitful, multiply, and fill the earth,
Subdue it, and throughout dominion hold
Over fish of the sea, and fowl of the air,
And every living thing that moves on th' earth.'
Wherever thus created, for no place
Is yet distinct by name, thence, as thou know'st
He brought thee into this delicious grove,
This garden, planted with the trees of God,
Delectable both to behold and taste;
And freely all their pleasant fruit for food　540
Gave thee, all sorts are here that all th' earth yields,
Variety without end; but of the tree
Which tasted works knowledge of good and evil,
Thou may'st not; in the day thou eat'st, thou di'st;
Death is the penalty imposed, beware,
And govern well thy appetite, lest Sin
Surprise thee, and her black attendant Death.
Here finished he, and all that he had made
Viewed, and behold all was entirely good;
So ev'n and morn accomplished the sixth day:　550
Yet not till the Creator from his work
Desisting, though unwearied, up returned
Up to the Heav'n of Heav'ns his high abode,
Thence to behold this new created world
Th' addition of his empire, how it showed
In prospect from his throne, how good, how fair,
Answering his great idea. Up he rode
Followed with acclamation and the sound
Symphonious of ten thousand harps that tuned
Angelic harmonies: the earth, the air　560
Resounded (thou remember'st, for thou heard'st)
The heav'ns and all the constellations rung,
The planets in their stations listening stood,
While the bright pomp ascended jubilant.
'Open, ye everlasting gates,' they sung,

---

564. *pomp:* procession.

'Open, ye Heav'ns, your living doors; let in
The great Creator from his work returned
Magnificent, his six days' work, a world;
Open, and henceforth oft; for God will deign
To visit oft the dwellings of just men   570
Delighted, and with frequent intercourse
Thither will send his wingéd messengers
On errands of supernal grace.' So sung
The glorious train ascending: he through Heav'n,
That opened wide her blazing portals, led
To God's eternal house direct the way,
A broad and ample road, whose dust is gold
And pavement stars, as stars to thee appear,
Seen in the galaxy, that milky way
Which nightly as a circling zone thou seest   580
Powdered with stars. And now on earth the seventh
Evening arose in Eden, for the sun
Was set, and twilight from the east came on,
Forerunning night; when at the holy mount
Of Heav'n's high-seated top, th' imperial throne
Of Godhead, fixed forever firm and sure,
The Filial Power arrived, and sat him down
With his great Father, for he also went
Invisible, yet stayed (such privilege
Hath omnipresence) and the work ordained,   590
Author and end of all things, and from work
Now resting, blessed and hallowed the seventh day,
As resting on that day from all his work,
But not in silence holy kept; the harp
Had work and rested not, the solemn pipe,
And dulcimer, all organs of sweet stop,
All sounds on fret by string or golden wire
Tempered soft tunings, intermixed with voice
Choral or unison: of incense clouds
Fuming from golden censers hid the mount.   600
Creation and the six days' acts they sung,
'Great are thy works, Jehovah, infinite
Thy power; what thought can measure thee or tongue
Relate thee; greater now in thy return

Than from the giant angels; thee that day
Thy thunders magnified; but to create
Is greater than created to destroy.
Who can impair thee, mighty King, or bound
Thy empire? Easily the proud attempt
Of spirits apostate and their counsels vain   610
Thou hast repelled, while impiously they thought
Thee to diminish, and from thee withdraw
The number of thy worshippers. Who seeks
To lessen thee, against his purpose serves
To manifest the more thy might: his evil
Thou usest, and from thence creat'st more good.
Witness this new-made world, another Heav'n
From Heaven gate not far, founded in view
On the clear hyaline, the glassy sea;
Of amplitude almost immense, with stars   620
Numerous, and every star perhaps a world
Of destined habitation; but thou know'st
Their seasons: among these the seat of men,
Earth with her nether ocean circumfused,
Their pleasant dwelling place. Thrice happy men,
And sons of men, whom God hath thus advanced,
Created in his image, there to dwell
And worship him, and in reward to rule
Over his works, on earth, in sea, or air,
And multiply a race of worshippers   630
Holy and just: thrice happy if they know
Their happiness, and persevere upright.'

"So sung they, and the empyrean rung,
With halleluiahs: thus was sabbath kept.
And thy request think now fulfilled, that asked
How first this world and face of things began,
And what before thy memory was done

---

605. *giant angels:* i.e., the rout of the rebel angels, which is here
paralleled with the creation; in Book VI it is paralleled with
the Redemption and the Last Judgment.
619. *hyaline:* a Greek word meaning "glassy"; i.e., the waters
above the firmament of VII, 261–271.
624. *nether ocean:* the waters below the firmament.

From the beginning, that posterity
Informed by thee might know; if else thou seek'st
Aught, not surpassing human measure, say."   6

BOOK VIII

THE ARGUMENT

Adam inquires concerning celestial motions, i
doubtfully answered, and exhorted to search rathe
things more worthy of knowledge: Adam assents, an
still desirous to detain Raphael, relates to him what h
remembered since his own creation, his placing in Para
dise, his talk with God concerning solitude and fit so
ciety, his first meeting and nuptials with Eve, his dis
course with the angel thereupon; who after admonition
repeated departs.

The angel ended, and in Adam's ear
So charming left his voice, that he a while

1–4. These four lines replace line 641 of Book VII of the 166
edition, which read "To whom thus Adam gratefully replied."
2. *charming:* laying under a spell.

Thought him still speaking, still stood fixed to hear;
Then as new waked thus gratefully replied.
"What thanks sufficient, or what recompense
Equal have I to render thee, divine
Historian, who thus largely hast allayed
The thirst I had of knowledge, and vouchsafed
This friendly condescension to relate
Things else by me unsearchable, now heard   10
With wonder, but delight, and, as is due,
With glory attributed to the high
Creator; something yet of doubt remains,
Which only thy solution can resolve.
When I behold this goodly frame, this world
Of heav'n and earth consisting, and compute
Their magnitudes, this earth a spot, a grain,
An atom, with the firmament compared
And all her numbered stars, that seem to roll
Spaces incomprehensible (for such   20
Their distance argues and their swift return
Diurnal) merely to officiate light
Round this opacous earth, this punctual spot,
One day and night; in all their vast survey
Useless besides, reasoning I oft admire,
How nature wise and frugal could commit
Such disproportions, with superfluous hand
So many nobler bodies to create,
Greater so manifold to this one use,
For aught appears, and on their orbs impose   30
Such restless revolution day by day
Repeated, while the sedentary earth,
That better might with far less compass move,
Served by more noble than herself, attains

---

3. *stood:* remained.
19. *numbered:* either "numerous" or an allusion to Psalm
147:4, "He telleth the number of the stars."
22. *officiate:* supply.
23. *opacous:* dark. *punctual:* no bigger than a point.
25. *admire:* wonder.
33. *far less compass:* a much shorter distance.

Her end without least motion, and receives,
As tribute such a sumless journey brought
Of incorporeal speed, her warmth and light;
Speed, to describe whose swiftness number fails."

   So spake our sire, and by his count'nance seemed
Entering on studious thoughts abstruse, which Eve   40
Perceiving where she sat retired in sight,
With lowliness majestic from her seat,
And grace that won who saw to wish her stay,
Rose, and went forth among her fruits and flow'rs,
To visit how they prospered, bud and bloom,
Her nursery; they at her coming sprung
And touched by her fair tendance gladlier grew.
Yet went she not, as not with such discourse
Delighted, or not capable her ear
Of what was high: such pleasure she reserved,   50
Adam relating, she sole auditress;
Her husband the relater she preferred
Before the angel, and of him to ask
Chose rather; he, she knew would intermix
Grateful digressions, and solve high dispute
With conjugal caresses, from his lip
Not words alone pleased her. O when meet now
Such pairs, in love and mutual honor joined?
With goddess-like demeanor forth she went;
Not unattended, for on her as queen   60
A pomp of winning graces waited still,
And from about her shot darts of desire
Into all eyes to wish her still in sight.
And Raphael now to Adam's doubt proposed
Benevolent and facile thus replied.

   "To ask or search I blame thee not, for heav'n
Is as the book of God before thee set,
Wherein to read his wondrous works, and learn
His seasons, hours, or days, or months, or years:

---

36. *sumless journey:* incalculable distance.
46. *nursery:* the objects of her nursing care.
61. *pomp:* train, procession.
65. *facile:* gracious.

This to attain, whether heav'n move or earth,   70
Imports not, if thou reckon right, the rest
From man or angel the great Architect
Did wisely to conceal, and not divulge
His secrets to be scanned by them who ought
Rather admire; or if they list to try
Conjecture, he his fabric of the heav'ns
Hath left to their disputes, perhaps to move
His laughter at their quaint opinions wide
Hereafter, when they come to model heav'n
And calculate the stars, how they will wield   80
The mighty frame, how build, unbuild, contrive
To save appearances, how gird the sphere
With centric and eccentric scribbled o'er,
Cycle and epicycle, orb in orb:
Already by thy reasoning this I guess,
Who art to lead thy offspring, and supposest
That bodies bright and greater should not serve
The less not bright, nor heav'n such journeys run,
Earth sitting still, when she alone receives
The benefit: consider first, that great   90
Or bright infers not excellence: the earth
Though, in comparison of heav'n, so small,
Nor glistering, may of solid good contain
More plenty than the sun that barren shines,
Whose virtue on itself works no effect,
But in the fruitful earth; there first received
His beams, unactive else, their vigor find.
Yet not to earth are those bright luminaries

---

78. *wide:* i.e., of the mark.

80–84. An allusion to the incredibly complex refinements of
the Ptolemaic system designed to *save appearances,* i.e., account
for the observed phenomena.

86. *who:* i.e., Adam, the antecedent being implied in "thy."
Raphael says that if Adam is foolish enough to suppose that
"great or bright" implies excellence, what can be expected of his
descendants? The burden of Raphael's discussion of astronomy is
that moral and religious wisdom is more valuable than scientific
knowledge.

Officious, but to thee earth's habitant.
And for the heav'n's wide circuit, let it speak   100
The Maker's high magnificence, who built
So spacious, and his line stretched out so far;
That man may know he dwells not in his own;
An edifice too large for him to fill,
Lodged in a small partition, and the rest
Ordained for uses to his Lord best known.
The swiftness of those circles attribute,
Though numberless, to his omnipotence,
That to corporeal substances could add
Speed almost spiritual; me thou think'st not slow,   110
Who since the morning hour set out from Heav'n
Where God resides, and ere mid-day arrived
In Eden, distance inexpressible
By numbers that have name. But this I urge,
Admitting motion in the heav'ns, to show
Invalid that which thee to doubt it moved;
Not that I so affirm, though so it seem
To thee who hast thy dwelling here on earth.
God to remove his ways from human sense,
Placed heav'n from earth so far, that earthly sight,   120
If it presume, might err in things too high,
And no advantage gain. What if the sun
Be center to the world, and other stars
By his attractive virtue and their own
Incited, dance about him various rounds?
Their wandering course now high, now low, then hid,
Progressive, retrograde, or standing still,
In six thou seest, and what if sev'nth to these
The planet earth, so steadfast though she seem,
Insensibly three different motions move?   130

99. *officious:* serviceable.
108. *numberless:* incalculable (modifies "swiftness").
124. *attractive virtue:* power of attraction.
130. *insensibly:* imperceptibly. *three different motions:* rotation
on its axis, rotation around the sun, and a slow motion of the
earth's axis, which was Copernicus' alternative to the theory of
"trepidation" (cf. III, 483n).

Which else to several spheres thou must ascribe,
Moved contrary with thwart obliquities,
Or save the sun his labor, and that swift
Nocturnal and diurnal rhomb supposed,
Invisible else above all stars, the wheel
Of day and night; which needs not thy belief,
If earth industrious of herself fetch day
Traveling east, and with her part averse
From the sun's beam meet night, her other part
Still luminous by his ray. What if that light   140
Sent from her through the wide transpicuous air,
To the terrestrial moon be as a star
Enlightening her by day, as she by night
This earth? reciprocal, if land be there,
Fields and inhabitants: her spots thou seest
As clouds, and clouds may rain, and rain produce
Fruits in her softened soil, for some to eat
Allotted there; and other suns perhaps
With their attendant moons thou wilt descry
Communicating male and female light,   150
Which two great sexes animate the world,
Stored in each orb perhaps with some that live.
For such vast room in nature unpossessed
By living soul, desert and desolate,
Only to shine, yet scarce to contribute
Each orb a glimpse of light, conveyed so far
Down to his habitable, which returns
Light back to them, is obvious to dispute.
But whether thus these things, or whether not,
Whether the sun predominant in heav'n   160

131–136. "You may attribute these three motions to spheres
moving in contrary directions and crossing each other obliquely,
or you may attribute them to the earth and save the sun his
labor and also dispense with the theory of the primum mobile
(the *wheel of day and night* or *nocturnal and diurnal rhomb*)."

153–158. "It is open to dispute whether this vast area of the
universe is deserted and desolate, uninhabited by living creatures,
the function of each orb being merely to provide from afar a
glimpse of light to this inhabited earth."

Rise on the earth, or earth rise on the sun,
He from the east his flaming road begin,
Or she from west her silent course advance
With inoffensive pace that spinning sleeps
On her soft axle, while she paces ev'n,
And bears thee soft with the smooth air along,
Solicit not thy thoughts with matters hid,
Leave them to God above, him serve and fear;
Of other creatures, as him pleases best,
Wherever placed, let him dispose: joy thou   170
In what he gives to thee, this Paradise
And thy fair Eve; heav'n is for thee too high
To know what passes there; be lowly wise:
Think only what concerns thee and thy being;
Dream not of other worlds, what creatures there
Live, in what state, condition or degree,
Contented that thus far hath been revealed
Not of earth only but of highest Heav'n."

    To whom thus Adam cleared of doubt, replied.
"How fully hast thou satisfied me, pure   180
Intelligence of Heav'n, angel serene,
And freed from intricacies, taught to live
The easiest way, nor with perplexing thoughts
To interrupt the sweet of life, from which
God hath bid dwell far off all anxious cares,
And not molest us, unless we ourselves
Seek them with wandering thoughts, and notions vain.
But apt the mind or fancy is to rove
Unchecked, and of her roving is no end;
Till warned, or by experience taught, she learn,   190
That not to know at large of things remote
From use, obscure and subtle, but to know
That which before us lies in daily life,
Is the prime wisdom; what is more, is fume,
Or emptiness, or fond impertinence,

---

164. *inoffensive:* not colliding with anything.
194. *fume:* smoke, vanity.
195. *fond impertinence:* foolish irrelevance.

And renders us in things that most concern
Unpractised, unprepared, and still to seek.
Therefore from this high pitch let us descend
A lower flight, and speak of things at hand
Useful, whence haply mention may arise   200
Of something not unseasonable to ask
By sufferance, and thy wonted favor deigned.
Thee I have heard relating what was done
Ere my remembrance: now hear me relate
My story, which perhaps thou hast not heard;
And day is yet not spent; till then thou seest
How subtly to detain thee I devise,
Inviting thee to hear while I relate,
Fond, were it not in hope of thy reply:
For while I sit with thee, I seem in Heav'n,   210
And sweeter thy discourse is to my ear
Than fruits of palm tree pleasantest to thirst
And hunger both, from labor, at the hour
Of sweet repast; they satiate, and soon fill,
Though pleasant, but thy words with grace divine
Imbued, bring to their sweetness no satiety."
    To whom thus Raphael answered heav'nly meek.
"Nor are thy lips ungraceful, sire of men,
Nor tongue ineloquent; for God on thee
Abundantly his gifts hath also poured   220
Inward and outward both, his image fair:
Speaking or mute all comeliness and grace
Attends thee, and each word, each motion forms.
Nor less think we in Heav'n of thee on earth
Than of our fellow servant, and inquire
Gladly into the ways of God with man:
For God we see hath honored thee, and set
On man his equal love: say therefore on;
For I that day was absent, as befell,

---

197. *still to seek:* always at a loss.
213. *from labor:* after labor.
224–225. "We in Heaven think of you as our fellow-servant,
no less."

Bound on a voyage uncouth and obscure,   230
Far on excursion toward the gates of Hell;
Squared in full legion (such command we had)
To see that none thence issued forth a spy,
Or enemy, while God was in his work,
Lest he incensed at such eruption bold,
Destruction with creation might have mixed.
Not that they durst without his leave attempt,
But us he sends upon his high behests
For state, as sovran King, and to enure
Our prompt obedience. Fast we found, fast shut   240
The dismal gates, and barricadoed strong;
But long ere our approaching heard within
Noise, other than the sound of dance or song,
Torment, and loud lament, and furious rage.
Glad we returned up to the coasts of light
Ere sabbath evening: so we had in charge.
But thy relation now; for I attend,
Pleased with thy words no less than thou with mine."
    So spake the godlike Power, and thus our sire.
"For man to tell how human life began   250
Is hard; for who himself beginning knew?
Desire with thee still longer to converse
Induced me. As new waked from soundest sleep
Soft on the flow'ry herb I found me laid
In balmy sweat, which with his beams the sun
Soon dried, and on the reeking moisture fed.
Straight toward Heav'n my wond'ring eyes I turned,
And gazed a while the ample sky, till raised
By quick instinctive motion up I sprung,
As thitherward endeavoring, and upright   260
Stood on my feet; about me round I saw
Hill, dale, and shady woods, and sunny plains,

----

    230. *uncouth:* unknown.
    239. *for state:* as evidence of his kingly state. *enure:* train.
    257. Adam instinctively looks upward toward "Heaven"; Eve looks down at the reflection of the "sky" in the water (IV, 456–459).
    260. *thitherward:* i.e., toward Heaven.

And liquid lapse of murmuring streams; by these,
Creatures that lived, and moved, and walked, or flew,
Birds on the branches warbling; all things smiled,
With fragrance and with joy my heart o'erflowed.
Myself I then perused, and limb by limb
Surveyed, and sometimes went, and sometimes ran
With supple joints, as lively vigor led:
But who I was, or where, or from what cause,　　　270
Knew not; to speak I tried, and forthwith spake,
My tongue obeyed and readily could name
Whate'er I saw. 'Thou sun,' said I, 'fair light,
And thou enlightened earth, so fresh and gay,
Ye hills and dales, ye rivers, woods, and plains,
And ye that live and move, fair creatures, tell,
Tell, if ye saw, how came I thus, how here?
Not of myself; by some great Maker then,
In goodness and in power preeminent;
Tell me, how may I know him, how adore,　　　280
From whom I have that thus I move and live,
And feel that I am happier than I know.'
While thus I called, and strayed I knew not whither,
From where I first drew air, and first beheld
This happy light, when answer none returned,
On a green shady bank profuse of flow'rs
Pensive I sat me down; there gentle sleep
First found me, and with soft oppression seized
My drowséd sense, untroubled, though I thought
I then was passing to my former state　　　290
Insensible, and forthwith to dissolve:
When suddenly stood at my head a dream,
Whose inward apparition gently moved
My fancy to believe I yet had being,
And lived: One came, methought, of shape divine,
And said, 'Thy mansion wants thee, Adam, rise,
First man, of men innumerable ordained
First father, called by thee I come thy guide

---

268. *went:* walked.
296. *mansion:* i.e., the Garden.

To the garden of bliss, thy seat prepared.'
So saying, by the hand he took me raised,   300
And over fields and waters, as in air
Smooth sliding without step, last led me up
A woody mountain; whose high top was plain,
A circuit wide, enclosed, with goodliest trees
Planted, with walks, and bow'rs, that what I saw
Of earth before scarce pleasant seemed. Each tree
Loaden with fairest fruit that hung to th' eye
Tempting, stirred in me sudden appetite
To pluck and eat; whereat I waked, and found
Before mine eyes all real, as the dream   310
Had lively shadowed. Here had new begun
My wandering, had not he who was my guide
Up hither, from among the trees appeared
Presence divine. Rejoicing, but with awe
In adoration at his feet I fell
Submiss: he reared me, and 'Whom thou sought'st I
     am,'
Said mildly, 'Author of all this thou seest
Above, or round about thee or beneath.
This Paradise I give thee, count it thine
To till and keep, and of the fruit to eat: 320
Of every tree that in the garden grows
Eat freely with glad heart; fear here no dearth:
But of the tree whose operation brings
Knowledge of good and ill, which I have set
The pledge of thy obedience and thy faith,
Amid the garden by the Tree of Life,
Remember what I warn thee, shun to taste,
And shun the bitter consequence: for know,
The day thou eat'st thereof, my sole command
Transgressed, inevitably thou shalt die;   330
From that day mortal, and this happy state
Shalt lose, expelled from hence into a world
Of woe and sorrow.' Sternly he pronounced
The rigid interdiction, which resounds

---

316. *submiss:* prostrate, cast down.

Yet dreadful in mine ear, though in my choice
Not to incur; but soon his clear aspéct
Returned and gracious purpose thus renewed.
'Not only these fair bounds, but all the earth
To thee and to thy race I give; as lords
Possess it, and all things that therein live,   340
Or live in sea, or air, beast, fish, and fowl.
In sign whereof each bird and beast behold
After their kinds; I bring them to receive
From thee their names, and pay thee fealty
With low subjection; understand the same
Of fish within their wat'ry residence,
Not hither summoned, since they cannot change
Their element to draw the thinner air.'
As thus he spake, each bird and beast behold
Approaching two and two, these cowering low   350
With blandishment, each bird stooped on his wing.
I named them, as they passed, and understood
Their nature, with such knowledge God endued
My sudden apprehension: but in these
I found not what methought I wanted still;
And to the heav'nly vision thus presumed.

   " 'O by what name, for thou above all these,
Above mankind, or aught than mankind higher,
Surpassest far my naming, how may I
Adore thee, Author of this universe,   360
And all this good to man, for whose well-being
So amply, and with hands so liberal
Thou hast provided all things: but with me
I see not who partakes. In solitude
What happiness, who can enjoy alone,
Or all enjoying, what contentment find?'
Thus I presumptuous; and the vision bright,
As with a smile more brightened, thus replied.

   " 'What call'st thou solitude? is not the earth

---

337. *purpose:* speech.
357. Adam could name the creatures because he understood their natures; he cannot name God.

With various living creatures, and the air   370
Replenished, and all these at thy command
To come and play before thee, know'st thou not
Their language and their ways? They also know,
And reason not contemptibly; with these
Find pastime, and bear rule; thy realm is large.'
So spake the universal Lord, and seemed
So ordering. I with leave of speech implored,
And humble deprecation thus replied.

   " 'Let not my words offend thee, heav'nly Power,
My Maker, be propitious while I speak.   380
Hast thou not made me here thy substitutê,
And these inferior far beneath me set?
Among unequals what society
Can sort, what harmony or true delight?
Which must be mutual, in proportion due
Giv'n and received; but in disparity
The one intense, the other still remiss
Cannot well suit with either, but soon prove
Tedious alike. Of fellowship I speak
Such as I seek, fit to participate   390
All rational delight, wherein the brute
Cannot be human consort; they rejoice
Each with their kind, lion with lioness;
So fitly them in pairs thou hast combined;
Much less can bird with beast, or fish with fowl
So well converse, nor with the ox the ape;
Worse then can man with beast, and least of all.'
   Whereto th' Almighty answered, not displeased.
'A nice and subtle happiness I see
Thou to thyself proposest, in the choice   400
Of thy associates, Adam, and wilt taste

---

   379. This is a genuine dialogue: God really listens to Adam.
Cf. the dialogue between God and Abraham in Genesis 18.

   384. *sort:* suit, be fitting.

   387. *intense* (taut, high-strung) and *remiss* (slack) continue the
musical metaphor begun with "harmony" (line 384).

   396. *converse:* have fellowship with.

   399. *nice:* fastidious.

No pleasure, though in pleasure, solitary.
What think'st thou then of me, and this my state,
Seem I to thee sufficiently possessed
Of happiness, or not? who am alone
From all eternity, for none I know
Second to me or like, equal much less.
How have I then with whom to hold converse
Save with the creatures which I made, and those
To me inferior, infinite descents   410
Beneath what other creatures are to thee?'
    "He ceased, I lowly answered. 'To attain
The highth and depth of thy eternal ways
All human thoughts come short, Supreme of things;
Thou in thyself art perfect, and in thee
Is no deficience found; not so is man,
But in degree, the cause of his desire
By conversation with his like to help,
Or solace his defects. No need that thou
Shouldst propagate, already infinite;   420
And through all numbers absolute, though one;
But man by number is to manifest
His single imperfection, and beget
Like of his like, his image multiplied,
In unity defective, which requires
Collateral love, and dearest amity.
Thou in thy secrecy although alone,
Best with thyself accompanied, seek'st not
Social communication, yet so pleased,
Canst raise thy creature to what highth thou wilt   430
Of union or communion, deified;
I by conversing cannot these erect
From prone, nor in their ways complacence find.'

---

417. *but in degree:* i.e., man is relative, not absolute like God.
421. *through all numbers absolute:* perfect in every respect.
422–423. "Man is to manifest his imperfection in being unwedded by increasing his numbers." The paradoxical wordplay in "infinite," "numbers," "one," "number," and "single" exhibits the fact that human thoughts and human language come short of comprehending God.

Thus I emboldened spake, and freedom used
Permissive, and acceptance found, which gained
This answer from the gracious voice divine.
  " 'Thus far to try thee, Adam, I was pleased,
And find thee knowing not of beasts alone,
Which thou hast rightly named, but of thyself,
Expressing well the spirit within thee free,   440
My image, not imparted to the brute,
Whose fellowship therefore unmeet for thee
Good reason was thou freely shouldst dislike,
And be so minded still; I, ere thou spak'st,
Knew it not good for man to be alone,
And no such company as then thou saw'st
Intended thee, for trial only brought,
To see how thou couldst judge of fit and meet:
What next I bring shall please thee, be assured,
Thy likeness, thy fit help, thy other self,   450
Thy wish exactly to thy heart's desire.'
  "He ended, or I heard no more, for now
My earthly by his heav'nly overpowered,
Which it had long stood under, strained to the highth
In that celestial colloquy sublime,
As with an object that excels the sense,
Dazzled and spent, sunk down, and sought repair
Of sleep, which instantly fell on me, called
By nature as in aid, and closed mine eyes.
Mine eyes he closed, but open left the cell   460
Of fancy my internal sight, by which
Abstract as in a trance methought I saw,
Though sleeping, where I lay, and saw the shape
Still glorious before whom awake I stood;
Who stooping opened my left side, and took
From thence a rib, with cordial spirits warm,
And life-blood streaming fresh; wide was the wound,
But suddenly with flesh filled up and healed:
The rib he formed and fashioned with his hands;

---

462. *abstract:* abstracted.
466. *cordial:* pertaining to the heart.

Under his forming hands a creature grew, 470
Manlike, but different sex, so lovely fair,
That what seemed fair in all the world, seemed now
Mean, or in her summed up, in her contained
And in her looks, which from that time infused
Sweetness into my heart, unfelt before,
And into all things from her air inspired
The spirit of love and amorous delight.
She disappeared, and left me dark, I waked
To find her, or forever to deplore
Her loss, and other pleasures all abjure: 480
When out of hope, behold her, not far off,
Such as I saw her in my dream, adorned
With what all earth or Heaven could bestow
To make her amiable. On she came,
Led by her heav'nly Maker, though unseen,
And guided by his voice, nor uninformed
Of nuptial sanctity and marriage rites:
Grace was in all her steps, Heav'n in her eye,
In every gesture dignity and love.
I overjoyed could not forbear aloud. 490
    " 'This turn hath made amends; thou hast fulfilled
Thy words, Creator bounteous and benign,
Giver of all things fair, but fairest this
Of all thy gifts, nor enviest. I now see
Bone of my bone, flesh of my flesh, my self
Before me; woman is her name, of man
Extracted; for this cause he shall forgo
Father and mother, and to his wife adhere;
And they shall be one flesh, one heart, one soul.'
    "She heard me thus, and though divinely
        brought, 500
Yet innocence and virgin modesty,
Her virtue and the conscience of her worth,
That would be wooed, and not unsought be won,
Not obvious, not obtrusive, but retired,

---

494. *nor enviest:* nor do you begrudge it me.
502. *conscience:* consciousness.
504. *obvious:* forward.

The more desirable, or to say all,
Nature herself, though pure of sinful thought,
Wrought in her so, that seeing me, she turned;
I followed her, she what was honor knew,
And with obsequious majesty approved
My pleaded reason. To the nuptial bow'r   51
I led her blushing like the morn: all heav'n,
And happy constellations on that hour
Shed their selectest influence; the earth
Gave sign of gratulation, and each hill;
Joyous the birds; fresh gales and gentle airs
Whispered it to the woods, and from their wings
Flung rose, flung odors from the spicy shrub,
Disporting, till the amorous bird of night
Sung spousal, and bid haste the evening star
On his hill top, to light the bridal lamp.   52
Thus I have told thee all my state, and brought
My story to the sum of earthly bliss
Which I enjoy, and must confess to find
In all things else delight indeed, but such
As used or not, works in the mind no change,
Nor vehement desire, these delicacies
I mean of taste, sight, smell, herbs, fruits, and flow'rs,
Walks, and the melody of birds; but here
Far otherwise, transported I behold,
Transported touch; here passion first I felt,   53
Commotion strange, in all enjoyments else
Superior and unmoved, here only weak
Against the charm of beauty's powerful glance.
Or nature failed in me, and left some part
Not proof enough such object to sustain,
Or from my side subducting, took perhaps
More than enough; at least on her bestowed
Too much of ornament, in outward show
Elaborate, of inward less exact.
For well I understand in the prime end   54

---

508. *honor:* cf. Hebrews 13:4, 'Marriage is honourable in all.'
518. *amorous bird of night:* nightingale.

Of nature her th' inferior, in the mind
And inward faculties, which most excel,
In outward also her resembling less
His image who made both, and less expressing
The character of that dominion giv'n
O'er other creatures; yet when I approach
Her loveliness, so absolute she seems
And in herself complete, so well to know
Her own, that what she wills to do or say,
Seems wisest, virtuousest, discreetest, best;   550
All higher knowledge in her presence falls
Degraded, wisdom in discourse with her
Loses discount'nanced, and like folly shows;
Authority and reason on her wait,
As one intended first, not after made
Occasionally; and to consummate all,
Greatness of mind and nobleness their seat
Build in her loveliest, and create an awe
About her, as a guard angelic placed."
To whom the angel with contracted brow.   560
    "Accuse not nature, she hath done her part;
Do thou but thine, and be not diffident
Of wisdom, she deserts thee not, if thou
Dismiss not her, when most thou need'st her nigh,
By áttributing overmuch to things
Less excellent, as thou thyself perceiv'st.
For what admir'st thou, what transports thee so,
An outside? fair no doubt, and worthy well
Thy cherishing, thy honoring, and thy love,
Not thy subjection: weigh with her thyself;   570
Then value: ofttimes nothing profits more
Than self esteem, grounded on just and right
Well managed; of that skill the more thou know'st,
The more she will acknowledge thee her head,
And to realities yield all her shows:

547. *absolute:* perfect.
556. *occasionally:* for some later need or occasion.
573. *that skill:* i.e., knowing how to manage self-esteem.

Made so adorn for thy delight the more,
So awful, that with honor thou may'st love
Thy mate, who sees when thou art seen least wise.
But if the sense of touch whereby mankind
Is propagated seem such dear delight   580
Beyond all other, think the same vouchsafed
To cattle and each beast; which would not be
To them made common and divulged, if aught
Therein enjoyed were worthy to subdue
The soul of man, or passion in him move.
What higher in her society thou find'st
Attractive, human, rational, love still;
In loving thou dost well, in passion not,
Wherein true love consists not; love refines
The thoughts, and heart enlarges, hath his seat   590
In reason, and is judicious, is the scale
By which to heav'nly love thou may'st ascend,
Not sunk in carnal pleasure, for which cause
Among the beasts no mate for thee was found."
    To whom thus half abashed Adam replied.
"Neither her outside formed so fair, nor aught
In procreation common to all kinds
(Though higher of the genial bed by far,
And with mysterious reverence I deem)
So much delights me as those graceful acts,   600
Those thousand decencies that daily flow
From all her words and actions mixed with love
And sweet compliance, which declare unfeigned
Union of mind, or in us both one soul;
Harmony to behold in wedded pair
More grateful than harmonious sound to th' ear.
Yet these subject not; I to thee disclose

---

591. *scale:* ladder. Raphael's Neoplatonic conception of the "ladder of love" is rather wide of the mark, since it is Adam's love for Eve in its fullest and most human sense that leads to his fall.

595. Adam, who knows more about human love than the angel Raphael, is only *half abashed*.

598. *genial:* nuptial, procreative.

601. *decencies:* graceful traits.

What inward thence I feel, not therefore foiled,
Who meet with various objects, from the sense
Variously representing; yet still free   610
Approve the best, and follow what I approve.
To love thou blam'st me not, for love thou say'st
Leads up to Heav'n, is both the way and guide;
Bear with me then, if lawful what I ask;
Love not the heav'nly spirits, and how their love
Express they, by looks only, or do they mix
Irradiance, virtual or immediate touch?"

 To whom the angel with a smile that glowed
Celestial rosy red, love's proper hue,
Answered. "Let it suffice thee that thou know'st   620
Us happy, and without love no happiness.
Whatever pure thou in the body enjoy'st
(And pure thou wert created) we enjoy
In eminence, and obstacle find none
Of membrane, joint, or limb, exclusive bars:
Easier than air with air, if spirits embrace,
Total they mix, union of pure with pure
Desiring; nor restrained conveyance need
As flesh to mix with flesh, or soul with soul.
But I can now no more; the parting sun   630
Beyond the earth's green cape and verdant isles
Hesperian sets, my signal to depart.
Be strong, live happy, and love, but first of all
Him whom to love is to obey, and keep
His great command; take heed lest passion sway
Thy judgment to do aught, which else free will
Would not admit; thine and of all thy sons
The weal or woe in thee is placed; beware.
I in thy persevering shall rejoice,

---

608. *not therefore foiled:* not overcome by those qualities (in Eve).

631. *green cape and verdant isles:* the Cape Verde Islands.

632. *Hesperian:* an oral reading of the sentence beginning with "the parting sun" demonstrates that "Hesperian" modifies "sun . . . sets" rather than "isles."

And all the blest: stand fast; to stand or fall   640
Free in thine own arbitrement it lies.
Perfect within, no outward aid require,
And all temptation to transgress repel."
   So saying, he arose; whom Adam thus
Followed with benediction. "Since to part,
Go heav'nly guest, ethereal messenger,
Sent from whose sovran goodness I adore.
Gentle to me and affable hath been
Thy condescension, and shall be honored ever
With grateful memory: thou to mankind   650
Be good and friendly still, and oft return."
   So parted they, the angel up to Heav'n
From the thick shade, and Adam to his bow'r.

BOOK IX �

THE ARGUMENT

   Satan having compassed the earth, with meditated
guile returns as a mist by night into Paradise, enters
into the serpent sleeping. Adam and Eve in the morning go forth to their labors, which Eve proposes to di-

vide in several places, each laboring apart: Adam consents not, alleging the danger, lest that enemy, of whom they were forewarned, should attempt her found alone: Eve loath to be thought not circumspect or firm enough, urges her going apart, the rather desirous to make trial of her strength; Adam at last yields. The serpent finds her alone; his subtle approach, first gazing, then speaking, with much flattery extolling Eve above all other creatures. Eve wondering to hear the serpent speak, asks how he attained to human speech and such understanding not till now; the serpent answers, that by tasting of a certain tree in the garden he attained both to speech and reason, till then void of both: Eve requires him to bring her to that tree, and finds it to be the Tree of Knowledge forbidden. The serpent now grown bolder, with many wiles and arguments induces her at length to eat; she pleased with the taste deliberates a while whether to impart thereof to Adam or not, at last brings him of the fruit, relates what persuaded her to eat thereof. Adam at first amazed, but perceiving her lost, resolves through vehemence of love to perish with her; and extenuating the trespass eats also of the fruit: the effects thereof in them both; they seek to cover their nakedness; then fall to variance and accusation of one another.

No more of talk where God or angel guest
With man, as with his friend, familiar used
To sit indulgent, and with him partake
Rural repast, permitting him the while
Venial discourse unblamed: I now must change
Those notes to tragic; foul distrust, and breach
Disloyal on the part of man, revolt,
And disobedience: on the part of Heav'n
Now alienated, distance and distaste,
Anger and just rebuke, and judgment giv'n,   10
That brought into this world a world of woe,
Sin and her shadow Death, and misery

Of muse and his choice not to write of war but of patience and heroic martyrdom

Death's harbinger: Sad task, yet argument
Not less but more heroic than the wrath
Of stern Achilles on his foe pursued
Thrice fugitive about Troy wall; or rage
Of Turnus for Lavinia disespoused,
Or Neptune's ire or Juno's, that so long
Perplexed the Greek and Cytherea's son;
If answerable style I can obtain   20
Of my celestial patroness, who deigns
Her nightly visitation unimplored,
And dictates to me slumbering, or inspires
Easy my unpremeditated verse: *Invocation again*
Since first this subject for heroic song
Pleased me long choosing, and beginning late;
React Not sedulous by nature to indite
Wars, hitherto the only argument
Heroic deemed, chief mast'ry to dissect
With long and tedious havoc fabled knights   30
In battles feigned; the better fortitude
Of patience and heroic martyrdom
Unsung; or to describe races and games,
Or tilting furniture, emblazoned shields,
Impreses quaint, caparisons and steeds;
Bases and tinsel trappings, gorgeous knights
At joust and tournament; then marshaled feast
Served up in hall with sewers, and seneschals;
The skill of artifice or office mean,
Not that which justly gives heroic name   40

Diligent

13-19. Once again M. asserts the superiority of Christian values to those of the classical epic. Since he has just spoken of the "anger and just rebuke" of God (line 10), he specifies the *wrath* of Achilles in the *Iliad*, the *rage* of Turnus in the *Aeneid*, and the *ire* of Neptune and Juno against Odysseus and Aeneas, respectively. *Cytherea* is Venus, the mother of Aeneas.

26. Cf. Introduction, above.

34. *tilting furniture:* the equipment of a tournament.

35. *impreses:* heraldic devices on shields.

36. *bases:* housings for horses (OED).

38. *sewers:* waiters.

To person or to poem. Me of these
Nor skilled nor studious, higher argument
Remains, sufficient of itself to raise
That name, unless an age too late, or cold
Climate, or years damp my intended wing
Depressed, and much they may, if all be mine,
Not hers who brings it nightly to my ear.

    The sun was sunk, and after him the star
Of Hesperus, whose office is to bring
Twilight upon the earth, short arbiter
'Twixt day and night, and now from end to end
Night's hemisphere had veiled th' horizon round:
When Satan who late fled before the threats
Of Gabriel out of Eden, now improved
In meditated fraud and malice, bent
On man's destruction, maugre what might hap
Of heavier on himself, fearless returned.
By night he fled, and at midnight returned
From compassing the earth, cautious of day,
Since Uriel regent of the sun descried
His entrance, and forewarned the Cherubim
That kept their watch; thence full of anguish driv'n,
The space of seven continued nights he rode
With darkness, thrice the equinoctial line
He circled, four times crossed the car of night
From pole to pole, traversing each colure;
On th' eighth returned, and on the coast averse
From entrance or Cherubic watch, by stealth

---

44. *that name:* referring to "heroic name" (line 40).

54. *improved:* Satan's discovery by the guardian angels when he was crudely attempting to seduce Eve by means of a dream has taught him that he must be more subtle and circumspect.

56. *maugre:* despite.

63–66. Satan rides around the earth for seven days, keeping always on the dark side of it. For three days he traverses the equator, and for each of the other four days he traverses half of the two "colures," which are great circles drawn through the poles at right angles to each other through the equinoxes and the solstices.

67. *coast averse:* opposite side.

Found unsuspected way. There was a place,
Now not, though sin, not time, first wrought the
    change,   70
Where Tigris at the foot of Paradise
Into a gulf shot under ground, till part
Rose up a fountain by the Tree of Life;
In with the river sunk, and with it rose
Satan involved in rising mist, then sought
Where to lie hid; sea he had searched and land
From Eden over Pontus, and the pool
Maeotis, up beyond the river Ob;
Downward as far Antarctic; and in length
West from Orontes to the ocean barred   80
At Darien, thence to the land where flows
Ganges and Indus: thus the orb he roamed
With narrow search; and with inspection deep
Considered every creature, which of all
Most opportune might serve his wiles, and found
The serpent subtlest beast of all the field.
Him after long debate, irresolute
Of thoughts revolved, his final sentence chose
Fit vessel, fittest imp of fraud, in whom
To enter, and his dark suggestions hide   90
From sharpest sight: for in the wily snake,
Whatever sleights none would suspicious mark,
As from his wit and native subtlety
Proceeding, which in other beasts observed
Doubt might beget of diabolic power
Active within beyond the sense of brute.
Thus he resolved, but first from inward grief
His bursting passion into plaints thus poured.
    "O earth, how like to Heav'n, if not preferred
More justly, seat worthier of gods, as built   100

77–82. Satan's seven-day journey around the earth is now described geographically.

87–88. *irresolute/ Of thoughts revolved:* turning it over in his
mind without reaching a decision.

88. *sentence:* decision.

95. *doubt:* suspicion.

Here comes Satan to destroy ---- but

With second thoughts, reforming what was old!
For what god after better worse would build?
Terrestrial heav'n, danced round by other heav'ns
That shine, yet bear their bright officious lamps,
Light above light, for thee alone, as seems,
In thee concentring all their precious beams
Of sacred influence: As God in Heav'n
Is center, yet extends to all, so thou
Centring receiv'st from all those orbs; in thee,
Not in themselves, all their known virtue appears
Productive in herb, plant, and nobler birth
Of creatures animate with gradual life
Of growth, sense, reason, all summed up in man.
With what delight could I have walked thee round,
If I could joy in aught, sweet interchange
Of hill and valley, rivers, woods and plains,
Now land, now sea, and shores with forest crowned,
Rocks, dens, and caves; but I in none of these
Find place or refuge; and the more I see
Pleasures about me, so much more I feel   120
Torment within me, as from the hateful siege
Of contraries; all good to me becomes
Bane, and in Heav'n much worse would be my state.
But neither here seek I, no nor in Heav'n
To dwell, unless by mastering Heav'n's Supreme;
Nor hope to be myself less miserable
By what I seek, but others to make such
As I, though thereby worse to me redound:
For only in destroying I find ease
To my relentless thoughts; and him destroyed,   130
Or won to what may work his utter loss,
For whom all this was made, all this will soon
Follow, as to him linked in weal or woe,
In woe then; that destruction wide may range:

Earth, not stars

Satan's love of earth

Read

his motive

his wish to destroy it

---

104. *officious:* serviceable.
121. *siege:* probably means "seat" rather than "conflict."
122. *contraries:* logical opposites, mutually exclusive conceptions such as hope-despair, light-dark, good-evil, Heaven-Hell.
123. *bane:* evil.

To me shall be the glory sole among
Th' infernal Powers, in one day to have marred
What he Almighty styled, six nights and days
Continued making, and who knows how long
Before had been contriving, though perhaps
Not longer than since I in one night freed   140
From servitude inglorious well-nigh half
Th' angelic name, and thinner left the throng
Of his adorers. He to be avenged,
And to repair his numbers thus impaired,
Whether such virtue spent of old now failed
More angels to create, if they at least
Are his created, or to spite us more,
Determined to advance into our room
A creature formed of earth, and him endow,
Exalted from so base original,   150
With heav'nly spoils, our spoils. What he decreed
He effected; man he made, and for him built
Magnificent this world, and earth his seat,
Him lord pronounced, and, O indignity!
Subjected to his service angel wings,
And flaming ministers to watch and tend
Their earthy charge. Of these the vigilance
I dread, and to elude, thus wrapped in mist
Of midnight vapor glide obscure, and pry
In every bush and brake, where hap may find   160
The serpent sleeping, in whose mazy folds
To hide me, and the dark intent I bring.
O foul descent! that I who erst contended
With gods to sit the highest, am now constrained
Into a beast, and mixed with bestial slime,
This essence to incarnate and imbrute,
That to the highth of Deity aspired;
But what will not ambition and revenge
Descend to? Who aspires must down as low

---

141. *well-nigh half:* Satan is now deceived by his own rhetoric.
166. *incarnate:* Satan's "foul descent" (line 163) is the diabolic
version of the Incarnation of Christ.

As high he soared, obnoxious first or last   170
To basest things. Revenge, at first though sweet,
Bitter ere long back on itself recoils;
Let it; I reck not, so it light well aimed,
Since higher I fall short, on him who next
Provokes my envy, this new favorite
Of Heav'n, this man of clay, son of despite,
Whom us the more to spite his Maker raised
From dust: spite then with spite is best repaid."
   So saying, through each thicket dank or dry,
Like a black mist low creeping, he held on   180
His midnight search, where soonest he might find
The serpent: him fast sleeping soon he found
In labyrinth of many a round self-rolled,
His head the midst, well stored with subtle wiles:
Not yet in horrid shade or dismal den,
Nor nocent yet, but on the grassy herb
Fearless unfeared he slept: in at his mouth
The devil entered, and his brutal sense,
In heart or head, possessing soon inspired
With act intelligential; but his sleep   190
Disturbed not, waiting close th' approach of morn.
Now whenas sacred light began to dawn
In Eden on the humid flow'rs, that breathed
Their morning incense, when all things that breathe,
From th' earth's great altar send up silent praise
To the Creator, and his nostrils fill
With grateful smell, forth came the human pair
And joined their vocal worship to the choir
Of creatures wanting voice, that done, partake
The season, prime for sweetest scents and airs: 200
Then commune how that day they best may ply
Their growing work: for much their work outgrew
The hands' dispatch of two gardening so wide.

_____

170. *obnoxious:* exposed.
186. *nocent:* harmful.
191. *close:* hidden.
199. *wanting:* lacking.

And Eve first to her husband thus began.
　"Adam, well may we labor still to dress
This garden, still to tend plant, herb and flow'r,
Our pleasant task enjoined, but till more hands
Aid us, the work under our labor grows,
Luxurious by restraint; what we by day
Lop overgrown, or prune, or prop, or bind,   210
One night or two with wanton growth derides
Tending to wild. Thou therefore now advise
Or hear what to my mind first thoughts present,
Let us divide our labors, thou where choice
Leads thee, or where most needs, whether to wind
The woodbine round this arbor, or direct
The clasping ivy where to climb, while I
In yonder spring of roses intermixed
With myrtle, find what to redress till noon:
For while so near each other thus all day   220
Our task we choose, what wonder if so near
Looks intervene and smiles, or object new
Casual discourse draw on, which intermits
Our day's work brought to little, though begun
Early, and th' hour of supper comes unearned."
　　To whom mild answer Adam thus returned.
"Sole Eve, associate sole, to me beyond
Compare above all living creatures dear,
Well hast thou motioned, well thy thoughts employed
How we might best fulfill the work which here   230
God hath assigned us, nor of me shalt pass
Unpraised: for nothing lovelier can be found
In woman, than to study household good,
And good works in her husband to promote.
Yet not so strictly hath our Lord imposed
Labor, as to debar us when we need
Refreshment, whether food, or talk between,
Food of the mind, or this sweet intercourse
Of looks and smiles, for smiles from reason flow,

----

218. *spring:* clump.
229. *motioned:* proposed.

To brute denied, and are of love the food,   240
Love not the lowest end of human life.
For not to irksome toil, but to delight
He made us, and delight to reason joined.   REASON
These paths and bow'rs doubt not but our joint hands
Will keep from wilderness with ease, as wide
As we need walk, till younger hands ere long
Assist us. But if much converse perhaps
Thee satiate, to short absence I could yield.
For solitude sometimes is best society,
And short retirement urges sweet return.   250
But other doubt possesses me, lest harm
Befall thee severed from me; for thou know'st
What hath been warned us, what malicious foe
Envying our happiness, and of his own
Despairing, seeks to work us woe and shame
By sly assault; and somewhere nigh at hand
Watches, no doubt, with greedy hope to find
His wish and best advantage, us asunder,
Hopeless to circumvent us joined, where each
To other speedy aid might lend at need;   260
Whether his first design be to withdraw
Our fealty from God, or to disturb
Conjugal love, than which perhaps no bliss
Enjoyed by us excites his envy more;
Or this, or worse, leave not the faithful side   265
That gave thee being, still shades thee and protects.
The wife, where danger or dishonor lurks,
Safest and seemliest by her husband stays,
Who guards her, or with her the worst endures."

    To whom the virgin majesty of Eve,   270
As one who loves, and some unkindness meets,
With sweet austere composure thus replied.

    "Offspring of Heav'n and earth, and all earth's lord,
That such an enemy we have, who seeks
Our ruin, both by thee informed I learn,

---

245. *wilderness:* wildness.
270. *virgin:* innocent.

And from the parting angel overheard
As in a shady nook I stood behind,
Just then returned at shut of evening flow'rs.
But that thou shouldst my firmness therefore doubt
To God or thee, because we have a foe   280
May tempt it, I expected not to hear.
His violence thou fear'st not, being such,
As we, not capable of death or pain,
Can either not receive, or can repel.
His fraud is then thy fear, which plain infers
Thy equal fear that my firm faith and love
Can by his fraud be shaken or seduced;
Thoughts, which how found they harbor in thy breast,
Adam, misthought of her to thee so dear?"

To whom with healing words Adam replied.   290
"Daughter of God and man, immortal Eve,
For such thou art, from sin and blame entire:
Not diffident of thee do I dissuade
Thy absence from my sight, but to avoid
Th' attempt itself, intended by our foe.
For he who tempts, though in vain, at least asperses
The tempted with dishonor foul, supposed
Not incorruptible of faith, not proof
Against temptation: thou thyself with scorn
And anger wouldst resent the offered wrong,   300
Though ineffectual found: misdeem not then,
If such affront I labor to avert
From thee alone, which on us both at once
The enemy, though bold, will hardly dare,
Or daring, first on me th' assault shall light.
Nor thou his malice and false guile contemn;
Subtle he needs must be, who could seduce
Angels, nor think superflous others' aid.
I from the influence of thy looks receive
Access in every virtue, in thy sight   310
More wise, more watchful, stronger, if need were

292. *entire:* whole, hence free from (sin and blame).
310. *access:* increase.

Of outward strength; while shame, thou looking on,
Shame to be overcome or over-reached
Would utmost vigor raise, and raised unite.
Why shouldst not thou like sense within thee feel
When I am present, and thy trial choose
With me, best witness of thy virtue tried."
  So spake domestic Adam in his care
And matrimonial love; but Eve, who thought
Less áttributed to her faith sincere,   320
Thus her reply with accent sweet renewed.
  "If this be our condition, thus to dwell
In narrow circuit straitened by a foe,
Subtle or violent, we not endued
Single with like defense, wherever met,
How are we happy, still in fear of harm?
But harm precedes not sin: only our foe
Tempting affronts us with his foul esteem
Of our integrity: his foul esteem
Sticks no dishonor on our front, but turns   330
Foul on himself; then wherefore shunned or feared
By us? who rather double honor gain
From his surmise proved false, find peace within,
Favor from Heav'n, our witness from th' event.
And what is faith, love, virtue unassayed
Alone, without exterior help sustained?
Let us not then suspect our happy state
Left so imperfect by the Maker wise,
As not secure to single or combined.
Frail is our happiness, if this be so,   340
And Eden were no Eden thus exposed."
  To whom thus Adam fervently replied.
  "O woman, best are all things as the will

Read
(Eve)

---

323. *straitened:* confined.
327–329. *only . . . integrity:* Eve is repeating Adam's argument,
which she tries to answer in the following lines.
334. *event:* outcome.
339. "as not to be safe either alone or together." Eve misrepre-
sents Adam's argument, since he had not suggested they were not
safe together.

Of God ordained them, his creating hand
Nothing imperfect or deficient left
Of all that he created, much less man,
Or aught that might his happy state secure,
Secure from outward force; within himself
The danger lies, yet lies within his power:
Against his will he can receive no harm.
But God left free the will, for what obeys
Reason, is free, and reason he made right,
But bid her well beware, and still erect,
Lest by some fair appearing good surprised
She dictate false, and misinform the will
To do what God expressly hath forbid.
Not then mistrust, but tender love enjoins,
That I should mind thee oft, and mind thou me.
Firm we subsist, yet possible to swerve,
Since reason not impossibly may meet
Some specious object by the foe suborned,
And fall into deception unaware,
Not keeping strictest watch, as she was warned.
Seek not temptation then, which to avoid
Were better, and most likely if from me
Thou sever not: trial will come unsought.
Wouldst thou approve thy constancy, approve
First thy obedience; th' other who can know,
Not seeing thee attempted, who attest?
But if thou think, trial unsought may find
Us both securer than thus warned thou seem'st,
Go; for thy stay, not free, absents thee more;
Go in thy native innocence, rely
On what thou hast of virtue, summon all,
For God towards thee hath done his part, do thine."
    So spake the patriarch of mankind, but Eve
Persisted, yet submiss, though last, replied.

---

353. *still erect:* always alert.
358. *mind:* remind.
367. *approve:* give proof of.
371. *securer:* less on our guard, with a false sense of security.

"With thy permission then, and thus forewarned
Chiefly by what thy own last reasoning words
Touched only, that our trial, when least sought,   380
May find us both perhaps far less prepared,
The willinger I go, nor much expect
A foe so proud will first the weaker seek;
So bent, the more shall shame him his repulse."
Thus saying, from her husband's hand her hand
Soft she withdrew, and like a wood-nymph light,
Oread or Dryad, or of Delia's train,
Betook her to the groves, but Delia's self
In gait surpassed and goddess-like deport,
Though not as she with bow and quiver armed,   390
But with such gardening tools as art yet rude,
Guiltless of fire had formed, or angels brought.
To Pales, or Pomona thus adorned,
Likest she seemed, Pomona when she fled
Vertumnus, or to Ceres in her prime,
Yet virgin of Proserpina from Jove.
Her long with ardent look his eye pursued
Delighted, but desiring more her stay.
Oft he to her his charge of quick return
Repeated, she to him as oft engaged   400
To be returned by noon amid the bow'r,
And all things in best order to invite
Noontide repast, or afternoon's repose.
O much deceived, much failing, hapless Eve,
Of thy presumed return! event perverse!
Thou never from that hour in Paradise
Found'st either sweet repast, or sound repose;
Such ambush hid among sweet flow'rs and shades

---

387. *Oread:* mountain nymph. *Dryad:* wood nymph. *Delia:* Diana, goddess of the chase.

393. *Pales:* goddess of flocks and pastures. *Pomona:* goddess of fruit. The story of her pursuit by Vertumnus, a wood-god, is told in Ovid, *Metamorphoses,* XIV, 623 ff.

395. *Ceres:* goddess of agriculture.

396. *yet virgin of:* i.e., before she had become the mother of Proserpine by Jupiter.

Waited with hellish rancor imminent
To intercept thy way, or send thee back   410
Despoiled of innocence, of faith, of bliss.
For now, and since first break of dawn the Fiend,
Mere serpent in appearance, forth was come,
And on his quest, where likeliest he might find
The only two of mankind, but in them
The whole included race, his purposed prey.
In bow'r and field he sought, where any tuft
Of grove or garden plot more pleasant lay,
Their tendance or plantation for delight,
By fountain or by shady rivulet   420
He sought them both, but wished his hap might find
Eve separate, he wished, but not with hope
Of what so seldom chanced, when to his wish,
Beyond his hope, Eve separate he spies,
Veiled in a cloud of fragrance, where she stood,
Half spied, so thick the roses bushing round
About her glowed, oft stooping to support
Each flow'r of slender stalk, whose head though gay
Carnation, purple, azure, or specked with gold,
Hung drooping unsustained, them she upstays   430
Gently with myrtle band, mindless the while,
Herself, though fairest unsupported flow'r,
From her best prop so far, and storm so nigh.
Nearer he drew, and many a walk traversed
Of stateliest covert, cedar, pine, or palm,
Then voluble and bold, now hid, now seen
Among thick-woven arborets and flow'rs
Embordered on each bank, the hand of Eve:
Spot more delicious than those gardens feigned

---

413. *mere serpent:* altogether a serpent, not half-serpent and
half-human as he was sometimes depicted.

419. *tendance:* object of care.

431. *mindless:* heedless.

436. *voluble:* rolling.

438. *embordered:* forming a border. *hand:* handiwork.

Or of revived Adonis, or renowned 440
Alcinous, host of old Laertes' son,
Or that, not mystic, where the sapient king
Held dalliance with his fair Egyptian spouse.
Much he the place admired, the person more.
As one who long in populous city pent,
Where houses thick and sewers annoy the air,
Forth issuing on a summer's morn to breathe
Among the pleasant villages and farms
Adjoined, from each thing met conceives delight,
The smell of grain, or tedded grass, or kine, 450
Or dairy, each rural sight, each rural sound;
If chance with nymphlike step fair virgin pass,
What pleasing seemed, for her now pleases more,
She most, and in her look sums all delight.
Such pleasure took the Serpent to behold
This flow'ry plat, the sweet recess of Eve
Thus early, thus alone; her heav'nly form
Angelic, but more soft, and feminine,
Her graceful innocence, her every air
Of gesture or least action overawed 460
His malice, and with rapine sweet bereaved
His fierceness of the fierce intent it brought:
That space the Evil One abstracted stood
From his own evil, and for the time remained
Stupidly good, of enmity disarmed,

---

440. Pliny, in *Natural History*, XIX, xix, says that "antiquity gave its highest admiration to the garden of the Hesperids and of the kings Adonis and Alcinous" (Loeb trans.).

441. *Alcinous:* cf. V, 340n.

442–443. An allusion to the garden of Solomon (*the sapient king*) in Song of Solomon 6:2. *Not mystic* means "historical" as opposed to the literary and mythological gardens of Alcinous and Adonis.

450. *tedded:* cut and spread out to dry.

453. *for her:* because of her.

456. *plat:* plot.

465. *stupidly good:* involuntarily and irrationally good, hence not really good at all.

Of guile, of hate, of envy, of revenge;
But the hot Hell that always in him burns,
Though in mid Heav'n, soon ended his delight,
And tortures him now more, the more he sees
Of pleasure not for him ordained: then soon   470
Fierce hate he recollects, and all his thoughts
Of mischief, gratulating, thus excites.
    "Thoughts, whither have ye led me, with what sweet
Compulsion thus transported to forget
What hither brought us, hate, not love, nor hope
Of Paradise for Hell, hope here to taste
Of pleasure, but all pleasure to destroy,
Save what is in destroying, other joy
To me is lost. Then let me not let pass
Occasion which now smiles, behold alone   480
The woman, opportune to all attempt,
Her husband, for I view far round, not nigh,
Whose higher intellectual more I shun,
And strength, of courage haughty, and of limb
Heroic built, though of terrestrial mold,
Foe not informidable, exempt from wound,
I not; so much hath Hell debased, and pain
Enfeebled me, to what I was in Heav'n.
She fair, divinely fair, fit love for gods,
Not terrible, though terror be in love   490
And beauty, not approached by stronger hate,
Hate stronger, under show of love well feigned,
The way which to her ruin now I tend."
    So spake the Enemy of mankind, enclosed
In serpent, inmate bad, and toward Eve
Addressed his way, not with indented wave,
Prone on the ground, as since, but on his rear,
Circular base of rising folds, that tow'red
Fold above fold a surging maze, his head
Crested aloft, and carbuncle his eyes;   500

---

472. *gratulating:* rejoicing.
485. *terrestrial mold:* formed of earth.
500. *carbuncle:* i.e., deep red.

With burnished neck of verdant gold, erect
Amidst his circling spires, that on the grass
Floated redundant: pleasing was his shape,
And lovely, never since of serpent kind
Lovelier, not those that in Illyria changed
Hermione and Cadmus, or the god
In Epidaurus; nor to which transformed
Ammonian Jove, or Capitoline was seen,
He with Olympias, this with her who bore
Scipio, the highth of Rome. With tract oblique   510
At first, as one who sought access, but feared
To interrupt, sidelong he works his way.
As when a ship by skilful steersman wrought
Nigh river's mouth or foreland, where the wind
Veers oft, as oft so steers, and shifts her sail;
So varied he, and of his tortuous train
Curled many a wanton wreath in sight of Eve,
To lure her eye; she busied heard the sound
Of rustling leaves, but minded not, as used
To such disport before her through the field,   520
From every beast, more duteous at her call,
Than at Circean call the herd disguised.
He bolder now, uncalled before her stood;
But as in gaze admiring: oft he bowed
His turret crest, and sleek enameled neck,
Fawning, and licked the ground whereon she trod.
His gentle dumb expression turned at length

---

502. *spires:* coils.
505–506. Ovid describes the metamorphosis of *Cadmus* and
Hermione in *Metamorphoses*, IV, 563–603.
507. *Epidaurus:* the seat of Aesculapius, god of medicine, who
came to Rome in the form of a serpent to stop a deadly pestilence.
Cf. Ovid, *Metamorphoses*, XV, 626–744.
508–510. *Ammonian Jove* is Jupiter Ammon (cf. IV, 277), who in
the form of a serpent, was the legendary father of Alexander the
Great, whose mother was *Olympias*. The Capitoline Jupiter simi-
larly fathered *Scipio Africanus*, the greatest Roman (*highth of
Rome*). M. thus calls attention to the serpent as a phallic symbol.
522. Circe was a sorceress who lured men and then turned them
into animals.

The eye of Eve to mark his play; he glad
Of her attention gained, with serpent tongue
Organic, or impulse of vocal air,   530
His fraudulent temptation thus began.

 flatters Eve

   "Wonder not, sovran mistress, if perhaps
Thou canst, who art sole wonder, much less arm
Thy looks, the heav'n of mildness, with disdain,
Displeased that I approach thee thus, and gaze
Insatiate, I thus single, nor have feared
Thy awful brow, more awful thus retired.
Fairest resemblance of thy Maker fair,
Thee all things living gaze on, all things thine
By gift, and thy celestial beauty adore   540
With ravishment beheld, there best beheld
Where universally admired; but here
In this enclosure wild, these beasts among,
Beholders rude, and shallow to discern
Half what in thee is fair, one man except,
Who sees thee? (and what is one?) who shouldst be seen
A goddess among gods, adored and served
By angels numberless, thy daily train."

   So glozed the Tempter, and his proem tuned;
Into the heart of Eve his words made way,   550
Though at the voice much marveling; at length
Not unamazed she thus in answer spake.
"What may this mean? Language of man pronounced
By tongue of brute, and human sense expressed?
The first at least of these I thought denied
To beasts, whom God on their creation-day
Created mute to all articulate sound;

   529–530. i.e., either he used the serpent's tongue as an actual organ of speech, or else he forced the air in such a way as to imitate a voice.

   538. With this fraudulent use of the word *fair*, cf. the reference to "manly grace/ And wisdom, which alone is truly fair" (IV, 490–491).

   544. *shallow:* lacking intelligence.

   549. *glozed:* flattered. *proem:* prelude.

Eve wonders that sense he was human and speech.

The latter I demur, for in their looks
Much reason, and in their actions oft appears.
Thee, serpent, subtlest beast of all the field   560
I knew, but not with human voice endued;
Redouble then this miracle, and say,
How cam'st thou speakable of mute, and how
To me so friendly grown above the rest
Of brutal kind, that daily are in sight?
Say, for such wonder claims attention due."
    To whom the guileful Tempter thus replied.
"Empress of this fair world, resplendent Eve,
Easy to me it is to tell thee all
What thou command'st, and right thou shouldst be
        obeyed: 570
I was at first as other beasts that graze
The trodden herb, of abject thoughts and low,
As was my food, nor aught but food discerned
Or sex, and apprehended nothing high:
Till on a day roving the field, I chanced
A goodly tree far distant to behold
Loaden with fruit of fairest colors mixed,
Ruddy and gold: I nearer drew to gaze;
When from the boughs a savory odor blown,
Grateful to appetite, more pleased my sense   580
Than smell of sweetest fennel or the teats
Of ewe or goat dropping with milk at ev'n,
Unsucked of lamb or kid, that tend their play.
To satisfy the sharp desire I had
Of tasting those fair apples, I resolved
Not to defer; hunger and thirst at once,
Powerful persuaders, quickened at the scent
Of that alluring fruit, urged me so keen.
About the mossy trunk I wound me soon,

REASON
SATAN answers how he speaks and reasons
Read how he speaks and reasons
apple first here? generic term for fruit, or specific?

---

558. *the latter I demur:* "I don't think 'sense' [line 554] was
denied to brutes."

563. *speakable of mute:* able to speak after being mute.

581. *fennel:* besides being thought a favorite food of snakes,
fennel was emblematic of dissembling and flattery.

For high from ground the branches would require   590
Thy utmost reach or Adam's: round the tree
All other beasts that saw, with like desire
Longing and envying stood, but could not reach.
Amid the tree now got, where plenty hung
Tempting so nigh, to pluck and eat my fill
I spared not, for such pleasure till that hour
At feed or fountain never had I found.
Sated at length, ere long I might perceive
Strange alteration in me, to degree
Of reason in my inward powers, and speech   600
Wanted not long, though to this shape retained.
Thenceforth to speculations high or deep
I turned my thoughts, and with capacious mind
Considered all things visible in heav'n,
Or earth, or middle, all things fair and good;
But all that fair and good in thy divine
Semblance, and in thy beauty's heav'nly ray
United I beheld; no fair to thine
Equivalent or second, which compelled
Me thus, though importune perhaps, to come   610
And gaze, and worship thee of right declared
Sovran of creatures, universal dame."

    So talked the spirited sly snake; and Eve
Yet more amazed unwary thus replied.

    "Serpent, thy overpraising leaves in doubt
The virtue of that fruit, in thee first proved:
But say, where grows the tree, from hence how far?
For many are the trees of God that grow
In Paradise, and various, yet unknown
To us, in such abundance lies our choice,   620
As leaves a greater store of fruit untouched
Still hanging incorruptible, till men

600–601. *speech . . . retained:* "and speech was not lacking for long, although I kept this shape."
605. *middle:* the air.
612. *universal dame:* mistress of all.
613. *spirited:* possessed by a spirit.

Grow up to their provision, and more hands
Help to disburden Nature of her birth."
    To whom the wily adder, blithe and glad.
"Empress, the way is ready, and not long,
Beyond a row of myrtles, on a flat,
Fast by a fountain, one small thicket past
Of blowing myrrh and balm; if thou accept
My conduct, I can bring thee thither soon."   630
    "Lead then," said Eve. He leading swiftly rolled
In tangles, and made intricate seem straight,
To mischief swift. Hope elevates, and joy
Brightens his crest, as when a wandering fire,
Compact of unctuous vapor, which the night
Condenses, and the cold environs round,
Kindled through agitation to a flame,
Which oft, they say, some evil spirit attends
Hovering and blazing with delusive light,
Misleads th' amazed night-wanderer from his way   640
To bogs and mires, and oft through pond or pool,
There swallowed up and lost, from succor far.
So glistered the dire snake, and into fraud
Led Eve our credulous mother, to the tree
Of prohibition, root of all our woe;
Which when she saw, thus to her guide she spake.
    "Serpent, we might have spared our coming hither,
Fruitless to me, though fruit be here to excess,
The credit of whose virtue rest with thee,
Wondrous indeed, if cause of such effects.   650
But of this tree we may not taste nor touch;
God so commanded, and left that command
Sole daughter of his voice; the rest, we live
Law to ourselves, our reason is our law."
    To whom the Tempter guilefully replied.

---

623. *to their provision:* i.e., to enjoy all that has been provided.
629. *blowing:* blossoming. *balm:* balsam.
634. *fire:* ignis fatuus.
644–645. *tree/ Of prohibition:* Hebraic locution for "pro-
hibited tree."

God's prohibition: don't eat
DON'T EVEN TOUCH

"Indeed? Hath God then said that of the fruit
Of all these garden trees ye shall not eat,
Yet lords declared of all in earth or air?"
   To whom thus Eve yet sinless. "Of the fruit
Of each tree in the garden we may eat,   660
But of the fruit of this fair tree amidst
The garden, God hath said, 'Ye shall not eat
Thereof, nor shall ye touch it, lest ye die.' "
   She scarce had said, though brief, when now more bold
The Tempter, but with show of zeal and love
To man, and indignation at his wrong,
New part puts on, and as to passion moved,
Fluctuates disturbed, yet comely, and in act
Raised, as of some great matter to begin.
As when of old some orator renowned   670
In Athens or free Rome, where eloquence
Flourished, since mute, to some great cause addressed,
Stood in himself collected, while each part,
Motion, each act won audience ere the tongue,
Sometimes in highth began, as no delay
Of preface brooking through his zeal of right.
So standing, moving, or to highth upgrown
The Tempter all impassioned thus began.
   "O sacred, wise, and wisdom-giving plant,
Mother of science, now I feel thy power   680
Within me clear, not only to discern
Things in their causes, but to trace the ways
Of highest agents, deemed however wise.
Queen of this universe, do not believe
Those rigid threats of death; ye shall not die:
How should ye? By the fruit? It gives you life

---

668. *fluctuates:* undulates.
674. *audience:* hearing.
675. *in highth:* in the middle of his subject.
680. *science:* knowledge. In the background is St. Augustine's distinction between mere secular knowledge (*scientia*) and religious wisdom (*sapientia*).

Satan lays it out

To knowledge. By the Threatener? Look on me,
Me who have touched and tasted, yet both live,
And life more perfect have attained than fate
Meant me, by vent'ring higher than my lot.   690
Shall that be shut to man, which to the beast
Is open? Or will God incense his ire
For such a petty trespass, and not praise
Rather your dauntless virtue, whom the pain
Of death denounced, whatever thing death be,
Deterred not from achieving what might lead
To happier life, knowledge of good and evil;
Of good, how just? Of evil, if what is evil
Be real, why not known, since easier shunned?
God therefore cannot hurt ye, and be just;   700
Not just, not God; not feared then, nor obeyed:
Your fear itself of death removes the fear.
Why then was this forbid? Why but to awe,
Why but to keep ye low and ignorant,
His worshippers; he knows that in the day
Ye eat thereof, your eyes that seem so clear,
Yet are but dim, shall perfectly be then
Opened and cleared, and ye shall be as gods,
Knowing both good and evil as they know.
That ye should be as gods, since I as man,   710
Internal man, is but proportion meet,
I of brute human, ye of human gods.
So ye shall die perhaps, by putting off
Human, to put on gods, death to be wished,

appeal to pride, desire to rise

serpent says he will be lifted proportionally: as snake became like man, Eve will become like god

---

687. *to knowledge:* in addition to knowledge.

700–702. Satan's sophistical argument is that it is illogical to
obey the command: Since a just God cannot hurt you, your fear
that he will hurt you implies that he is unjust, and if he is unjust
he is not God and therefore need not be feared or obeyed.

701. *not feared:* not to be feared.

711. *internal man:* i.e., in his "inward powers" (line 600), though
still a serpent externally.

713–714. Satan unwittingly states the paradox of the fortunate
fall. Cf. III, 281–317, and the many references to putting on the
new man in the New Testament.

pride!

Though threatened, which no worse than this can
    bring.
And what are gods that man may not become
As they, participating godlike food?
The gods are first, and that advantage use
On our belief, that all from them proceeds;
I question it, for this fair earth I see,   720
Warmed by the sun, producing every kind,
Them nothing. If they all things, who enclosed
Knowledge of good and evil in this tree,
That whoso eats thereof, forthwith attains
Wisdom without their leave? And wherein lies
Th' offense, that man should thus attain to know?
What can your knowledge hurt him, or this tree
Impart against his will if all be his?
Or is it envy, and can envy dwell
In heav'nly breasts? These, these and many more   730
Causes import your need of this fair fruit.
Goddess humane, reach then, and freely taste."

    He ended, and his words replete with guile
Into her heart too easy entrance won:
Fixed on the fruit she gazed, which to behold
Might tempt alone, and in her ears the sound
Yet rung of his persuasive words, impregned
With reason, to her seeming, and with truth;
Meanwhile the hour of noon drew on, and waked
An eager appetite, raised by the smell   740
So savory of that fruit, which with desire,
Inclinable now grown to touch or taste,
Solicited her longing eye; yet first
Pausing a while, thus to herself she mused.

---

    718. *the gods are first:* This was the argument of the Epicureans.
Satan has modulated easily from the singular "God" to the plural
"gods."

    722. *if they all things:* if they produced all things.

    732. *humane:* either "gracious" or "human."

    742. *inclinable now grown:* Eve's desire for the fruit has now
developed to the extent that she is inclined to touch and taste (as
well as see and smell).

"Great are thy virtues, doubtless, best of fruits,
Though kept from man, and worthy to be admired,
Whose taste, too long forborne, at first assay
Gave elocution to the mute, and taught
The tongue not made for speech to speak thy praise:
Thy praise he also who forbids thy use,   750
Conceals not from us, naming thee the Tree
Of Knowledge, knowledge both of good and evil;
Forbids us then to taste, but his forbidding
Commends thee more, while it infers the good
By thee communicated, and our want:
For good unknown, sure is not had, or had
And yet unknown, is as not had at all.
In plain then, what forbids he but to know,
Forbids us good, forbids us to be wise?
Such prohibitions bind not. But if Death   760
Bind us with after-bands, what profits then
Our inward freedom? In the day we eat
Of this fair fruit, our doom is, we shall die.
How dies the serpent? He hath eat'n and lives,
And knows, and speaks, and reasons, and discerns,
Irrational till then. For us alone
Was death invented? Or to us denied
This intellectual food, for beasts reserved?
For beasts it seems: yet that one beast which first
Hath tasted, envies not, but brings with joy   770
The good befall'n him, author unsuspect,
Friendly to man, far from deceit or guile.
What fear I then, rather what know to fear
Under this ignorance of good and evil,
Of God or death, of law or penalty?
Here grows the cure of all, this fruit divine,
Fair to the eye, inviting to the taste,
Of virtue to make wise: what hinders then
To reach, and feed at once both body and mind?"
    So saying, her rash hand in evil hour   780

---

758. *in plain:* in short.
771. *author unsuspect:* informant not to be suspected.

[handwritten annotations: "Milton confirms her motives: 789-90", "EVE'S MOTIVES LINE 781", "EVE EATS", "read", "MOTIVES", "high", "EFFECT"]

Forth reaching to the fruit, she plucked, she eat:
Earth felt the wound, and Nature from her seat
Sighing through all her works gave signs of woe,
That all was lost. Back to the thicket slunk
The guilty serpent, and well might, for Eve
Intent now wholly on her taste, naught else
Regarded, such delight till then, as seemed,
In fruit she never tasted, whether true
Or fancied so, through expectation high
Of knowledge, nor was godhead from her thought.   790
Greedily she engorged without restraint,
And knew not eating death: satiate at length,
And heightened as with wine, jocund and boon,
Thus to herself she pleasingly began.

    "O sovran, virtuous, precious of all trees
In Paradise, of operation blest
To sapience, hitherto obscured, infamed,
And thy fair fruit let hang, as to no end
Created; but henceforth my early care,
Not without song, each morning, and due praise   800
Shall tend thee, and the fertile burden ease
Of thy full branches offered free to all;
Till dieted by thee I grow mature
In knowledge, as the gods who all things know;
Though others envy what they cannot give;
For had the gift been theirs, it had not here
Thus grown. Experience, next to thee I owe,
Best guide; not following thee, I had remained
In ignorance, thou open'st wisdom's way,
And giv'st access, though secret she retire.   810
And I perhaps am secret; Heav'n is high,
High and remote to see from thence distinct
Each thing on earth; and other care perhaps
May have diverted from continual watch

---

781. *eat:* ate.

792. *knew not eating death:* knew not that she was eating death.

795. *virtuous, precious:* the positive used as the superlative.

797. *sapience: scientia* has now become *sapientia.* Cf. line 680*n*
above. *infamed:* unknown.

Our great Forbidder, safe with all his spies
About him. But to Adam in what sort
Shall I appear? Shall I to him make known
As yet my change, and give him to partake
Full happiness with me, or rather not,
But keep the odds of knowledge in my power　　　820
Without copartner? so to add what wants
In female sex, the more to draw his love,
And render me more equal, and perhaps,
A thing not undesirable, sometime
Superior; for inferior who is free?
This may be well: but what if God have seen,
And death ensue? Then I shall be no more,
And Adam wedded to another Eve,
Shall live with her enjoying, I extinct;
A death to think. Confirmed then I resolve,　　　830
Adam shall share with me in bliss or woe:
So dear I love him, that with him all deaths
I could endure, without him live no life."

　So saying, from the tree her step she turned,
But first low reverence done, as to the power
That dwelt within, whose presence had infused
Into the plant sciential sap, derived
From nectar, drink of gods. Adam the while
Waiting desirous her return, had wove
Of choicest flow'rs a garland to adorn　　　840
Her tresses, and her rural labors crown,
As reapers oft are wont their harvest queen.
Great joy he promised to his thoughts, and new
Solace in her return, so long delayed;
Yet oft his heart, divine of something ill,
Misgave him; he the faltering measure felt;
And forth to meet her went, the way she took
That morn when first they parted; by the Tree

　823–825. Cf. IV, 295–296, "though both/ Not equal, as their sex
not equal seemed."

　845. *divine of:* foreboding, foreseeing.

　846. *faltering measure:* the irregular beat (of his heart).

Eve
contains motive

Of Knowledge he must pass; there he her met,
Scarce from the tree returning; in her hand   8
A bough of fairest fruit that downy smiled,
New gathered, and ambrosial smell diffused.
To him she hasted, in her face excuse
Came prologue, and apology to prompt,
Which with bland words at will she thus addressed.
    "Hast thou not wondered, Adam, at my stay?
Thee I have missed, and thought it long, deprived
Thy presence, agony of love till now
Not felt, nor shall be twice, for never more

Read

Mean I to try, what rash untried I sought,   86
The pain of absence from thy sight. But strange
Hath been the cause, and wonderful to hear:

Eve persuades ADAM

This tree is not as we are told, a tree
Of danger tasted, nor to evil unknown

MOTIVE

Opening the way, but of divine effect
To open eyes, and make them gods who taste;
And hath been tasted such: the serpent wise,
Or not restrained as we, or not obeying,
Hath eaten of the fruit, and is become,
Not dead, as we are threatened, but thenceforth   87
Endued with human voice and human sense,
Reasoning to admiration, and with me
Persuasively hath so prevailed, that I
Have also tasted, and have also found

Read

Th' effects to correspond, opener mine eyes,
Dim erst, dilated spirits, ampler heart,
And growing up to godhead; which for thee
Chiefly I sought, without thee can despise.
For bliss, as thou hast part, to me is bliss,
Tedious, unshared with thee, and odious soon.   88

Read

Thou therefore also taste, that equal lot
May join us, equal joy, as equal love;

853–854. *Excuse* came as a *prologue* to lead on (*prompt*) he
apology (*apologia:* a formal defense).
    860. *what . . . sought:* what I rashly sought to try because i
was untried.
    864. *tasted:* if tasted.

Lest thou not tasting, different degree
Disjoin us, and I then too late renounce
Deity for thee, when fate will not permit."
    Thus Eve with count'nance blithe her story told;
But in her cheek distemper flushing glowed.
On th' other side, Adam, soon as he heard
The fatal trespass done by Eve, amazed,
Astonied stood and blank, while horror chill
Ran through his veins, and all his joints relaxed;
From his slack hand the garland wreathed for Eve
Down dropped, and all the faded roses shed:
Speechless he stood and pale, till thus at length
First to himself he inward silence broke.
    "O fairest of creation, last and best
Of all God's works, creature in whom excelled
Whatever can to sight or thought be formed,
Holy, divine, good, amiable, or sweet!
How art thou lost, how on a sudden lost,
Defaced, deflow'red, and now to death devote?
Rather how hast thou yielded to transgress
The strict forbiddance, how to violate
The sacred fruit forbidd'n! Some cursèd fraud
Of enemy hath beguiled thee, yet unknown,
And me with thee hath ruined, for with thee
Certain my resolution is to die;
How can I live without thee, how forgo
Thy sweet converse and love so dearly joined,
To live again in these wild woods forlorn?
Should God create another Eve, and I
Another rib afford, yet loss of thee
Would never from my heart; no no, I feel
The link of nature draw me: flesh of flesh,
Bone of my bone thou art, and from thy state
Mine never shall be parted, bliss or woe."
    So having said, as one from sad dismay

———————————

901. *devote:* doomed.
916. *bliss or woe:* Adam unwittingly echoes Eve's words of line
831 above.

Recomforted, and after thoughts disturbed
Submitting to what seemed remediless,
Thus in calm mood his words to Eve he turned.   920
    "Bold deed thou hast presumed, advent'rous Eve,
And peril great provoked, who thus hast dared
Had it been only coveting to eye
That sacred fruit, sacred to abstinence,
Much more to taste it under ban to touch.
But past who can recall, or done undo?
Not God omnipotent, nor fate, yet so
Perhaps thou shalt not die, perhaps the fact
Is not so heinous now, foretasted fruit,
Profaned first by the serpent, by him first   930
Made common and unhallowed ere our taste;
Nor yet on him found deadly, he yet lives,
Lives, as thou saidst, and gains to live as man
Higher degree of life, inducement strong
To us, as likely tasting to attain
Proportional ascent, which cannot be
But to be gods, or angels demi-gods.
Nor can I think that God, Creator wise,
Though threatening, will in earnest so destroy
Us his prime creatures, dignified so high,   940
Set over all his works, which in our fall,
For us created, needs with us must fail,
Dependent made; so God shall uncreate,
Be frustrate, do, undo, and labor lose,
Not well conceived of God, who though his power
Creation could repeat, yet would be loth
Us to abolish, lest the Adversary
Triumph and say, 'Fickle their state whom God
Most favors, who can please him long? Me first
He ruined, now mankind; whom will he next?'   950
Matter of scorn, not to be giv'n the Foe.
However I with thee have fixed my lot,
Certain to undergo like doom, if death

---

928. *fact:* deed.
953. *certain:* resolved.

Consort with thee, death is to me as life;
So forcible within my heart I feel
The bond of nature draw me to my own,
My own in thee, for what thou art is mine;
Our state cannot be severed, we are one,
One flesh; to lose thee were to lose myself."
    So Adam, and thus Eve to him replied.   960
"O glorious trial of exceeding love,
Illustrious evidence, example high!
Engaging me to emulate, but short
Of thy perfection, how shall I attain,
Adam, from whose dear side I boast me sprung,
And gladly of our union hear thee speak,
One heart, one soul in both; whereof good proof
This day affords, declaring thee resolved,
Rather than death or aught than death more dread   970
Shall separate us, linked in love so dear,
To undergo with me one guilt, one crime,
If any be, of tasting this fair fruit,
Whose virtue, for of good still good proceeds,
Direct, or by occasion hath presented
This happy trial of thy love, which else
So eminently never had been known.
Were it I thought death menaced would ensue
This my attempt, I would sustain alone
The worst, and not persuade thee, rather die   980
Deserted, than oblige thee with a fact
Pernicious to thy peace, chiefly assured
Remarkably so late of thy so true,
So faithful love unequaled; but I feel
Far otherwise th' event, not death, but life
Augmented, opened eyes, new hopes, new joys,
Taste so divine, that what of sweet before
Hath touched my sense, flat seems to this, and harsh.
On my experience, Adam, freely taste,
And fear of death deliver to the winds."

---

974. *by occasion:* indirectly.
980. *oblige:* involve in guilt.

So saying, she embraced him, and for joy   990
Tenderly wept, much won that he his love
Had so ennobled, as of choice to incur
Divine displeasure for her sake, or death.
In recompense (for such compliance bad
Such recompense best merits) from the bough
She gave him of that fair enticing fruit
With liberal hand: he scrupled not to eat
Against his better knowledge, not deceived,
But fondly overcome with female charm.
Earth trembled from her entrails, as again   1000
In pangs, and Nature gave a second groan,
Sky loured, and muttering thunder, some sad drops
Wept at completing of the mortal sin
Original; while Adam took no thought,
Eating his fill, nor Eve to iterate
Her former trespass feared, the more to soothe
Him with her loved society, that now
As with new wine intoxicated both
They swim in mirth, and fancy that they feel
Divinity within them breeding wings   1010
Wherewith to scorn the earth: but that false fruit
Far other operation first displayed,
Carnal desire inflaming, he on Eve
Began to cast lascivious eyes, she him
As wantonly repaid; in lust they burn:
Till Adam thus 'gan Eve to dalliance move.

  "Eve, now I see thou art exact of taste,
And elegant, of sapience no small part,
Since to each meaning savor we apply,
And palate call judicious; I the praise   1020
Yield thee, so well this day thou hast purveyed.
Much pleasure we have lost, while we abstained
From this delightful fruit, nor known till now

1017–1020. *sapience* and *savor* both derive ultimately from the
Latin *sapere*, which means both "to taste" and "to be wise."
Adam's tasteless pun is a measure of his now fallen condition.

True relish, tasting; if such pleasure be
In things to us forbidd'n, it might be wished,
For this one tree had been forbidden ten.
But come, so well refreshed, now let us play,
As meet is, after such delicious fare;
For never did thy beauty since the day
I saw thee first and wedded thee, adorned   1030
With all perfections, so inflame my sense
With ardor to enjoy thee, fairer now
Than ever, bounty of this virtuous tree."
     So said he, and forbore not glance or toy
Of amorous intent, well understood
Of Eve, whose eye darted contagious fire.
Her hand he seized, and to a shady bank,
Thick overhead with verdant roof embow'red
He led her nothing loth; flow'rs were the couch,
Pansies, and violets, and asphodel,
And hyacinth, earth's freshest softest lap.   1040
There they their fill of love and love's disport
Took largely, of their mutual guilt the seal,
The solace of their sin, till dewy sleep
Oppressed them, wearied with their amorous play.
Soon as the force of that fallacious fruit,
That with exhilarating vapor bland
About their spirits had played, and inmost powers
Made err, was now exhaled, and grosser sleep
Bred of unkindly fumes, with conscious dreams
Encumbered, now had left them, up they rose   1050
As from unrest, and each the other viewing,
Soon found their eyes how opened, and their minds
How darkened; innocence, that as a veil
Had shadowed them from knowing ill, was gone,
Just confidence, and native righteousness
And honor from about them, naked left

1037–1041. This passage gains in ironic overtones when placed
in juxtaposition to IV, 697–703, and the *Iliad*, XIV, 292–353.
1050. *unkindly:* unnatural.

To guilty shame; he covered, but his robe
Uncovered more. So rose the Danite strong
Herculean Samson from the harlot-lap   1060
Of Philistean Dalilah, and waked
Shorn of his strength, they destitute and bare
Of all their virtue: silent, and in face
Confounded long they sat, as stricken mute,
Till Adam, though not less than Eve abashed,
At length gave utterance to these words constrained.
   "O Eve, in evil hour thou didst give ear
To that false worm, of whomsoever taught
To counterfeit man's voice, true in our fall,
False in our promised rising; since our eyes   1070
Opened we find indeed, and find we know
Both good and evil, good lost, and evil got,
Bad fruit of knowledge, if this be to know,
Which leaves us naked thus, of honor void,
Of innocence, of faith, of purity,
Our wonted ornaments now soiled and stained,
And in our faces evident the signs
Of foul concupiscence; whence evil store;
Even shame, the last of evils; of the first
Be sure then. How shall I behold the face   1080
Henceforth of God or angel, erst with joy
And rapture so oft beheld? Those heav'nly shapes
Will dazzle now this earthly, with their blaze
Insufferably bright. O might I here
In solitude live savage, in some glade
Obscured, where highest woods impenetrable
To star or sunlight, spread their umbrage broad
And brown as evening! Cover me ye pines,
Ye cedars, with innumerable boughs
Hide me, where I may never see them more.   1090

  1059–1061. The story of how *Samson*, who was of the tribe of
Dan, betrayed to *Dalilah* the secret that his strength lay in his
hair is told in Judges 16:4–20.

  1068. *worm*: serpent.

  1088. *brown*: dark. *cover me*: cf. VI, 842–843, and Revelation
6:15–16.

But let us now, as in bad plight, devise
What best may for the present serve to hide
The parts of each from other, that seem most
To shame obnoxious, and unseenliest seen,
Some tree whose broad smooth leaves together sewed,
And girded on our loins, may cover round
Those middle parts, that this newcomer, shame,
There sit not, and reproach us as unclean."

So counseled he, and both together went
Into the thickest wood, there soon they chose   1100
The fig tree, not that kind for fruit renowned,
But such as at this day to Indians known
In Malabar or Decan spreads her arms
Branching so broad and long, that in the ground
The bended twigs take root, and daughters grow
About the mother tree, a pillared shade
High overarched, and echoing walks between;
There oft the Indian herdsman shunning heat
Shelters in cool, and tends his pasturing herds   1109
At loopholes cut through thickest shade: those leaves
They gathered, broad as Amazonian targe,
And with what skill they had, together sewed,
To gird their waist, vain covering if to hide
Their guilt and dreaded shame; O how unlike
To that first naked glory! Such of late
Columbus found th' American so girt
With feathered cincture, naked else and wild
Among the trees on isles and woody shores.
Thus fenced, and as they thought, their shame in part
Covered, but not at rest or ease of mind,   1120
They sat them down to weep, nor only tears
Rained at their eyes, but high winds worse within
Began to rise, high passions, anger, hate,

1101–1111. M. mistakenly gives to the banyan or Indian fig tree,
which has small leaves, the large leaves of the banana tree. It
seems fitting that Adam and Eve should cover their shame with
leaves from a fig tree that bears no fruit and that grows downward
instead of upward.

[handwritten margin notes: "sensual appetite (+ thus emotion) now rules reason (BUT why?)"]

[handwritten margin note: "Read"]

Mistrust, suspicion, discord, and shook sore
Their inward state of mind, calm region once
And full of peace, now tossed and turbulent:
For understanding ruled not, and the will
Heard not her lore, both in subjection now
To sensual appetite, who from beneath
Usurping over sovran reason claimed
Superior sway: from thus distempered breast, 1130
Adam, estranged in look and altered style,
Speech intermitted thus to Eve renewed.

[handwritten margin note: "Adam: I told you so"]

    "Would thou hadst hearkened to my words, and
        stayed
With me, as I besought thee, when that strange
Desire of wandering this unhappy morn,
I know not whence possessed thee; we had then
Remained still happy, not as now, despoiled
Of all our good, shamed, naked, miserable.
Let none henceforth seek needless cause to approve 1140
The faith they owe; when earnestly they seek
Such proof, conclude they then begin to fail."

[handwritten margin note: "Bickering continues"]

    To whom soon moved with touch of blame thus Eve.

[handwritten margin note: "Eve's counter argument"]

"What words have passed thy lips, Adam severe,
Imput'st thou that to my default, or will
Of wandering, as thou call'st it, which who knows
But might as ill have happened thou being by,
Or to thyself perhaps: hadst thou been there,
Or here th' attempt, thou couldst not have discerned
Fraud in the serpent, speaking as he spake; 1150
No ground of enmity between us known,
Why he should mean me ill, or seek to harm.
Was I to have never parted from thy side?
As good have grown there still a lifeless rib.
Being as I am, why didst not thou the head
Command me absolutely not to go,

1132. *altered style:* with a changed manner of speech (e.g., he
doesn't even address Eve by name).

1140. *approve:* give proof of.

1141. *owe:* possess.

Going into such danger as thou saidst?
Too facile then thou didst not much gainsay,
Nay didst permit, approve, and fair dismiss.
Hadst thou been firm and fixed in thy dissent,   1160
Neither had I transgressed, nor thou with me."

    To whom then first incensed Adam replied.
"Is this the love, is this the recompense
Of mine to thee, ingrateful Eve, expressed
Immutable when thou wert lost, not I,
Who might have lived and joyed immortal bliss,
Yet willingly chose rather death with thee?
And am I now upbraided, as the cause
Of thy transgressing? not enough severe,
It seems, in thy restraint: what could I more?   1170
I warned thee, I admonished thee, foretold
The danger, and the lurking Enemy
That lay in wait; beyond this had been force,
And force upon free will hath here no place.
But confidence then bore thee on, secure
Either to meet no danger, or to find
Matter of glorious trial; and perhaps
I also erred in overmuch admiring
What seemed in thee so perfect, that I thought
No evil durst attempt thee, but I rue   1180
That error now, which is become my crime,
And thou th' accuser. Thus it shall befall
Him who to worth in women overtrusting
Lets her will rule; restraint she will not brook,
And left to herself, if evil thence ensue,
She first his weak indulgence will accuse."

    Thus they in mutual accusation spent
The fruitless hours, but neither self-condemning,
And of their vain contest appeared no end.

1164–1165. *expressed/ Immutable:* shown to be unchangeable.
1183. *women:* many editors accept Bentley's emendation,
"woman."

BOOK X ❧

THE ARGUMENT

Man's transgression known, the guardian angels forsake Paradise, and return up to Heaven to approve their vigilance, and are approved, God declaring that the entrance of Satan could not be by them prevented. He sends his Son to judge the transgressors, who descends and gives sentence accordingly; then in pity clothes them both, and reascends. Sin and Death sitting till then at the gates of Hell, by wondrous sympathy feeling the success of Satan in this new world, and the sin by man there committed, resolve to sit no longer confined in Hell, but to follow Satan their sire up to the place of man. To make the way easier from Hell to this world to and fro, they pave a broad highway or bridge over chaos, according to the track that Satan first made; then preparing for earth, they meet him proud of his success returning to Hell; their mutual gratulation. Satan arrives at Pandemonium, in full assembly relates with boasting his success against man; instead of applause is entertained with a general hiss by all his audience, transformed with himself also suddenly into serpents, according to his doom given in Paradise; then deluded with a show of the forbidden tree springing up before them, they greedily reaching to take of the fruit, chew dust and bitter ashes. The proceedings of Sin and Death;

God foretells the final victory of his Son over them, and
the renewing of all things; but for the present commands his angels to make several alterations in the heavens and elements. Adam more and more perceiving his
fallen condition heavily bewails, rejects the condole-
ment of Eve; she persists and at length appeases him:
then to evade the curse likely to fall on their offspring,
proposes to Adam violent ways which he approves not,
but conceiving better hope, puts her in mind of the late
promise made them, that her seed should be revenged
on the serpent, and exhorts her with him to seek peace
of the offended Deity, by repentance and supplication.

    Meanwhile the heinous and despiteful act
Of Satan done in Paradise, and how
He in the serpent had perverted Eve,
Her husband she, to taste the fatal fruit,
Was known in Heav'n; for what can scape the eye
Of God all-seeing, or deceive his heart
Omniscient, who in all things wise and just,
Hindered not Satan to attempt the mind
Of man, with strength entire, and free will armed,
Complete to have discovered and repulsed   10
Whatever wiles of foe or seeming friend.
For still they knew, and ought to have still remembered
The high injunction not to taste that fruit,
Whoever tempted; which they not obeying,
Incurred, what could they less, the penalty,
And manifold in sin, deserved to fall.
Up into Heav'n from Paradise in haste
Th' angelic guards ascended, mute and sad
For man, for of his state by this they knew,
Much wondering how the subtle Fiend had stol'n   20
Entrance unseen. Soon as th' unwelcome news
From earth arrived at Heaven gate, displeased
All were who heard, dim sadness did not spare

---

10. *complete to:* fully able (modifies "mind," line 8).
19. *by this:* by this time.

That time celestial visages, yet mixed
With pity, violated not their bliss.
About the new-arrived, in multitudes
Th' ethereal people ran, to hear and know
How all befell: they towards the throne supreme
Accountable made haste to make appear
With righteous plea, their utmost vigilance,   30
And easily approved; when the Most High
Eternal Father, from his secret cloud
Amidst, in thunder uttered thus his voice.
     "Assembled angels, and ye powers returned
From unsuccessful charge, be not dismayed,
Nor troubled at these tidings from the earth,
Which your sincerest care could not prevent,
Foretold so lately what would come to pass,
When first this tempter crossed the gulf from Hell.
I told ye then he should prevail and speed   40
On his bad errand, man should be seduced
And flattered out of all, believing lies
Against his Maker; no decree of mine
Concurring to necessitate his fall,
Or touch with lightest moment of impulse
His free will, to her own inclining left
In even scale. But fall'n he is, and now
What rests but that the mortal sentence pass
On his transgression, death denounced that day,
Which he presumes already vain and void,   50
Because not yet inflicted, as he feared,
By some immediate stroke; but soon shall find
Forbearance no acquittance ere day end.
Justice shall not return as bounty scorned.

29–30. i.e., made haste to justify their utmost vigilance.
40. *speed:* succeed.
45. *moment:* force.
48. *rests:* remains.
53. *acquittance:* exoneration.
54. "Justice shall not return scorned as my bounty has been scorned."

But whom send I to judge them? whom but thee
Vicegerent Son, to thee I have transferred
All judgment, whether in Heav'n, or earth, or Hell.
Easy it may be seen that I intend
Mercy colleague with justice, sending thee
Man's friend, his Mediator, his designed   60
Both ransom and Redeemer voluntary,
And destined man himself to judge man fall'n."

So spake the Father, and unfolding bright
Toward the right hand his glory, on the Son
Blazed forth unclouded Deity; he full
Resplendent all his Father manifest
Expressed, and thus divinely answered mild.

"Father eternal, thine is to decree,
Mine both in Heav'n and earth to do thy will
Supreme, that thou in me thy Son beloved   70
May'st ever rest well pleased. I go to judge
On earth these thy transgressors, but thou know'st,
Whoever judged, the worst on me must light,
When time shall be, for so I undertook
Before thee; and not repenting, this obtain
Of right, that I may mitigate their doom
On me derived, yet I shall temper so
Justice with mercy, as may illustrate most
Them fully satisfied, and thee appease.
Attendance none shall need nor train, where none   80
Are to behold the judgment, but the judged,
Those two; the third best absent is condemned,
Convict by flight, and rebel to all law;
Conviction to the serpent none belongs."

Thus saying, from his radiant seat he rose

55-57. Cf. John 5:22, "For the Father judgeth no man, but hath committed all judgment unto the Son."
77. *derived:* turned aside.
78. *illustrate:* glorify.
79. *them:* i.e., justice and mercy.
83. *convict:* convicted.
84. *conviction:* proof of guilt.

Son finds Adam & Eve hiding in the garden.

Of high collateral glory: him Thrones and Powers,
Princedoms, and Dominations ministrant
Accompanied to Heaven gate, from whence
Eden and all the coast in prospect lay.
Down he descended straight; the speed of gods   90
Time counts not, though with swiftest minutes winged.
Now was the sun in western cadence low
From noon, and gentle airs due at their hour
To fan the earth now waked, and usher in
The evening cool when he from wrath more cool
Came the mild Judge and Intercessor both
To sentence man: the voice of God they heard
Now walking in the garden, by soft winds
Brought to their ears, while day declined, they heard,
And from his presence hid themselves among   100
The thickest trees, both man and wife, till God
Approaching, thus to Adam called aloud.
    "Where art thou Adam, wont with joy to meet
My coming seen far off? I miss thee here,
Not pleased, thus entertained with solitude,
Where obvious duty erewhile appeared unsought:
Or come I less conspicuous, or what change
Absents thee, or what chance detains? Come forth."
He came, and with him Eve, more loth, though first
To offend, discount'nanced both, and discomposed;   110
Love was not in their looks, either to God
Or to each other, but apparent guilt,
And shame, and perturbation, and despair,
Anger, and obstinacy, and hate, and guile.
Whence Adam faltering long, thus answered brief.
    "I heard thee in the garden, and of thy voice
Afraid, being naked, hid myself." To whom
The gracious Judge without revile replied.
    "My voice thou oft hast heard, and hast not feared,

---

89. *coast:* region.
92. *cadence:* falling, setting.
106. *obvious duty:* your duty in coming to meet me.
112. *apparent:* manifest.

But still rejoiced; how is it now become   120
So dreadful to thee? that thou are naked, who
Hath told thee? hast thou eaten of the tree
Whereof I gave thee charge thou shouldst not eat?"
   To whom thus Adam sore beset replied.
"O Heav'n! in evil strait this day I stand
Before my Judge, either to undergo
Myself the total crime, or to accuse
My other self, the partner of my life;
Whose failing, while her faith to me remains,
I should conceal, and not expose to blame   130
By my complaint; but strict necessity
Subdues me, and calamitous constraint
Lest on my head both sin and punishment,
However insupportable, be all
Devolved; though should I hold my peace, yet thou
Wouldst easily detect what I conceal.
This woman whom thou mad'st to be my help,
And gav'st me as thy perfect gift, so good,
So fit, so acceptáble, so divine,
That from her hand I could suspect no ill,   140
And what she did, whatever in itself,
Her doing seemed to justify the deed;
She gave me of the tree, and I did eat."
   To whom the sovran Presence thus replied.
"Was she thy God, that her thou didst obey
Before his voice, or was she made thy guide,
Superior, or but equal, that to her
Thou didst resign thy manhood, and the place
Wherein God set thee above her made of thee,
And for thee, whose perfection far excelled   150
Hers in all real dignity: adorned
She was indeed, and lovely to attract
Thy love, not thy subjection, and her gifts
Were such as under government well seemed,
Unseemly to bear rule, which was thy part

---

154. "such as were seemly as long as they were ruled."
155-156. *part/ And person:* role and character (metaphors from
the stage).

And person, hadst thou known thyself aright."
  So having said, he thus to Eve in few:
"Say woman, what is this which thou hast done?"
  To whom sad Eve with shame nigh overwhelmed,
Confessing soon, yet not before her Judge   16
Bold or loquacious, thus abashed replied.
  "The serpent me beguiled and I did eat."
  Which when the Lord God heard, without delay
To judgment he proceeded on th' accused
Serpent though brute, unable to transfer
The guilt on him who made him instrument
Of mischief, and polluted from the end
Of his creation; justly then accursed,
As vitiated in nature: more to know
Concerned not man (since he no further knew)   17
Nor altered his offense; yet God at last
To Satan first in sin his doom applied,
Though in mysterious terms, judged as then best:
And on the serpent thus his curse let fall.
  "Because thou hast done this, thou art accursed
Above all cattle, each beast of the field;
Upon thy belly groveling thou shalt go,
And dust shalt eat all the days of thy life.
Between thee and the woman I will put
Enmity, and between thine and her seed;   18
Her seed shall bruise thy head, thou bruise his heel."
  So spake this oracle, then verified
When Jesus son of Mary second Eve,
Saw Satan fall like lightning down from heav'n,
Prince of the air; then rising from his grave
Spoiled Principalities and Powers, triumphed

---

  165. *unable:* modifies *serpent.*
  167. *end:* purpose.
  173. *mysterious:* having a hidden significance.
  184. Cf. Luke 10:18, "And he said unto them, I beheld Satan
as lightning fall from heaven."
  185. Cf. Ephesians 2:2, "the prince of the power of the air."
  186–187. Cf. Colossians 2:15, "And having spoiled principalities and powers, he made a shew of them openly, triumphing over
them in it."

In open show, and with ascension bright
Captivity led captive through the air,
The realm itself of Satan long usurped,
Whom he shall tread at last under our feet;   190
Ev'n he who now foretold his fatal bruise,
And to the woman thus his sentence turned.
    "Thy sorrow I will greatly multiply
By thy conception; children thou shalt bring
In sorrow forth, and to thy husband's will
Thine shall submit, he over thee shall rule."
    On Adam last thus judgment he pronounced.
"Because thou hast hearkened to the voice of thy wife,
And eaten of the tree concerning which
I charged thee, saying: Thou shalt not eat thereof,   200
Cursed is the ground for thy sake, thou in sorrow
Shalt eat thereof all the days of thy life;
Thorns also and thistles it shall bring thee forth
Unbid, and thou shalt eat th' herb of the field,
In the sweat of thy face shalt thou eat bread,
Till thou return unto the ground, for thou
Out of the ground wast taken, know thy birth,
For dust thou art, and shalt to dust return."
    So judged he man, both Judge and Saviour sent,
And th' instant stroke of death denounced that day   210
Removed far off; then pitying how they stood
Before him naked to the air, that now
Must suffer change, disdained not to begin
Thenceforth the form of servant to assume,
As when he washed his servants' feet, so now
As father of his family he clad
Their nakedness with skins of beasts, or slain,

187–188. Cf. Psalm 68:18, "Thou hast ascended on high, thou
hast led captivity captive."

190. Cf. Romans 16:20, "And the God of peace shall bruise
[marg. note, "tread"] Satan under your feet shortly."

214. Cf. Philippians 2:7, "and took upon him the form of a
servant."

217–218. *or . . . repaid:* either the animals were slain for their
skins, or else they were given new skins, like snakes.

Or as the snake with youthful coat repaid;
And thought not much to clothe his enemies:
Nor he their outward only with the skins   220
Of beasts, but inward nakedness, much more
Opprobrious, with his robe of righteousness,
Arraying covered from his Father's sight.
To him with swift ascent he up returned,
Into his blissful bosom reassumed
In glory as of old, to him appeased
All, though all-knowing, what had passed with man
Recounted, mixing intercession sweet.
Meanwhile ere thus was sinned and judged on earth,
Within the gates of Hell sat Sin and Death,   230
In counterview within the gates, that now
Stood open wide, belching outrageous flame
Far into chaos, since the Fiend passed through,
Sin opening, who thus now to Death began.
    "O son, why sit we here each other viewing
Idly, while Satan our great author thrives
In other worlds, and happier seat provides
For us his offspring dear? It cannot be
But that success attends him; if mishap,
Ere this he had returned, with fury driv'n   240
By his avengers, since no place like this
Can fit his punishment, or their revenge.
Methinks I feel new strength within me rise,
Wings growing, and dominion giv'n me large
Beyond this deep; whatever draws me on,
Or sympathy, or some connatural force
Powerful at greatest distance to unite
With secret amity things of like kind
By secretest conveyance. Thou my shade
Inseparable must with me along: 250

---

219. *thought not much:* did not think it was too much.
222. Cf. Isaiah 61:10, "he hath covered me with the robe of righteousness."
231. *in counterview:* opposite each other.
246. *sympathy:* attraction (as in line 263 below).

For Death from Sin no power can separate.
But lest the difficulty of passing back
Stay his return perhaps over this gulf
Impassable, impervious, let us try
Advent'rous work, yet to thy power and mine
Not unagreeable, to found a path
Over this main from Hell to that new world
Where Satan now prevails, a monument
Of merit high to all th' infernal host,
Easing their passage hence, for intercourse,　　260
Or transmigration, as their lot shall lead.
Nor can I miss the way, so strongly drawn
By this new-felt attraction and instinct."
　　Whom thus the meager shadow answered soon.
"Go whither fate and inclination strong
Leads thee, I shall not lag behind, nor err
The way, thou leading, such a scent I draw
Of carnage, prey innumerable, and taste
The savor of death from all things there that live:
Nor shall I to the work thou enterprisest　　270
Be wanting, but afford thee equal aid."
　　So saying, with delight he snuffed the smell
Of mortal change on earth. As when a flock
Of ravenous fowl, though many a league remote,
Against the day of battle, to a field
Where armies lie encamped, come flying, lured
With scent of living carcasses designed
For death, the following day, in bloody fight.
So scented the grim feature, and upturned
His nostril wide into the murky air,　　280
Sagacious of his quarry from so far.
Then both from out Hell gates into the waste
Wide anarchy of chaos damp and dark
Flew diverse, and with power (their power was great)

---

256. *found:* lay the foundation of.
260. *intercourse:* going back and forth.
261. *transmigration:* going to stay.
281. *sagacious of:* scenting.

Hovering upon the waters; what they met
Solid or slimy, as in raging sea
Tossed up and down, together crowded drove
From each side shoaling towards the mouth of Hell.
As when two polar winds blowing adverse
Upon the Cronian Sea, together drive   290
Mountains of ice, that stop th' imagined way
Beyond Petsora eastward, to the rich
Cathaian coast. The aggregated soil
Death with his mace petrific, cold and dry,
As with a trident smote, and fixed as firm
As Delos floating once; the rest his look
Bound with Gorgonian rigor not to move,
And with asphaltic slime; broad as the gate,
Deep to the roots of Hell the gathered beach
They fastened, and the mole immense wrought on   300
Over the foaming deep high arched, a bridge
Of length prodigious joining to the wall
Immovable of this now fenceless world
Forfeit to Death; from hence a passage broad,
Smooth, easy, inoffensive down to Hell.
So, if great things to small may be compared,

285–305. Cf. the account of the Creation in Book VII.

288. *shoaling:* making it into a shoal or bank.

290. *Cronian Sea:* Arctic Ocean.

291. *imagined way:* i.e., the northeast passage.

292. *Petsora:* Pechora, name of a river and a bay in Siberia.

293. M. thought of Cathay as an empire distinct from China
and stretching northward to the Arctic Ocean.

293–298. With his *mace* Death petrifies the *cold and dry* elements of the *aggregated soil,* as Neptune caused to rise from the
bottom of the sea with a stroke of his trident the island of *Delos,*
which was later anchored in place by Zeus; *the rest* of the elements
he binds together with asphaltic slime and with a look like that
of the Gorgons, who had the power to turn anyone who looked
at them into stone.

300. *mole:* massive structure.

303. *fenceless:* defenseless.

305. *inoffensive:* presenting no obstacles.

Xerxes, the liberty of Greece to yoke,
From Susa his Memnonian palace high
Came to the sea, and over Hellespont
Bridging his way, Europe with Asia joined,　　　310
And scourged with many a stroke th' indignant waves.
Now had they brought the work by wondrous art
Pontifical, a ridge of pendent rock
Over the vexed abyss, following the track
Of Satan, to the selfsame place where he
First lighted from his wing, and landed safe
From out of chaos to the outside bare
Of this round world: with pins of adamant
And chains they made all fast, too fast they made
And durable; and now in little space　　　　　320
The confines met of empyrean Heav'n
And of this world, and on the left hand Hell
With long reach interposed; three sev'ral ways
In sight, to each of these three places led.
And now their way to earth they had descried,
To Paradise first tending, when behold
Satan in likeness of an angel bright
Betwixt the Centaur and the Scorpion steering
His zenith, while the sun in Aries rose:
Disguised he came, but those his children dear　330
Their parent soon discerned, though in disguise.
He, after Eve seduced, unminded slunk

307-311. Herodotus tells the story of how *Xerxes* caused the
Hellespont to be scourged three hundred times when a storm destroyed his bridge of boats. *Susa,* the winter residence of the Persian kings, was said to have been founded by Tithonus, father of
Memnon.

313. *Pontifical:* literally, "bridge-making," no doubt with a sarcastic allusion to the Roman Pontiff or Pope.

314. *vexed:* storm-tossed.

323. The *three sev'ral ways* are the causeway to Hell, the stairs
to Heaven (II, 502-503), and the passage to earth (II, 528).

328-329. i.e., Satan flies straight upward, keeping away from
the sun. Scorpio is opposite Aries.

332. *after Eve seduced:* after the seduction of Eve.

Into the wood fast by, and changing shape
To observe the sequel, saw his guileful act
By Eve, though all unweeting, seconded
Upon her husband, saw their shame that sought
Vain covertures; but when he saw descend
The Son of God to judge them, terrified
He fled, not hoping to escape, but shun
The present, fearing guilty what his wrath   340
Might suddenly inflict; that past, returned
By night, and listening where the hapless pair
Sat in their sad discourse, and various plaint,
Thence gathered his own doom, which understood
Not instant, but of future time. With joy
And tidings fraught, to Hell he now returned,
And at the brink of chaos, near the foot
Of this new wondrous pontifice, unhoped
Met who to meet him came, his offspring dear.
Great joy was at their meeting, and at sight   350
Of that stupendious bridge his joy increased.
Long he admiring stood, till Sin, his fair
Enchanting daughter, thus the silence broke.
    "O parent, these are thy magnific deeds,
Thy trophies, which thou view'st as not thine own,
Thou art their author and prime architect:
For I no sooner in my heart divined,
My heart, which by a secret harmony
Still moves with thine, joined in connection sweet, 359
That thou on earth hadst prospered, which thy looks
Now also evidence, but straight I felt
Though distant from thee worlds between, yet felt
That I must after thee with this thy son;
Such fatal consequence unites us three:

335. *unweeting:* unaware.
344. *which understood:* which being understood.
345–346. *joy/ And tidings:* joyful tidings.
347–348. Satan meets them at the *foot* of the bridge (*pontifice*) where it joins the universe.
364. *consequence:* connection, interdependence.

Hell could no longer hold us in her bounds,
Nor this unvoyageable gulf obscure
Detain from following thy illustrious track.
Thou hast achieved our liberty, confined
Within Hell gates till now, thou us empowered
To fortify thus far, and overlay   370
With this portentous bridge the dark abyss.
Thine now is all this world, thy virtue hath won
What thy hands builded not, thy wisdom gained
With odds what war hath lost, and fully avenged
Our foil in Heav'n; here thou shalt monarch reign,
There didst not; there let him still victor sway,
As battle hath adjudged, from this new world
Retiring, by his own doom alienated,
And henceforth monarchy with thee divide
Of all things parted by th' empyreal bounds,   380
His quadrature, from thy orbicular world,
Or try thee now more dangerous to his throne."
　　Whom thus the Prince of Darkness answered glad.
"Fair daughter, and thou son and grandchild both,
High proof ye now have giv'n to be the race
Of Satan (for I glory in the name,
Antagonist of Heav'n's Almighty King)
Amply have merited of me, of all
Th' infernal empire, that so near Heav'n's door
Triumphal with triumphal act have met,   390
Mine with this glorious work, and made one realm
Hell and this world, one realm, one continent
Of easy thoroughfare. Therefore while I
Descend through darkness, on your road with ease
To my associate powers, them to acquaint
With these successes, and with them rejoice,

---

370. *fortify:* build.
378. *doom:* judgment (on man).
381. Heaven is square (*quadrature*) in Revelation 21:16.
382. *try:* put to the test (and find).
386–387. *Satan* means "adversary."
390. Sin and Death have met Satan's triumphal act of seducing
man with their own triumphal act of building the bridge.

You two this way, among these numerous orbs
All yours, right down to Paradise descend;
There dwell and reign in bliss, thence on the earth
Dominion exercise and in the air,   400
Chiefly on man, sole lord of all declared,
Him first make sure your thrall, and lastly kill.
My substitutes I send ye, and create
Plenipotent on earth, of matchless might
Issuing from me: on your joint vigor now
My hold of this new kingdom all depends,
Through Sin to Death exposed by my exploit.
If your joint power prevail, th' affairs of Hell
No detriment need fear, go and be strong."
  So saying he dismissed them, they with speed   410
Their course through thickest constellations held
Spreading their bane; the blasted stars looked wan,
And planets, planet-struck, real eclipse
Then suffered. Th' other way Satan went down
The causey to Hell gate; on either side
Disparted chaos overbuilt exclaimed,
And with rebounding surge the bars assailed,
That scorned his indignation: through the gate,
Wide open and unguarded, Satan passed,
And all about found desolate; for those   420
Appointed to sit there, had left their charge,
Flown to the upper world; the rest were all
Far to th' inland retired, about the walls
Of Pandemonium, city and proud seat
Of Lucifer, so by allusion called,
Of that bright star to Satan paragoned.
There kept their watch the legions, while the grand
In council sat, solicitous what chance
Might intercept their emperor sent; so he
Departing gave command, and they observed.   430
As when the Tartar from his Russian foe

---

413. *planet-struck:* cf. "moon-struck." The planets themselves
are under the evil influence of Sin and Death.

415. *causey:* causeway.

426. *paragoned:* compared. Cf. VII, 131n above.

By Astracan over the snowy plains
Retires, or Bactrian Sophi from the horns
Of Turkish crescent, leaves all waste beyond
The realm of Aladule, in his retreat
To Tauris or Casbeen. So these the late
Heav'n-banished host, left desert utmost Hell
Many a dark league, reduced in careful watch
Round their metropolis, and now expecting
Each hour their great adventurer from the search   440
Of foreign worlds: he through the midst unmarked,
In show plebeian angel militant
Of lowest order, passed; and from the door
Of that Plutonian hall, invisible
Ascended his high throne, which under state
Of richest texture spread, at th' upper end
Was placed in regal luster. Down a while
He sat, and round about him saw unseen:
At last as from a cloud his fulgent head
And shape star-bright appeared, or brighter, clad   450
With what permissive glory since his fall
Was left him or false glitter: all amazed
At that so sudden blaze the Stygian throng
Bent their aspéct, and whom they wished beheld,
Their mighty chief returned: loud was th' acclaim:
Forth rushed in haste the great consulting peers,
Raised from their dark divan, and with like joy
Congratulant approached him, who with hand
Silence, and with these words attention won.
   "Thrones, Dominations, Princedoms, Virtues,
      Powers,   460

---

432. *Astracan:* Russian town on the Volga.
433. *Bactrian Sophi:* Persian Shah.
435. *Aladule:* last king of Greater Armenia.
436. *Tauris:* modern Tabriz. *Casbeen:* modern Kazvin, near Teheran.
438. *reduced:* led back.
445. *state:* canopy.
451. *permissive:* permitted (by God).
457. *divan:* Turkish council of state.

For in possession such, not only of right,
I call ye and declare ye now, returned
Successful beyond hope, to lead ye forth
Triumphant out of this infernal pit
Abominable, accurst, the house of woe,
And dungeon of our tyrant: now possess,
As lords, a spacious world, to our native Heav'n
Little inferior, by my adventure hard
With peril great achieved. Long were to tell
What I have done, what suffered, with what pain   470
Voyaged th' unreal, vast, unbounded deep
Of horrible confusion, over which
By Sin and Death a broad way now is paved
To expedite your glorious march; but I
Toiled out my uncouth passage, forced to ride
Th' untractable abyss, plunged in the womb
Of unoriginal Night and Chaos wild,
That jealous of their secrets fiercely opposed
My journey strange, with clamorous uproar
Protesting fate supreme; thence how I found   480
The new created world, which fame in Heav'n
Long had foretold, a fabric wonderful
Of absolute perfection, therein man
Placed in a Paradise, by our exile
Made happy: him by fraud I have seduced
From his Creator, and the more to increase
Your wonder, with an apple; he thereat
Offended, worth your laughter, hath giv'n up
Both his beloved man and all his world,
To Sin and Death a prey, and so to us,   490
Without our hazard, labor, or alarm,
To range in, and to dwell, and over man
To rule, as over all he should have ruled.
True is, me also he hath judged, or rather

---

461. i.e., "these titles are yours not only by right but also by
virtue of your possession of the world."

480. *protesting fate:* protesting that fate objected. Satan exag-
gerates his exploits; Chaos actually helped him on his way.

Me not, but the brute serpent in whose shape
Man I deceived: that which to me belongs,
Is enmity, which he will put between
Me and mankind; I am to bruise his heel;
His seed, when is not set, shall bruise my head:
A world who would not purchase with a bruise,   500
Or much more grievous pain? Ye have th' account
Of my performance: what remains, ye gods,
But up and enter now into full bliss."
    So having said, a while he stood, expecting
Their universal shout and high applause
To fill his ear, when contrary he hears
On all sides, from innumerable tongues
A dismal universal hiss, the sound
Of public scorn; he wondered, but not long
Had leisure, wondering at himself now more;   510
His visage drawn he felt to sharp and spare,
His arms clung to his ribs, his legs entwining
Each other, till supplanted down he fell
A monstrous serpent on his belly prone,
Reluctant, but in vain, a greater power
Now ruled him, punished in the shape he sinned,
According to his doom: he would have spoke,
But hiss for hiss returned with forkéd tongue
To forkéd tongue, for now were all transformed
Alike, to serpents all, as accessories   520
To his bold riot: dreadful was the din
Of hissing through the hall, thick swarming now
With complicated monsters, head and tail,
Scorpion and asp, and amphisbaena dire,
Cerastes horned, hydrus, and ellops drear,
And dipsas (not so thick swarmed once the soil
Bedropped with blood of Gorgon, or the isle

---

513. *supplanted:* tripped up.
515. *reluctant:* struggling against.
521. *riot:* rebellion.
523. *complicated:* twisted together.
524–526. *amphisbaena . . . dipsas:* names of various serpent-monsters, chosen mainly for their sound values.

Ophiusa) but still greatest he the midst,
Now dragon grown, larger than whom the sun
Engendered in the Pythian vale on slime,   530
Huge Python, and his power no less he seemed
Above the rest still to retain; they all
Him followed issuing forth to th' open field,
Where all yet left of that revolted rout
Heav'n-fall'n, in station stood or just array,
Sublime with expectation when to see
In triumph issuing forth their glorious chief;
They saw, but other sight instead, a crowd
Of ugly serpents; horror on them fell,
And horrid sympathy; for what they saw,   540
They felt themselves now changing; down their arms,
Down fell both spear and shield, down they as fast,
And the dire hiss renewed, and the dire form
Catched by contagion, like in punishment,
As in their crime. Thus was th' applause they meant,
Turned to exploding hiss, triumph to shame
Cast on themselves from their own mouths. There stood
A grove hard by, sprung up with this their change,
His will who reigns above, to aggravate
Their penance, laden with fair fruit like that   550
Which grew in Paradise, the bait of Eve
Used by the Tempter: on that prospect strange
Their earnest eyes they fixed, imagining
For one forbidden tree a multitude
Now ris'n, to work them further woe or shame;
Yet parched with scalding thirst and hunger fierce,
Though to delude them sent, could not abstain,
But on they rolled in heaps, and up the trees
Climbing, sat thicker than the snaky locks
That curled Megaera: greedily they plucked   560
The fruitage fair to sight, like that which grew

528: *Ophiusa* ("snaky"): one of the Balearic Islands.
535. *in station:* on guard, at their posts.
536. *sublime:* uplifted.
560. *Megaera:* one of the Furies.

Near that bituminous lake where Sodom flamed;
This more delusive, not the touch, but taste
Deceived; they fondly thinking to allay
Their appetite with gust, instead of fruit
Chewed bitter ashes, which th' offended taste
With spattering noise rejected: oft they assayed,
Hunger and thirst constraining, drugged as oft,
With hatefullest disrelish writhed their jaws
With soot and cinders filled; so oft they fell   570
Into the same illusion, not as man,
Whom they triumphed, once lapsed. Thus were they
        plagued
And worn with famine, long and ceaseless hiss,
Till their lost shape, permitted, they resumed,
Yearly enjoined, some say, to undergo
This annual humbling certain numbered days,
To dash their pride, and joy for man seduced.
However some tradition they dispersed
Among the heathen of their purchase got,
And fabled how the serpent, whom they called   580
Ophion with Eurynome, the wide-
Encroaching Eve perhaps, had first the rule
Of high Olympus, thence by Saturn driv'n
And Ops, ere yet Dictaean Jove was born.

---

562. *bituminous lake:* the Dead Sea. The destruction of *Sodom*
is described in Genesis 19:24-25.

565. *gust:* gusto.

568. *drugged:* nauseated.

572. *triumphed:* triumphed over.

579. *purchase:* prey.

579-584. In *PL* the pagan gods are really fallen angels (I, 507-521), and many classical myths are corrupted versions of sacred history (cf. the allusion to Mulciber in I, 739-748). Here M. boldly suggests that Satan's rebellion and subsequent seduction of Eve was corrupted in the myth of the Titan *Ophion* ("serpent"), who first ruled *Olympus* and who was overthrown by *Saturn* and his wife *Ops* (or Rhea) before the birth of Cretan ("Dictaean") *Jove*. Ophion's wife was *Eurynome*, and the similarity between her and *Eve* lies in the meaning of Eurynome, "wide-ruling" or "wide-encroaching," since Eve tried to extend her dominion further than she should.

Meanwhile in Paradise the hellish pair
Too soon arrived, Sin there in power before,
Once actual, now in body, and to dwell
Habitual habitant; behind her Death
Close following pace for pace, not mounted yet
On his pale horse: to whom Sin thus began.   590
  "Second of Satan sprung, all-conquering Death,
What think'st thou of our empire now, though earned
With travail difficult, not better far
Than still at Hell's dark threshold to have sat watch,
Unnamed, undreaded, and thyself half starved?"
  Whom thus the Sin-born monster answered soon.
"To me, who with eternal famine pine,
Alike is Hell, or Paradise, or Heav'n,
There best, where most with ravin I may meet;
Which here, though plenteous, all too little seems   600
To stuff this maw, this vast unhidebound corpse."
  To whom th' incestuous mother thus replied.
"Thou therefore on these herbs, and fruits, and flow'rs
Feed first, on each beast next, and fish, and fowl,
No homely morsels, and whatever thing
The scythe of time mows down, devour unspared,
Till I in man residing through the race,
His thoughts, his looks, words, actions all infect,
And season him thy last and sweetest prey."
  This said, they both betook them several ways,   610
Both to destroy, or unimmortal make
All kinds, and for destruction to mature
Sooner or later; which th' Almighty seeing,
From his transcendent seat the saints among,
To those bright orders uttered thus his voice.
  "See with what heat these dogs of Hell advance

586–587. *in power* and *actual* are probably synonymous, meaning that before Sin arrived in body, her power was present in the
actual sin of Adam and Eve.

590. Cf. Revelation 6:8, "And I looked, and behold a pale
horse: and his name that sat on him was Death, and Hell followed with him."

601. *unhidebound:* with loosely hanging skin.

To waste and havoc yonder world, which I
So fair and good created, and had still
Kept in that state, had not the folly of man
Let in these wasteful furies, who impute   620
Folly to me, so doth the Prince of Hell
And his adherents, that with so much ease
I suffer them to enter and possess
A place so heav'nly, and conniving seem
To gratify my scornful enemies,
That laugh, as if transported with some fit
Of passion I to them had quitted all,
At random yielded up to their misrule;
And know not that I called and drew them thither
My Hell-hounds, to lick up the draff and filth   630
Which man's polluting sin with taint hath shed
On what was pure, till crammed and gorged, nigh
     burst
With sucked and glutted offal, at one sling
Of thy victorious arm, well-pleasing Son,
Both Sin, and Death, and yawning grave at last
Through chaos hurled, obstruct the mouth of Hell
Forever, and seal up his ravenous jaws.
Then heav'n and earth renewed shall be made pure
To sanctity that shall receive no stain:
Till then the curse pronounced on both precedes."   640
     He ended, and the heav'nly audience loud
Sung halleluiah, as the sound of seas,
Through multitude that sung: "Just are thy ways,
Righteous are thy decrees on all thy works;
Who can extenuate thee? Next, to the Son,
Destined restorer of mankind, by whom
New heav'n and earth shall to the ages rise,
Or down from Heav'n descend." Such was their song,

---

617. *havoc:* "cry havoc" was the signal for soldiers to plunder and slaughter indiscriminately.
624. *conniving:* literally, "shutting the eyes."
640. *precedes:* takes precedence.
645. *extenuate:* disparage.

While the Creator calling forth by name
His mighty angels gave them several charge,   6
As sorted best with present things. The sun
Had first his precept so to move, so shine,
As might affect the earth with cold and heat
Scarce tolerable, and from the north to call
Decrepit winter, from the south to bring
Solstitial summer's heat. To the blank moon
Her office they prescribed, to th' other five
Their planetary motions and aspécts
In sextile, square, and trine, and opposite,
Of noxious efficacy, and when to join   66
In synod unbenign, and taught the fixed
Their influence malignant when to show'r;
Which of them rising with the sun, or falling,
Should prove tempestuous: to the winds they set
Their corners, when with bluster to confound
Sea, air, and shore, the thunder when to roll
With terror through the dark aereal hall.
Some say he bid his angels turn askance
The poles of earth twice ten degrees and more
From the sun's axle; they with labor pushed   67
Oblique the centric globe: some say the sun

---

651. *sorted:* corresponded.

658–661. Astrologers distinguished five *aspects* or relative positions of planets: *synod* or conjunction when two planets are con-
joined, and *sextile, square, trine,* and *opposite* when they are
respectively 60, 90, 120, and 180 degrees apart.

661. *fixed:* fixed stars.

668–678. M. suggests that before the Fall the ecliptic or path of
the sun lay in the plane of the equator (*th' equinoctial road*) and
that the present obliquity of 23 1/2 degrees was caused either by
tilting the earth's axis (lines 668–671) or by changing the course
of the sun (lines 671–672), which is then described in terms of
its northernmost distance from the equatorial line at the sign
of the *Crab* in the Tropic of Cancer and its southernmost distance in the Tropic of *Capricorn*. The signs of the zodiac through
which it passes in the spring and summer months of the northern
hemisphere are specified in lines 673–676.

Was bid turn reins from th' equinoctial road
Like distant breadth to Taurus with the sev'n
Atlantic Sisters, and the Spartan Twins
Up to the Tropic Crab; thence down amain
By Leo and the Virgin and the Scales,
As deep as Capricorn, to bring in change
Of seasons to each clime; else had the spring
Perpetual smiled on earth with vernant flow'rs,
Equal in days and nights, except to those —680
Beyond the polar circles; to them day
Had unbenighted shone, while the low sun
To recompense his distance, in their sight
Had rounded still th' horizon, and not known
Or east or west, which had forbid the snow
From cold Estotiland, and south as far
Beneath Magellan. At that tasted fruit
The sun, as from Thyestean banquet, turned
His course intended; else how had the world
Inhabited, though sinless, more than now, 690
Avoided pinching cold and scorching heat?
These changes in the heav'ns, though slow, produced
Like change on sea and land, sideral blast,
Vapor, and mist, and exhalation hot,
Corrupt and pestilent: now from the north
Of Norumbega, and the Samoed shore
Bursting their brazen dungeon, armed with ice

680–687. i.e., if the sun followed the path of the equator, people living in the polar circles would have no night and no way of distinguishing east and west, since the sun would always be low on the horizon (lines 680–685), nor would it be cold enough for snow between the northern part of North America (*Estotiland*) and the Straits of *Magellan* (lines 685–687).

688. *Thyestean:* To get revenge on his brother Thyestes, Atreus killed Thyestes' two sons and served him their flesh at a banquet. The sun was said to have turned aside in horror.

693. *sideral blast:* blasting "influence" from the stars.

696. *Norumbega:* southern Canada and northern New England. *Samoed:* Siberian.

And snow and hail and stormy gust and flaw,
Boreas and Caecias and Argestes loud
And Thrascias rend the woods and seas upturn;   700
With adverse blast upturns them from the south
Notus and Afer black with thunderous clouds
From Serraliona; thwart of these as fierce
Forth rush the Levant and the Ponent winds
Eurus and Zephyr with their lateral noise,
Sirocco, and Libecchio. Thus began
Outrage from lifeless things; but discord first
Daughter of Sin, among th' irrational,
Death introduced through fierce antipathy:
Beast now with beast gan war, and fowl with fowl,   710
And fish with fish; to graze the herb all leaving,
Devoured each other; nor stood much in awe
Of man, but fled him, or with count'nance grim
Glared on him passing: these were from without
The growing miseries, which Adam saw
Already in part, though hid in gloomiest shade,
To sorrow abandoned, but worse felt within,
And in a troubled sea of passion tossed,
Thus to disburden sought with sad complaint.

      "O miserable of happy! Is this the end   720
Of this new glorious world, and me so late
The glory of that glory, who now, become

699–706. It is probably not necessary to know precisely that
Boreas, Caecias, Argestes, Thrascias, Notus, Afer, Eurus (*Levant*)
and *Zephyr* (*Ponent*), *Sirocco,* and *Libecchio* are the N, NE, NW,
NNW, S, SW, E, W, SE, and SW winds respectively. The point is
that in contrast to the one wind that is mentioned in Paradise,
"cool Zephyr" (IV, 329), all the "warring winds" of Chaos (II, 905)
have been let loose on the earth. Cf. the "high winds" of passion
in IX, 1122.

703. *Serraliona:* Sierra Leone.

718. Cf. Isaiah 57:20, "The wicked are like the troubled sea,
when it cannot rest," and the description of Chaos in VII, 212,
"Outrageous as a sea, dark, wasteful, wild."

719. *disburden:* i.e., disburden himself, as a ship is unladen in
a tempest to keep it from sinking.

Accurst of blesséd, hide me from the face
Of God, whom to behold was then my highth
Of happiness: yet well, if here would end
The misery, I deserved it, and would bear
My own deservings; but this will not serve;
All that I eat or drink, or shall beget,
Is propagated curse. O voice once heard
Delightfully, 'Increase and multiply,'   730
Now death to hear! for what can I increase
Or multiply, but curses on my head?
Who of all ages to succeed, but feeling
The evil on him brought by me, will curse
My head, 'Ill fare our ancestor impure,
For this we may thank Adam'; but his thanks
Shall be the execration; so besides
Mine own that bide upon me, all from me
Shall with a fierce reflux on me redound,
On me as on their natural center light   740
Heavy, though in their place. O fleeting joys
Of Paradise, dear bought with lasting woes!
Did I request thee, Maker, from my clay
To mold me man, did I solicit thee
From darkness to promote me, or here place
In this delicious garden? As my will
Concurred not to my being, it were but right
And equal to reduce me to my dust,
Desirous to resign, and render back
All I received, unable to perform   750
Thy terms too hard, by which I was to hold

---

738. *mine own:* i.e., curses (line 732).
740–741. *light/Heavy:* Adam engages in grim, tortured wordplay. He alludes to the notion that when a thing is in its proper
place in the universe it has no weight, heaviness being merely
the tendency of certain things to move to the center of the
universe, the earth. He says that even though the curses which
light on his head will have found their natural place, they will
still be *heavy*.
748. *equal:* fair, just.

The good I sought not. To the loss of that,
Sufficient penalty, why hast thou added
The sense of endless woes? Inexplicable
Thy justice seems; yet to say truth, too late
I thus contest; then should have been refused
Those terms whatever, when they were proposed:
Thou didst accept them; wilt thou enjoy the good,
Then cavil the conditions? And though God
Made thee without thy leave, what if thy son   760
Prove disobedient, and reproved, retort,
'Wherefore didst thou beget me? I sought it not.'
Wouldst thou admit for his contempt of thee
That proud excuse? Yet him not thy election,
But natural necessity begot.
God made thee of choice his own, and of his own
To serve him, thy reward was of his grace,
Thy punishment then justly is at his will.
Be it so, for I submit, his doom is fair;
That dust I am, and shall to dust return: 770
O welcome hour whenever! Why delays
His hand to execute what his decree
Fixed on this day? Why do I overlive,
Why am I mocked with death, and lengthened out
To deathless pain? How gladly would I meet
Mortality my sentence, and be earth
Insensible, how glad would lay me down
As in my mother's lap? There I should rest
And sleep secure; his dreadful voice no more
Would thunder in my ears, no fear of worse   780
To me and to my offspring would torment me
With cruel expectation. Yet one doubt
Pursues me still, lest all I cannot die,
Lest that pure breath of life, the spirit of man
Which God inspired, cannot together perish
With this corporeal clod; then in the grave,
Or in some other dismal place, who knows
But I shall die a living death? O thought

---

785. *inspired:* used in its literal sense of "breathed."

Horrid, if true! Yet why? It was but breath
Of life that sinned; what dies but what had life   790
And sin? The body properly hath neither.
All of me then shall die: let this appease
The doubt, since human reach no further knows.
For though the Lord of all be infinite,
Is his wrath also? Be it, man is not so,
But mortal doomed. How can he exercise
Wrath without end on man whom death must end?
Can he make deathless death? That were to make
Strange contradiction, which to God himself
Impossible is held, as argument   800
Of weakness, not of power. Will he draw out,
For anger's sake, finite to infinite
In punished man, to satisfy his rigor
Satisfied never; that were to extend
His sentence beyond dust and nature's law,
By which all causes else according still
To the reception of their matter act,
Not to th' extent of their own sphere. But say
That death be not one stroke, as I supposed,
Bereaving sense, but endless misery   810
From this day onward, which I feel begun
Both in me, and without me, and so last
To perpetuity. Ay me, that fear

789–793. In *The Christian Doctrine*, I, 13, M. accepts the
"mortalist" heresy that the soul dies with the body, to be resurrected with the body at the Second Coming. Here he avoids offending his orthodox readers by putting the doctrine in the
mouth of the fallen Adam, who is "in wandering mazes lost,"
like the fallen angels.

806–808. *By which . . . sphere:* "according to the law of nature
all causes, no matter how powerful in themselves, can only affect
other things to the extent that these things are capable of re-
ceiving them." Adam thus comforts himself with the thought
that although God's anger is infinite, man is finite. In the following lines, however, he tortures himself with the thought that
perhaps "death" is a kind of metaphor for "endless misery." It
is not until Michael tells him of the Messiah that he learns that
"to the faithful death [is] the gate of life" (XII, 571).

810. *bereaving sense:* depriving (me) of sensation.

Comes thundering back with dreadful revolution
On my defenseless head; both death and I
Am found eternal, and incorporate both,
Nor I on my part single, in me all
Posterity stands cursed: fair patrimony
That I must leave ye, sons; O were I able
To waste it all myself, and leave ye none!   820
So disinherited how would ye bless
Me now your curse! Ah, why should all mankind
For one man's fault thus guiltless be condemned,
If guiltless? But from me what can proceed,
But all corrupt, both mind and will depraved,
Not to do only, but to will the same
With me? How can they then acquitted stand
In sight of God? Him after all disputes
Forced I absolve: all my evasions vain,
And reasonings, though through mazes, lead me still   830
But to my own conviction: first and last
On me, me only, as the source and spring
Of all corruption, all the blame lights due;
So might the wrath. Fond wish! Couldst thou support
That burden heavier than the earth to bear,
Than all the world much heavier, though divided
With that bad woman? Thus what thou desir'st
And what thou fear'st, alike destroys all hope
Of refuge, and concludes thee miserable
Beyond all past example and future,   840
To Satan only like, both crime and doom.
O conscience, into what abyss of fears
And horrors hast thou driv'n me; out of which
I find no way, from deep to deeper plunged!"
    Thus Adam to himself lamented loud
Through the still night, not now, as ere man fell,
Wholesome and cool, and mild, but with black air
Accompanied, with damps and dreadful gloom,
Which to his evil conscience represented

---

816. *incorporate both:* both in one body.
832. With the repetition of *me* cf. the words of Christ in III,
236–238, and of Eve in X, 935–936.

All things with double terror: on the ground 850
Outstretched he lay, on the cold ground, and oft
Cursed his creation, death as oft accused
Of tardy execution, since denounced
The day of his offense. "Why comes not death,"
Said he, "with one thrice ácceptáble stroke
To end me? Shall Truth fail to keep her word,
Justice divine not hasten to be just?
But death comes not at call, justice divine
Mends not her slowest pace for prayers or cries.
O woods, O fountains, hillocks, dales and bow'rs, 860
With other echo late I taught your shades
To answer, and resound far other song."
Whom thus afflicted when sad Eve beheld,
Desolate where she sat, approaching nigh,
Soft words to his fierce passion she assayed:
But her with stern regard he thus repelled.

　"Out of my sight, thou serpent, that name best
Befits thee with him leagued, thyself as false
And hateful; nothing wants, but that thy shape,
Like his, and color serpentine may show 870
Thy inward fraud, to warn all creatures from thee
Henceforth; lest that too heav'nly form, pretended
To hellish falsehood, snare them. But for thee
I had persisted happy, had not thy pride
And wandering vanity, when least was safe,
Rejected my forewarning, and disdained
Not to be trusted, longing to be seen
Though by the Devil himself, him overweening
To overreach, but with the serpent meeting
Fooled and beguiled, by him thou, I by thee, 880
To trust thee from my side, imagined wise,
Constant, mature, proof against all assaults,
And understood not all was but a show
Rather than solid virtue, all but a rib
Crooked by nature, bent, as now appears,

872–873. *pretended/ To:* literally, "stretched before," hence "masking."

Adam's complaint

More to the part sinister from me drawn,
Well if thrown out, as supernumerary
To my just number found. O why did God,
Creator wise, that peopled highest Heav'n
With spirits masculine, create at last   890
This novelty on earth, this fair defect
Of nature, and not fill the world at once
With men as angels without feminine,
Or find some other way to generate
Mankind? This mischief had not then befall'n,
And more that shall befall, innumerable
Disturbances on earth through female snares,
And strait conjunction with this sex: for either
He never shall find out fit mate, but such
As some misfortune brings him, or mistake,   900
Or whom he wishes most shall seldom gain
Through her perverseness, but shall see her gained
By a far worse, or if she love, withheld
By parents, or his happiest choice too late
Shall meet, already linked and wedlock-bound
To a fell adversary, his hate or shame:
Which infinite calamity shall cause
To human life, and household peace confound."

      He added not, and from her turned, but Eve
Not so repulsed, with tears that ceased not flowing,   910
And tresses all disordered, at his feet
Fell humble, and embracing them, besought
His peace, and thus proceeded in her plaint.

      "Forsake me not thus, Adam, witness Heav'n
What love sincere and reverence in my heart
I bear thee, and unweeting have offended,
Unhappily deceived; thy suppliant
I beg, and clasp thy knees; bereave me not,
Whereon I live, thy gentle looks, thy aid,

---

886. *sinister:* a play on the meanings "left" and "unlucky."
887. *supernumerary:* referring to the belief that Adam originally
had thirteen ribs on his left side.

Thy counsel in this uttermost distress,   920
My only strength and stay: forlorn of thee,
Whither shall I betake me, where subsist?
While yet we live, scarce one short hour perhaps,
Between us two let there be peace, both joining,
As joined in injuries, one enmity
Against a foe by doom express assigned us,
That cruel serpent: on me exercise not
Thy hatred for this misery befall'n,
On me already lost, me than thyself
More miserable; both have sinned, but thou   930
Against God only, I against God and thee,
And to the place of judgment will return,
There with my cries importune Heav'n, that all
The sentence from thy head removed may light
On me, sole cause to thee of all this woe,
Me, me only, just object of his ire."

   She ended weeping, and her lowly plight,
Immovable till peace obtained from fault
Acknowledged and deplored, in Adam wrought
Commiseration; soon his heart relented   940
Towards her, his life so late and sole delight,
Now at his feet submissive in distress,
Creature so fair his reconcilement seeking,
His counsel whom she had displeased, his aid;
As one disarmed, his anger all he lost,
And thus with peaceful words upraised her soon.

   "Unwary, and too desirous, as before,
So now of what thou know'st not, who desir'st
The punishment all on thyself; alas,
Bear thine own first, ill able to sustain   950
His full wrath whose thou feel'st as yet least part,
And my displeasure bear'st so ill. If prayers
Could alter high decrees, I to that place
Would speed before thee, and be louder heard,
That on my head all might be visited,
Thy frailty and infirmer sex forgiv'n,
To me committed and by me exposed.

[Marginalia, handwritten:] Eve offers to take all guilt

[Marginalia, handwritten:] Adam, moved likewise wishes

But rise, let us no more contend, nor blame
Each other, blamed enough elsewhere, but strive
In offices of love, how we may light'n   960
Each other's burden in our share of woe;
Since this day's death denounced, if aught I see,
Will prove no sudden, but a slow-paced evil,
A long day's dying to augment our pain,
And to our seed (O hapless seed!) derived."
    To whom thus Eve, recovering heart, replied.
"Adam, by sad experiment I know
How little weight my words with thee can find,
Found so erroneous, thence by just event
Found so unfortunate; nevertheless,   970
Restored by thee, vile as I am, to place
Of new acceptance, hopeful to regain
Thy love, the sole contentment of my heart
Living or dying, from thee I will not hide
What thoughts in my unquiet breast are ris'n,
Tending to some relief of our extremes,
Or end, though sharp and sad, yet tolerable,
As in our evils, and of easier choice.
If care of our descent perplex us most,
Which must be born to certain woe, devoured   980
By Death at last, and miserable it is
To be to others cause of misery,
Our own begott'n, and of our loins to bring
Into this curséd world a woeful race,
That after wretched life must be at last
Food for so foul a monster, in thy power
It lies, yet ere conception to prevent
The race unblest, to being yet unbegot.
Childless thou art, childless remain: so Death
Shall be deceived his glut, and with us two   990
Be forced to satisfy his ravenous maw.

---

959. *elsewhere:* i.e., at the place where they were judged.
978. *as in our evils:* considering that we are in such evil straits.
979. *descent:* descendants.
987. *prevent:* forestall.

(handwritten margin note: to deprive Death of his glut. If you can't give up sex, we say give up life and defeat Death that way)

But if thou judge it hard and difficult,
Conversing, looking, loving, to abstain
From love's due rites, nuptial embraces sweet,
And with desire to languish without hope,
Before the present object languishing
With like desire, which would be misery
And torment less than none of what we dread,
Then both ourselves and seed at once to free
From what we fear for both, let us make short,   1000
Let us seek Death, or he not found, supply
With our own hands his office on ourselves;
Why stand we longer shivering under fears,
That show no end but death, and have the power,
Of many ways to die the shortest choosing,
Destruction with destruction to destroy."
    She ended here, or vehement despair
Broke off the rest; so much of death her thoughts
Had entertained, as dyed her cheeks with pale.
But Adam with such counsel nothing swayed,   1010
To better hopes his more attentive mind
Laboring had raised, and thus to Eve replied.
    "Eve, thy contempt of life and pleasure seems
To argue in thee something more sublime
And excellent than what thy mind contemns;
But self-destruction therefore sought, refutes
That excellence thought in thee, and implies,
Not thy contempt, but anguish and regret
For loss of life and pleasure overloved.
Or if thou covet death, as utmost end   1020
Of misery, so thinking to evade
The penalty pronounced, doubt not but God
Hath wiselier armed his vengeful ire than so
To be forestalled; much more I fear lest death
So snatched will not exempt us from the pain
We are by doom to pay; rather such acts
Of contumacy will provoke the Highest
To make death in us live: then let us seek

---

996. *present object:* the object of your love who is present.

Some safer resolution, which methinks
I have in view, calling to mind with heed   1030
Part of our sentence, that thy seed shall bruise
The serpent's head; piteous amends, unless
Be meant, whom I conjecture, our grand foe
Satan, who in the serpent hath contrived
Against us this deceit: to crush his head
Would be revenge indeed; which will be lost
By death brought on ourselves, or childless days
Resolved, as thou proposest; so our foe
Shall scape his punishment ordained, and we
Instead shall double ours upon our heads.   1040
No more be mentioned then of violence
Against ourselves, and wilful barrenness,
That cuts us off from hope, and savors only
Rancor and pride, impatience and despite,
Reluctance against God and his just yoke
Laid on our necks. Remember with what mild
And gracious temper he both heard and judged
Without wrath or reviling; we expected
Immediate dissolution, which we thought
Was meant by death that day, when lo, to thee   1050
Pains only in child-bearing were foretold,
And bringing forth, soon recompensed with joy,
Fruit of thy womb: on me the curse aslope
Glanced on the ground, with labor I must earn
My bread; what harm? Idleness had been worse;
My labor will sustain me; and lest cold
Or heat should injure us, his timely care
Hath unbesought provided, and his hands
Clothed us unworthy, pitying while he judged;
How much more, if we pray him, will his ear   1060
Be open, and his heart to pity incline,
And teach us further by what means to shun
Th' inclement seasons, rain, ice, hail and snow,
Which now the sky with various face begins

1045. *reluctance:* struggling.
1053–1054. Cf. X, 200–201 above.

To show us in this mountain, while the winds
Blow moist and keen, shattering the graceful locks
Of these fair spreading trees; which bids us seek
Some better shroud, some better warmth to cherish
Our limbs benumbed, ere this diurnal star
Leave cold the night, how we his gathered beams   1070
Reflected, may with matter sere foment,
Or by collision of two bodies grind
The air attrite to fire, as late the clouds
Justling or pushed with winds rude in their shock
Tine the slant lightning, whose thwart flame driv'n
      down
Kindles the gummy bark of fir or pine,
And sends a comfortable heat from far,
Which might supply the sun: such fire to use,
And what may else be remedy or cure
To evils which our own misdeeds have wrought,   1080
He will instruct us praying, and of grace
Beseeching him, so as we need not fear
To pass commodiously this life, sustained
By him with many comforts, till we end
In dust, our final rest and native home.
What better can we do, than to the place
Repairing where he judged us, prostrate fall
Before him reverent, and there confess
Humbly our faults, and pardon beg, with tears
Watering the ground, and with our sighs the air   1090
Frequenting, sent from hearts contrite, in sign
Of sorrow unfeigned, and humiliation meek.
Undoubtedly he will relent and turn
From his displeasure; in whose look serene,
When angry most he seemed and most severe,
What else but favor, grace, and mercy shone?"

1069. *diurnal star:* the sun.
1073. *attrite:* rubbed, worn by friction.
1075. *tine:* kindle.
1081. *praying:* i.e., if we pray.
1091. *frequenting:* filling.

So spake our father penitent, nor Eve
Felt less remorse: they forthwith to the place
Repairing where he judged them prostrate fell
Before him reverent, and both confessed   1100
Humbly their faults, and pardon begged, with tears
Watering the ground, and with their sighs the air
Frequenting, sent from hearts contrite, in sign
Of sorrow unfeigned, and humiliation meek.

BOOK XI

THE ARGUMENT

The Son of God presents to his Father the prayers
of our first parents now repenting, and intercedes for
them: God accepts them, but declares that they must
no longer abide in Paradise; sends Michael with a band
of Cherubim to dispossess them; but first to reveal to
Adam future things: Michael's coming down. Adam
shows to Eve certain ominous signs; he discerns Michael's approach, goes out to meet him: the angel de-
nounces their departure. Eve's lamentation. Adam
pleads, but submits: the angel leads him up to a high
hill, sets before him in vision what shall happen till
the Flood.

Thus they in lowliest plight repentant stood
Praying, for from the mercy-seat above
Prevenient grace descending had removed
The stony from their hearts, and made new flesh
Regenerate grow instead, that sighs now breathed
Unutterable, which the spirit of prayer
Inspired, and winged for Heav'n with speedier flight
Than loudest oratory: yet their port
Not of mean suitors, nor important less
Seemed their petition, than when th' ancient pair   10
In fables old, less ancient yet than these,
Deucalion and chaste Pyrrha to restore
The race of mankind drowned, before the shrine
Of Themis stood devout. To Heav'n their prayers
Flew up, nor missed the way, by envious winds
Blown vagabond or frustrate: in they passed
Dimensionless through heav'nly doors; then clad
With incense, where the golden altar fumed,
By their great Intercessor, came in sight
Before the Father's throne: them the glad Son   20
Presenting, thus to intercede began.

"See Father, what first fruits on earth are sprung
From thy implanted grace in man, these sighs
And prayers, which in this golden censer, mixed
With incense, I thy priest before thee bring,
Fruits of more pleasing savor from thy seed
Sown with contrition in his heart, than those
Which his own hand manuring all the trees
Of Paradise could have produced, ere fall'n

---

1. *stood:* continued.

3. *prevenient grace:* grace that "comes before" repentance and
makes it possible.

10–14. *Deucalion* and *Pyrrha,* The classical counterparts of
Noah and his family, prayed to Themis, the goddess of justice,
after surviving a flood.

18. The imagery of incense and altars comes from Psalm
141:2 and Revelation 8:3–4.

28. *manuring:* cultivating.

From innocence. Now therefore bend thine ear   3
To supplication, hear his sighs though mute;
Unskilful with what words to pray, let me
Interpret for him, me his advocate
And propitiation, all his works on me
Good or not good ingraft, my merit those
Shall perfect, and for these my death shall pay.
Accept me, and in me from these receive
The smell of peace toward mankind, let him live
Before thee reconciled, at least his days
Numbered, though sad, till death, his doom (which I   4
To mitigate thus plead, not to reverse)
To better life shall yield him, where with me
All my redeemed may dwell in joy and bliss,
Made one with me as I with thee am one."
    To whom the Father, without cloud, serene.
"All thy request for man, accepted Son,
Obtain, all thy request was my decree:
But longer in that Paradise to dwell,
The law I gave to nature him forbids:
Those pure immortal elements that know   5
No gross, no unharmonious mixture foul,
Eject him tainted now, and purge him off
As a distemper, gross to air as gross,
And mortal food, as may dispose him best
For dissolution wrought by sin, that first
Distempered all things, and of incorrupt
Corrupted. I at first with two fair gifts
Created him endowed, with happiness
And immortality: that fondly lost,
This other served but to eternize woe;   6
Till I provided death; so death becomes
His final remedy, and after life
Tried in sharp tribulation, and refined
By faith and faithful works, to second life,
Waked in the renovation of the just,
Resigns him up with heav'n and earth renewed.
But let us call to synod all the blest

Through Heav'n's wide bounds; from them I will not
   hide
My judgments, how with mankind I proceed,
As how with peccant angels late they saw;   70
And in their state, though firm, stood more con-
   firmed."
   He ended, and the Son gave signal high
To the bright minister that watched; he blew
His trumpet, heard in Oreb since perhaps
When God descended, and perhaps once more
To sound at general Doom. Th' angelic blast
Filled all the regions: from their blissful bow'rs
Of amarantine shade, fountain or spring,
By the waters of life, where'er they sat
In fellowships of joy, the sons of light   80
Hasted, resorting to the summons high,
And took their seats; till from his throne supreme
Th' Almighty thus pronounced his sovran will.
   "O sons, like one of us man is become
To know both good and evil, since his taste
Of that defended fruit; but let him boast
His knowledge of good lost, and evil got,
Happier, had it sufficed him to have known
Good by itself, and evil not at all.
He sorrows now, repents, and prays contrite,   90
My motions in him; longer than they move,
His heart I know, how variable and vain
Self-left. Lest therefore his now bolder hand
Reach also of the Tree of Life, and eat,

74–76. M. says that this may be the same trumpet that was after-
wards heard when God gave the Ten Commandments (Exodus
19:16–19) and will be heard again on Judgment Day (1 Corinthians
15:52).

78. *amarantine:* cf. III, 353–359 above.

86. *defended:* forbidden.

91–93. *longer . . ./ Self-left:* "I know how changeable and vain
man's heart is once my motions (the 'prevenient grace' of line 3
above) cease to influence it and it is left to itself."

And live forever, dream at least to live
Forever, to remove him I decree,
And send him from the Garden forth to till
The ground whence he was taken, fitter soil.
    "Michael, this my behest have thou in charge,
Take to thee from among the Cherubim   100
Thy choice of flaming warriors, lest the Fiend
Or in behalf of man, or to invade
Vacant possession, some new trouble raise:
Haste thee, and from the Paradise of God
Without remorse drive out the sinful pair,
From hallowed ground th' unholy, and denounce
To them and to their progeny from thence
Perpetual banishment. Yet lest they faint
At the sad sentence rigorously urged,
For I behold them softened and with tears   110
Bewailing their excess, all terror hide.
If patiently thy bidding they obey,
Dismiss them not disconsolate; reveal
To Adam what shall come in future days,
As I shall thee enlighten, intermix
My cov'nant in the woman's seed renewed;
So send them forth, though sorrowing, yet in peace:
And on the east side of the garden place,
Where entrance up from Eden easiest climbs,
Cherubic watch, and of a sword the flame   120
Wide waving, all approach far off to fright,
And guard all passage to the Tree of Life:
Lest Paradise a receptácle prove
To spirits foul, and all my trees their prey,
With whose stol'n fruit man once more to delude."
    He ceased, and th' Archangelic Power prepared
For swift descent, with him the cohort bright
Of watchful Cherubim; four faces each

---

95. *dream at least to live/ Forever* is M.'s rationalistic addition
to Genesis 3:22–23.
102. *in behalf of:* with regard to.
105. *remorse:* pity.

Had, like a double Janus, all their shape
Spangled with eyes more numerous than those   130
Of Argus, and more wakeful than to drowse,
Charmed with Arcadian pipe, the pastoral reed
Of Hermes, or his opiate rod. Meanwhile
To resalute the world with sacred light
Leucothea waked, and with fresh dews embalmed
The earth, when Adam and first matron Eve
Had ended now their orisons, and found
Strength added from above, new hope to spring
Out of despair, joy, but with fear yet linked;
Which thus to Eve his welcome words renewed.   140
    "Eve, easily may faith admit, that all
The good which we enjoy, from Heav'n descends;
But that from us aught should ascend to Heav'n
So prevalent as to concern the mind
Of God high-blest, or to incline his will,
Hard to belief may seem; yet this will prayer,
Or one short sigh of human breath, upborne
Ev'n to the seat of God. For since I sought
By prayer th' offended Deity to appease,
Kneeled and before him humbled all my heart,   150
Methought I saw him placable and mild,
Bending his ear; persuasion in me grew
That I was heard with favor; peace returned
Home to my breast, and to my memory
His promise, that thy seed shall bruise our foe;
Which then not minded in dismay, yet now
Assures me that the bitterness of death

129–130. The *Cherubim* of Ezekiel's vision (Ezekiel 1) also have four faces. They are like a *double Janus* because Janus, the Roman god of gates, was usually represented with two faces.

131–133. *Argus*, the hundred-eyed monster, was set by Juno to watch over Io, of whom she was jealous. Jupiter sent Mercury to lull Argus to sleep with his shepherd's pipe (*pastoral reed*) and caduceus (*opiate rod*).

135. *Leucothea:* Greek sea-goddess whose name means "bright goddess" and who was identified by the Romans with Matuta, goddess of the dawn.

Is past, and we shall live. Whence hail to thee,
Eve rightly called, mother of all mankind,
Mother of all things living, since by thee   160
Man is to live, and all things live for man."
    To whom thus Eve with sad demeanor meek.
"Ill worthy I such title should belong
To me transgressor, who for thee ordained
A help, became thy snare; to me reproach
Rather belongs, distrust and all dispraise:
But infinite in pardon was my Judge,
That I who first brought death on all, am graced
The source of life; next favorable thou,
Who highly thus to entitle me vouchsaf'st,   170
Far other name deserving. But the field
To labor calls us now with sweat imposed,
Though after sleepless night; for see the morn,
All unconcerned with our unrest, begins
Her rosy progress smiling; let us forth,
I never from thy side henceforth to stray,
Where'er our day's work lies, though now enjoined
Laborious, till day droop; while here we dwell,
What can be toilsome in these pleasant walks?
Here let us live, though in fall'n state, content."   180
    So spake, so wished much-humbled Eve, but fate
Subscribed not; nature first gave signs, impressed
On bird, beast, air, air suddenly eclipsed
After short blush of morn; nigh in her sight
The bird of Jove, stooped from his aery tow'r,
Two birds of gayest plume before him drove:
Down from a hill the beast that reigns in woods,
First hunter then, pursued a gentle brace,
Goodliest of all the forest, hart and hind;
Direct to th' eastern gate was bent their flight.   190

---

162. *sad:* serious.
182. *subscribed:* assented.
185. "The eagle, having swooped down from his lofty position
in the air." "Stoop" was a technical term in falconry.
188. *brace:* pair.

Adam observed, and with his eye the chase
Pursuing, not unmoved to Eve thus spake.
   "O Eve, some further change awaits us nigh,
Which Heav'n by these mute signs in nature shows
Forerunners of his purpose, or to warn
Us haply too secure of our discharge
From penalty, because from death released
Some days; how long, and what till then our life,
Who knows, or more than this, that we are dust,
And thither must return and be no more.   200
Why else this double object in our sight
Of flight pursued in th' air and o'er the ground
One way the selfsame hour? Why in the east
Darkness ere day's mid-course, and morning light
More orient in yon western cloud that draws
O'er the blue firmament a radiant white,
And slow descends, with something heav'nly fraught."
   He erred not, for by this the heav'nly bands
Down from a sky of jasper lighted now
In Paradise, and on a hill made alt,   210
A glorious apparition, had not doubt
And carnal fear that day dimmed Adam's eye.
Not that more glorious, when the angels met
Jacob in Mahanaim, where he saw
The field pavilioned with his guardians bright;
Nor that which on the flaming mount appeared
In Dothan, covered with a camp of fire,
Against the Syrian king, who to surprise
One man, assassin-like had levied war,
War unproclaimed. The princely hierarch   220
In their bright stand, there left his powers to seize
Possession of the garden; he alone,
To find where Adam sheltered, took his way,

---

196. *too secure of:* i.e., feeling secure because too assured of.
213–215. Cf. Genesis 32:1–2.
216–220. In 2 Kings 6:13–18, the soldiers of the king of Syria, sent to *Dothan* to capture Elisha, were blinded by God, who had surrounded Elisha with "horses and chariots of fire."

Not unperceived of Adam, who to Eve,
While the great visitant approached, thus spake.
　　"Eve, now expect great tidings, which perhaps
Of us will soon determine, or impose
New laws to be observed; for I descry
From yonder blazing cloud that veils the hill
One of the heav'nly host, and by his gait   230
None of the meanest, some great potentate
Or of the Thrones above, such majesty
Invests him coming; yet not terrible,
That I should fear, nor sociably mild,
As Raphael, that I should much confide,
But solemn and sublime, whom not to offend,
With reverence I must meet, and thou retire."
He ended; and th' Archangel soon drew nigh,
Not in his shape celestial, but as man
Clad to meet man; over his lucid arms   240
A military vest of purple flowed
Livelier than Meliboean, or the grain
Of Sarra, worn by kings and heroes old
In time of truce; Iris had dipped the woof;
His starry helm unbuckled showed him prime
In manhood where youth ended; by his side
As in a glistering zodiac hung the sword,
Satan's dire dread, and in his hand the spear.
Adam bowed low, he kingly from his state
Inclined not, but his coming thus declared.   250
　　"Adam, Heav'n's high behest no preface needs:
Sufficient that thy prayers are heard, and Death,
Then due by sentence when thou didst transgress,
Defeated of his seizure many days
Giv'n thee of grace, wherein thou may'st repent,
And one bad act with many deeds well done

---

　227. *determine:* make an end (of us).
　242–243. *Livelier . . . Sarra:* more vivid than purple from Meli-
boea or Tyre, towns that were proverbial for their dyes or "grain."
　244. *Iris:* goddess of the rainbow.
　247. *zodiac:* literally, "belt."
　254. *defeated:* deprived.

May'st cover: well may then thy Lord appeased
Redeem thee quite from Death's rapacious claim;
But longer in this Paradise to dwell
Permits not; to remove thee I am come,   260
And send thee from the garden forth to till
The ground whence thou wast taken, fitter soil."

    He added not, for Adam at the news
Heart-struck with chilling gripe of sorrow stood,
That all his senses bound; Eve, who unseen
Yet all had heard, with audible lament
Discovered soon the place of her retire.

    "O unexpected stroke, worse than of Death!
Must I thus leave thee Paradise? thus leave
Thee native soil, these happy walks and shades,   270
Fit haunt of gods? where I had hope to spend,
Quiet though sad, the respite of that day
That must be mortal to us both. O flow'rs,
That never will in other climate grow,
My early visitation, and my last
At ev'n, which I bred up with tender hand
From the first opening bud, and gave ye names,
Who now shall rear ye to the sun, or rank
Your tribes, and water from th' ambrosial fount?
Thee lastly nuptial bow'r, by me adorned   280
With what to sight or smell was sweet; from thee
How shall I part, and whither wander down
Into a lower world, to this obscure
And wild, how shall we breathe in other air
Less pure, accustomed to immortal fruits?"

    Whom thus the angel interrupted mild.
"Lament not Eve, but patiently resign
What justly thou hast lost; nor set thy heart,
Thus over-fond, on that which is not thine;
Thy going is not lonely, with thee goes   290

---

267. *discovered:* revealed.

272. *respite of that day:* respite from that day (i.e., the time granted as a reprieve from the sentence of immediate death).

283. *to this:* compared to this.

Thy husband, him to follow thou art bound;
Where he abides, think there thy native soil."
    Adam by this from the cold sudden damp
Recovering, and his scattered spirits returned,
To Michael thus his humble words addressed.
    "Celestial, whether among the Thrones, or named
Of them the highest, for such of shape may seem
Prince above princes, gently hast thou told
Thy message, which might else in telling wound,
And in performing end us; what besides   300
Of sorrow and dejection and despair
Our frailty can sustain, thy tidings bring,
Departure from this happy place, our sweet
Recess, and only consolation left
Familiar to our eyes, all places else
Inhospitable appear and desolate,
Nor knowing us nor known: and if by prayer
Incessant I could hope to change the will
Of him who all things can, I would not cease
To weary him with my assiduous cries: 310
But prayer against his absolute decree
No more avails than breath against the wind,
Blown stifling back on him that breathes it forth:
Therefore to his great bidding I submit.
This most afflicts me, that departing hence,
As from his face I shall be hid, deprived
His blesséd count'nance; here I could frequent,
With worship, place by place where he vouchsafed
Presence divine, and to my sons relate,
'On this mount he appeared, under this tree   320
Stood visible, among these pines his voice
I heard, here with him at this fountain talked.'
So many grateful altars I would rear
Of grassy turf, and pile up every stone
Of luster from the brook, in memory,

---

293. *damp:* depression.
309. *can:* can do. "Can" was not then a mere auxiliary verb.
310. *weary:* importune.

Or monument to ages, and thereon
Offer sweet smelling gums and fruits and flow'rs:
In yonder nether world where shall I seek
His bright appearances, or footstep trace?
For though I fled him angry, yet recalled   330
To life prolonged and promised race, I now
Gladly behold though but his utmost skirts
Of glory, and far off his steps adore."
   To whom thus Michael with regard benign.
"Adam, thou know'st heav'n his, and all the earth,
Not this rock only; his omnipresence fills
Land, sea, and air, and every kind that lives,
Fomented by his virtual power and warmed:
All th' earth he gave thee to possess and rule,
No despicable gift; surmise not then   340
His presence to these narrow bounds confined
Of Paradise or Eden: this had been
Perhaps thy capital seat, from whence had spread
All generations, and had hither come
From all the ends of th' earth, to celebrate
And reverence thee their great progenitor.
But this preeminence thou hast lost, brought down
To dwell on even ground now with thy sons:
Yet doubt not but in valley and in plain
God is as here, and will be found alike   350
Present, and of his presence many a sign
Still following thee, still compassing thee round
With goodness and paternal love, his face
Express, and of his steps the track divine.
Which that thou may'st believe, and be confirmed
Ere thou from hence depart, know I am sent
To show thee what shall come in future days
To thee and to thy offspring; good with bad
Expect to hear, supernal grace contending
With sinfulness of men; thereby to learn   360
True patience, and to temper joy with fear
And pious sorrow, equally inured

---

338. *virtual:* effective.

By moderation either state to bear,
Prosperous or adverse: so shalt thou lead
Safest thy life, and best prepared endure
Thy mortal passage when it comes. Ascend
This hill; let Eve (for I have drenched her eyes)
Here sleep below while thou to foresight wak'st,
As once thou slep'st, while she to life was formed."
   To whom thus Adam gratefully replied.   370
"Ascend, I follow thee, safe guide, the path
Thou lead'st me, and to the hand of Heav'n submit,
However chastening, to the evil turn
My obvious breast, arming to overcome
By suffering, and earn rest from labor won,
If so I may attain." So both ascend
In the visions of God: it was a hill
Of Paradise the highest, from whose top
The hemisphere of earth in clearest ken
Stretched out to amplest reach of prospect lay.   380
Not higher that hill nor wider looking round,
Whereon for different cause the Tempter set
Our second Adam in the wilderness,
To show him all earth's kingdoms and their glory.
His eye might there command wherever stood
City of old or modern fame, the seat
Of mightiest empire, from the destined walls
Of Cambalu, seat of Cathaian Can
And Samarchand by Oxus, Temir's throne,
To Paquin of Sinaean kings, and thence   390

---

374. *obvious:* lying in the way of (the evil).

385–411. The reader is no doubt expected to have the same contempt for these *seat[s] of mightiest empire* that Christ in *Paradise
Regained* had for "all earth's kingdoms and their glory." Part of
their (false) claim to glory lay in their high-sounding names, which
M. supplies in purposely bewildering profusion. In the notes that
follow the places referred to are identified, but no attempt is made
to explain every proper name.

388. Cathay.

389. The realm of Tamburlaine.

390. China.

To Agra and Lahor of great Mogul
Down to the golden Chersonese, or where
The Persian in Ecbatan sat, or since
In Hispahan, or where the Russian Ksar
In Moscow, or the Sultan in Bizance,
Turkestan-born; nor could his eye not ken
Th' empire of Negus to his utmost port
Ercoco and the less maritime kings
Mombaza, and Quiloa, and Melind,
And Sofala thought Ophir, to the realm   400
Of Congo, and Angola farthest south;
Or thence from Niger flood to Atlas mount
The kingdoms of Almansor, Fez and Sus,
Marocco and Algiers, and Tremisen;
On Europe thence, and where Rome was to sway
The world: in spirit perhaps he also saw
Rich Mexico the seat of Motezume,
And Cusco in Peru, the richer seat
Of Atabalipa, and yet unspoiled
Guiana, whose great city Geryon's sons   410
Call El Dorado: but to nobler sights
Michael from Adam's eyes the film removed
Which that false fruit that promised clearer sight
Had bred; then purged with euphrasy and rue
The visual nerve, for he had much to see;

---

391. India.
392. Malay peninsula.
393. Persia.
394. Russia.
395. Constantinople.
397. Abyssinia.
399–400. East Africa.
401. West Africa.
402–404. North Africa.
405. Rome (for all of Europe).
407–411. South America.
411–414. Adam has surveyed the pagan kingdoms with eyes still
covered by the film *"Which that false fruit. ... ./ Had bred";* his
eyes must now be purged for the *nobler sights* of the salvation history of the Chosen People.

And from the well of life three drops instilled.
So deep the power of these ingredients pierced,
Ev'n to the inmost seat of mental sight,
That Adam now enforced to close his eyes,
Sunk down and all his spirits became entranced: 420
But him the gentle angel by the hand
Soon raised, and his attention thus recalled.
    "Adam, now ope thine eyes, and first behold
Th' effects which thy original crime hath wrought
In some to spring from thee, who never touched
Th' excepted tree, nor with the snake conspired,
Nor sinned thy sin, yet from that sin derive
Corruption to bring forth more violent deeds."
    His eyes he opened, and beheld a field,
Part arable and tilth, whereon were sheaves   430
New-reaped, the other part sheep-walks and folds;
I' th' midst an altar as the landmark stood
Rustic, of grassy sord; thither anon
A sweaty reaper from his tillage brought
First fruits, the green ear, and the yellow sheaf,
Unculled, as came to hand; a shepherd next
More meek came with the firstlings of his flock
Choicest and best; then sacrificing, laid
The inwards and their fat, with incense strewed,
On the cleft wood, and all due rites performed.   440
His offering soon propitious fire from heav'n
Consumed with nimble glance, and grateful steam;
The other's not, for his was not sincere;
Whereat he inly raged, and as they talked,
Smote him into the midriff with a stone
That beat out life; he fell, and deadly pale
Groaned out his soul with gushing blood effused.
Much at that sight was Adam in his heart

---

    416. Cf. Psalm 26:9, "For with thee is the fountain of life: in
thy light shall we see light."
    430. *tilth:* under cultivation.
    433. *sord:* sward.
    436 *unculled:* unselected, not "choicest and best" (line 438) like
Abel's.

Dismayed, and thus in haste to th' angel cried.

  "O teacher, some great mischief hath befall'n   450
To that meek man, who well had sacrificed;
Is piety thus and pure devotion paid?"

  T' whom Michael thus, he also moved, replied.
"These two are brethren, Adam, and to come
Out of thy lions; th' unjust the just hath slain,
For envy that his brother's offering found
From Heav'n acceptance; but the bloody fact
Will be avenged, and th' other's faith approved
Lose no reward, though here thou see him die,
Rolling in dust and gore." To which our sire.   460

  "Alas, both for the deed and for the cause!
But have I now seen Death? Is this the way
I must return to native dust? O sight
Of terror, foul and ugly to behold,
Horrid to think, how horrible to feel!"

  To whom thus Michael. "Death thou hast seen
In his first shape on man; but many shapes
Of Death, and many are the ways that lead
To his grim cave, all dismal; yet to sense
More terrible at th' entrance than within.   470
Some, as thou saw'st, by violent stroke shall die,
By fire, flood, famine, by intemperance more
In meats and drinks, which on the earth shall bring
Diseases dire, of which a monstrous crew
Before thee shall appear; that thou may'st know
What misery th' inabstinence of Eve
Shall bring on men." Immediately a place
Before his eyes appeared, sad, noisome, dark,
A lazar-house it seemed, wherein were laid
Numbers of all diseased, all maladies   480
Of ghastly spasm, or racking torture, qualms
Of heart-sick agony, all feverous kinds,
Convulsions, epilepsies, fierce catarrhs,
Intestine stone and ulcer, colic pangs,

---

457. *fact:* deed.
479. *lazar-house:* place for lepers.

Demoniac frenzy, moping melancholy
And moon-struck madness, pining atrophy,
Marasmus, and wide-wasting pestilence,
Dropsies, and asthmas, and joint-racking rheums.
Dire was the tossing, deep the groans, despair
Tended the sick busiest from couch to couch;   490
And over them triumphant Death his dart
Shook, but delayed to strike, though oft invoked
With vows, as their chief good, and final hope.
Sight so deform what heart of rock could long
Dry-eyed behold? Adam could not, but wept,
Though not of woman born; compassion quelled
His best of man, and gave him up to tears
A space, till firmer thoughts restrained excess,
And scarce recovering words his plaint renewed.

   "O miserable mankind, to what fall   500
Degraded, to what wretched state reserved!
Better end here unborn. Why is life giv'n
To be thus wrested from us? rather why
Obtruded on us thus? who if we knew
What we receive, would either not accept
Life offered, or soon beg to lay it down,
Glad to be so dismissed in peace. Can thus
Th' image of God in man created once
So goodly and erect, though faulty since,
To such unsightly sufferings be debased   510
Under inhuman pains? Why should not man,
Retaining still divine similitude
In part, from such deformities be free,
And for his Maker's image sake exempt?"

   "Their Maker's image," answered Michael, "then
Forsook them, when themselves they vilified
To serve ungoverned appetite, and took
His image whom they served, a brutish vice,
Inductive mainly to the sin of Eve.

---

487. *Marasmus:* consumption.

Therefore so abject is their punishment,   520
Disfiguring not God's likeness, but their own,
Or if his likeness, by themselves defaced
While they pervert pure nature's healthful rules
To loathsome sickness; worthily, since they
God's image did not reverence in themselves."
   "I yield it just," said Adam, "and submit.
But is there yet no other way, besides
These painful passages, how we may come
To death, and mix with our connatural dust?"
   "There is," said Michael, "if thou well observe   530
The rule of not too much, by temperance taught
In what thou eat'st and drink'st, seeking from thence
Due nourishment, not gluttonous delight,
Till many years over thy head return:
So may'st thou live, till like ripe fruit thou drop
Into thy mother's lap, or be with ease
Gathered, not harshly plucked, for death mature:
This is old age; but then thou must outlive
Thy youth, thy strength, thy beauty, which will
     change
To withered weak and gray; thy senses then   540
Obtuse, all taste of pleasure must forgo,
To what thou hast, and for the air of youth
Hopeful and cheerful, in thy blood will reign
A melancholy damp of cold and dry
To weigh thy spirits down, and last consume
The balm of life." To whom our ancestor.
   "Henceforth I fly not death, nor would prolong
Life much, bent rather how I may be quit
Fairest and easiest of this cumbrous charge,
Which I must keep till my appointed day   550
Of rendering up, and patiently attend
My dissolution." Michael replied,
   "Nor love thy life, nor hate; but what thou liv'st
Live well, how long or short permit to Heav'n:
And now prepare thee for another sight."
   He looked and saw a spacious plain, whereon

Were tents of various hue; by some were herds
Of cattle grazing: others, whence the sound
Of instruments that made melodious chime
Was heard, of harp and organ; and who moved   5●
Their stops and chords was seen: his volant touch
Instinct through all proportions low and high
Fled and pursued transverse the resonant fugue.
In other part stood one who at the forge
Laboring, two massy clods of iron and brass
Had melted (whether found where casual fire
Had wasted woods on mountain or in vale,
Down to the veins of earth, thence gliding hot
To some cave's mouth, or whether washed by stream
From underground) the liquid ore he drained   5?
Into fit molds prepared; from which he formed
First his own tools; then, what might else be wrought
Fusile or grav'n in metal. After these,
But on the hither side a different sort
From the high neighboring hills, which was their seat,
Down to the plain descended: by their guise
Just men they seemed, and all their study bent
To worship God aright, and know his works
Not hid, nor those things last which might preserve
Freedom and peace to men: they on the plain   58●
Long had not walked, when from the tents behold
A bevy of fair women, richly gay
In gems and wanton dress; to th' harp they sung
Soft amorous ditties, and in dance came on:
The men though grave, eyed them, and let their eyes

577–558. An allusion to Jabal, "the father of such as dwell i
tents, and of such as have cattle" (Genesis 4:20).

560. *who:* Jabal, "the father of all such as handle the harp an●
organ" (Genesis 4:21).

561. *volant:* flying.

562. *instinct:* instinctively.

564. *one:* Tubal-cain, "an instructor of every artificer in bra♯
and iron" (Genesis 4:22).

573. *fusile:* cast in molds.

573–592. Genesis 6:1–2.

Rove without rein, till in the amorous net
Fast caught, they liked, and each his liking chose;
And now of love they treat till th' evening star
Love's harbinger appeared; then all in heat
They light the nuptial torch, and bid invoke   590
Hymen, then first to marriage rites invoked;
With feast and music all the tents resound.
Such happy interview and fair event
Of love and youth not lost, songs, garlands, flow'rs,
And charming symphonies attached the heart
Of Adam, soon inclined to admit delight,
The bent of nature; which he thus expressed.

    "True opener of mine eyes, prime angel blest,
Much better seems this vision, and more hope
Of peaceful days portends, than those two past;   600
Those were of hate and death, or pain much worse,
Here nature seems fulfilled in all her ends."

    To whom thus Michael. "Judge not what is best
By pleasure, though to nature seeming meet,
Created, as thou art, to nobler end
Holy and pure, conformity divine.
Those tents thou saw'st so pleasant, were the tents
Of wickedness, wherein shall dwell his race
Who slew his brother; studious they appear
Of arts that polish life, inventors rare,   610
Unmindful of their Maker, though his spirit
Taught them, but they his gifts acknowledged none,
Yet they a beauteous offspring shall beget;
For that fair female troop thou saw'st, that seemed
Of goddesses, so blithe, so smooth, so gay,
Yet empty of all good wherein consists
Woman's domestic honor and chief praise;
Bred only and completed to the taste
Of lustful appetence, to sing, to dance,
To dress, and troll the tongue, and roll the eye.   620

---

591. *Hymen:* god of marriage.
595. *symphonies:* harmonies.
620. *troll:* roll, wag.

To these that sober race of men, whose lives
Religious titled them the sons of God,
Shall yield up all their virtue, all their fame
Ignobly, to the trains and to the smiles
Of these fair atheists, and now swim in joy,
(Erelong to swim at large) and laugh; for which
The world ere long a world of tears must weep."

    To whom thus Adam of short joy bereft.
"O pity and shame, that they who to live well
Entered so fair, should turn aside to tread   630
Paths indirect, or in the mid way faint!
But still I see the tenor of man's woe
Holds on the same from woman to begin."

    "From man's effeminate slackness it begins,"
Said th' angel, "who should better hold his place
By wisdom, and superior gifts received.
But now prepare thee for another scene."

    He looked and saw wide territory spread
Before him, towns, and rural works between,
Cities of men with lofty gates and tow'rs,   640
Concourse in arms, fierce faces threatening war,
Giants of mighty bone, and bold emprise;
Part wield their arms, part curb the foaming steed,
Single or in array of battle ranged
Both horse and foot, nor idly mustering stood;
One way a band select from forage drives
A herd of beeves, fair oxen and fair kine,
From a fat meadow ground; or fleecy flock,
Ewes and their bleating lambs over the plain,
Their booty; scarce with life the shepherds fly,   650
But call in aid, which makes a bloody fray;
With cruel tournament the squadrons join;

---

    624. *trains:* wiles.

    625. *swim in joy:* Cf. "swim in mirth" (IX, 1009). In line 626, "swim" in its literal sense is a grim allusion to the Flood.

    638–673. This passage is both an imitation of the description of the shield of Achilles in the *Iliad,* XVIII, 478–616, and a comment on pagan "heroic" values.

Where cattle pastured late, now scattered lies
With carcasses and arms th' ensanguined field
Deserted: others to a city strong
Lay siege, encamped; by battery, scale, and mine,
Assaulting; others from the wall defend
With dart and jav'lin, stones and sulphurous fire;
On each hand slaughter and gigantic deeds.
In other part the sceptered heralds call　　　　　660
To council in the city gates: anon
Gray-headed men and grave, with warriors mixed,
Assemble, and harangues are heard, but soon
In factious opposition, till at last
Of middle age one rising, eminent
In wise deport, spake much of right and wrong,
Of justice, of religion, truth and peace,
And judgment from above: him old and young
Exploded and had seized with violent hands,
Had not a cloud descending snatched him thence　　　　　670
Unseen amid the throng: so violence
Proceeded, and oppression, and sword-law
Through all the plain, and refuge none was found.
Adam was all in tears, and to his guide
Lamenting turned full sad; "O what are these,
Death's ministers, not men, who thus deal death
Inhumanly to men, and multiply
Ten thousandfold the sin of him who slew
His brother; for of whom such massacre
Make they but of their brethren, men of men?　　　　　680
But who was that just man, whom had not Heav'n
Rescued, had in his righteousness been lost?"
　　To whom thus Michael. "These are the product
Of those ill-mated marriages thou saw'st:
Where good with bad were matched, who of them-
　　selves
Abhor to join; and by imprudence mixed,
Produce prodigious births of body or mind.

---

665. *one:* Enoch. Cf. Genesis 5:22–24 and Hebrews 11:5.
669. *exploded:* hissed.

Such were these giants, men of high renown;
For in those days might only shall be admired,
And valor and heroic virtue called;   690
To overcome in battle, and subdue
Nations, and bring home spoils with infinite
Manslaughter, shall be held the highest pitch
Of human glory, and for glory done
Of triumph, to be styled great conquerors,
Patrons of mankind, gods, and sons of gods,
Destroyers rightlier called and plagues of men.
Thus fame shall be achieved, renown on earth,
And what most merits fame in silence hid.
But he the seventh from thee, whom thou beheld'st   700
The only righteous in a world perverse,
And therefore hated, therefore so beset
With foes for daring single to be just,
And utter odious truth, that God would come
To judge them with his saints: him the Most High
Rapt in a balmy cloud with wingéd steeds
Did, as thou saw'st, receive, to walk with God
High in salvation and the climes of bliss,
Exempt from death; to show thee what reward
Awaits the good, the rest what punishment;   710
Which now direct thine eyes and soon behold."
    He looked, and saw the face of things quite
          changed;
The brazen throat of war had ceased to roar,
All now was turned to jollity and game,
To luxury and riot, feast and dance,
Marrying or prostituting, as befell,
Rape or adultery, where passing fair
Allured them; thence from cups to civil broils.
At length a reverend sire among them came,
And of their doings great dislike declared,   720

---

688. *giants:* Cf. Genesis 6:4.
715. *luxury:* lust.
717. *fair:* i.e., fair women.
719. *reverend sire:* Noah.

And testified against their ways; he oft
Frequented their assemblies, whereso met,
Triumphs or festivals, and to them preached
Conversion and repentance, as to souls
In prison under judgments imminent:
But all in vain: which when he saw, he ceased
Contending, and removed his tents far off;
Then from the mountain hewing timber tall,
Began to build a vessel of huge bulk,
Measured by cubit, length, and breadth, and highth,   730
Smeared round with pitch, and in the side a door
Contrived, and of provisions laid in large
For man and beast: when lo a wonder strange!
Of every beast, and bird, and insect small
Came sev'ns, and pairs, and entered in, as taught
Their order; last the sire, and his three sons
With their four wives; and God made fast the door.
Meanwhile the south wind rose, and with black wings
Wide hovering, all the clouds together drove
From under heav'n; the hills to their supply   740
Vapor, and exhalation dusk and moist,
Sent up amain; and now the thickened sky
Like a dark ceiling stood; down rushed the rain
Impetuous, and continued till the earth
No more was seen; the floating vessel swum
Uplifted; and secure with beakéd prow
Rode tilting o'er the waves; all dwellings else
Flood overwhelmed, and them with all their pomp
Deep under water rolled; sea covered sea,
Sea without shore; and in their palaces   750
Where luxury late reigned, sea-monsters whelped
And stabled; of mankind, so numerous late,
All left, in one small bottom swum embarked.
How didst thou grieve then, Adam, to behold
The end of all thy offspring, end so sad,
Depopulation; thee another flood,
Of tears and sorrow a flood thee also drowned,

---

723. *triumphs:* public shows.

And sunk thee as thy sons; till gently reared
By th' angel, on thy feet thou stood'st at last,
Though comfortless, as when a father mourns   760
His children, all in view destroyed at once;
And scarce to th' angel utter'dst thus thy plaint.
    "O visions ill foreseen! better had I
Lived ignorant of future, so had borne
My part of evil only, each day's lot
Enough to bear; those now, that were dispensed
The burd'n of many ages, on me light
At once, by my foreknowledge gaining birth
Abortive, to torment me ere their being,
With thought that they must be. Let no man seek   770
Henceforth to be foretold what shall befall
Him or his children, evil he may be sure,
Which neither his foreknowing can prevent,
And he the future evil shall no less
In apprehension than in substance feel
Grievous to bear: but that care now is past,
Man is not whom to warn: those few escaped
Famine and anguish will at last consume
Wandering that wat'ry desert: I had hope
When violence was ceased, and war on earth,   780
All would have then gone well, peace would have
          crowned
With length of happy days the race of man;
But I was far deceived; for now I see
Peace to corrupt no less than war to waste.
How comes it thus? unfold, celestial guide,
And whether here the race of man will end."
          To whom thus Michael. "Those whom last thou
                    saw'st
In triumph and luxurious wealth, are they
First seen in acts of prowess eminent
And great exploits, but of true virtue void;   790
Who having spilt much blood, and done much waste
Subduing nations, and achieved thereby
Fame in the world, high titles, and rich prey,

Shall change their course to pleasure, ease, and sloth,
Surfeit, and lust, till wantonness and pride
Raise out of friendship hostile deeds in peace.
The conquered also, and enslaved by war
Shall with their freedom lost all virtue lose
And fear of God, from whom their piety feigned
In sharp contést of battle found no aid   800
Against invaders; therefore cooled in zeal
Thenceforth shall practise how to live secure,
Worldly or dissolute, on what their lords
Shall leave them to enjoy; for th' earth shall bear
More than enough, that temperance may be tried.
So all shall turn degenerate, all depraved,
Justice and temperance, truth and faith forgot;
One man except, the only son of light
In a dark age, against example good,
Against allurement, custom and a world   810
Offended; fearless of reproach and scorn,
Or violence, he of their wicked ways
Shall them admonish, and before them set
The paths of righteousness, how much more safe,
And full of peace, denouncing wrath to come
On their impenitence; and shall return
Of them derided, but of God observed
The one just man alive; by his command
Shall build a wondrous ark, as thou beheldst,
To save himself and household from amidst   820
A world devote to universal rack.
No sooner he with them of man and beast
Select for life shall in the ark be lodged,
And sheltered round, but all the cataracts
Of heav'n set open on the earth shall pour
Rain day and night, all fountains of the deep
Broke up, shall heave the ocean to usurp
Beyond all bounds, till inundation rise
Above the highest hills: then shall this mount
Of Paradise by might of waves be moved   830
Out of this place, pushed by the hornéd flood,

With all his verdure spoiled, and trees adrift
Down the great river to the opening gulf,
And there take root an island salt and bare,
The haunt of seals and orcs, and sea-mews' clang,
To teach thee that God áttributes to place
No sanctity, if none be thither brought
By men who there frequent, or therein dwell.
And now what further shall ensue, behold."

    He looked, and saw the ark hull on the flood,   840
Which now abated, for the clouds were fled,
Driv'n by a keen north wind, that blowing dry
Wrinkled the face of deluge, as decayed;
And the clear sun on his wide wat'ry glass
Gazed hot, and of the fresh wave largely drew,
As after thirst, which made their flowing shrink
From standing lake to tripping ebb, that stole
With soft foot towards the deep, who now had stopped
His sluices, as the heav'n his windows shut.
The ark no more now floats, but seems on ground   850
Fast on the top of some high mountain fixed.
And now the tops of hills as rocks appear;
With clamor thence the rapid currents drive
Towards the retreating sea their furious tide.
Forthwith from out the ark a raven flies,
And after him, the surer messenger,
A dove sent forth once and again to spy
Green tree or ground whereon his foot may light;
The second time returning, in his bill
An olive leaf he brings, pacific sign: 860
Anon dry ground appears, and from his ark
The ancient sire descends with all his train;
Then with uplifted hands, and eyes devout,
Grateful to Heav'n, over his head beholds
A dewy cloud, and in the cloud a bow
Conspicuous with three listed colors gay,

---

833. *great river:* Euphrates.
835. *orcs:* whales.
840. *hull:* toss.
866. *listed:* striped. The three colors are red, yellow, and blue.

Betokening peace from God, and cov'nant new.
Whereat the heart of Adam erst so sad
Greatly rejoiced, and thus his joy broke forth.
   "O thou who future things canst represent   870
As present, heav'nly instructor, I revive
At this last sight, assured that man shall live
With all the creatures, and their seed preserve.
Far less I now lament for one whole world
Of wicked sons destroyed, than I rejoice
For one man found so perfect and so just,
That God vouchsafes to raise another world
From him, and all his anger to forget.
But say, what mean those colored streaks in heav'n,
Distended as the brow of God appeased,   880
Or serve they as a flow'ry verge to bind
The fluid skirts of that same wat'ry cloud,
Lest it again dissolve and show'r the earth?"
   To whom th' Archangel. "Dextrously thou aim'st;
So willingly doth God remit his ire,
Though late repenting him of man depraved,
Grieved at his heart, when looking down he saw
The whole earth filled with violence, and all flesh
Corrupting each their way; yet those removed,
Such grace shall one just man find in his sight,   890
That he relents, not to blot out mankind,
And makes a cov'nant never to destroy
The earth again by flood, nor let the sea
Surpass his bounds, nor rain to drown the world
With man therein or beast; but when he brings
Over the earth a cloud, will therein set
His triple-colored bow, whereon to look
And call to mind his cov'nant: day and night,
Seed time and harvest, heat and hoary frost
Shall hold their course, till fire purge all things new,   900
Both heav'n and earth, wherein the just shall dwell."

BOOK XII ❧

THE ARGUMENT

The angel Michael continues from the Flood to relate what shall succeed; then, in the mention of Abraham, comes by degrees to explain, who that Seed of the woman shall be, which was promised Adam and Eve in the Fall; his incarnation, death, resurrection, and ascension; the state of the church till his second coming. Adam greatly satisfied and recomforted by these relations and promises descends the hill with Michael; wakens Eve, who all this while had slept, but with gentle dreams composed to quietness of mind and submission. Michael in either hand leads them out of Paradise, the fiery sword waving behind them, and the Cherubim taking their stations to guard the place.

As one who in his journey bates at noon,
Though bent on speed, so here th' Archangel paused
Betwixt the world destroyed and world restored,
If Adam aught perhaps might interpose;
Then with transition sweet new speech resumes.
    "Thus thou hast seen one world begin and end;
And man as from a second stock proceed.

1–5. These five lines were added when the original Book X was divided into the present Books XI and XII.
1. *bates:* abates, slackens.

Much thou hast yet to see, but I perceive
Thy mortal sight to fail; objects divine
Must needs impair and weary human sense: 10
Henceforth what is to come I will relate,
Thou therefore give due audience, and attend.
This second source of men, while yet but few,
And while the dread of judgment past remains
Fresh in their minds, fearing the Deity,
With some regard to what is just and right
Shall lead their lives, and multiply apace,
Laboring the soil, and reaping plenteous crop,
Corn wine and oil; and from the herd or flock,
Oft sacrificing bullock, lamb, or kid,   20
With large wine-offerings poured, and sacred feast,
Shall spend their days in joy unblamed, and dwell
Long time in peace by families and tribes
Under paternal rule; till one shall rise
Of proud ambitious heart, who not content
With fair equality, fraternal state,
Will arrogate dominion undeserved
Over his brethren, and quite dispossess
Concord and law of nature from the earth,
Hunting (and men not beasts shall be his game)   30
With war and hostile snare such as refuse
Subjection to his empire tyrannous:
A mighty hunter thence he shall be styled
Before the Lord, as in despite of Heav'n,
Or from Heav'n claiming second sovranty;

9–11. The shift from vision to narration is occasioned partly by the increasing complexity of the material and Adam's own growth in understanding, but a more important consideration is suggested by St. Paul's dicta, "For we walk by faith, not by sight" (2 Corinthians 5:7) and "faith cometh by hearing, and hearing by the word of God" (Romans 10:17). Michael is about to begin the account of salvation history, which begins with Abraham (lines 113 ff.) and culminates in Christ, and Adam must learn this the way every Christian does, by hearing the Word of God.

24. *one:* i.e., Nimrod, "a mighty hunter before the Lord" (Genesis 10:9).

And from rebellion shall derive his name,
Though of rebellion others he accuse.
He with a crew, whom like ambition joins
With him or under him to tyrannize,
Marching from Eden towards the west, shall find   40
The plain, wherein a black bituminous gurge
Boils out from under ground, the mouth of Hell;
Of brick, and of that stuff they cast to build
A city and tow'r, whose top may reach to heav'n;
And get themselves a name, lest far dispersed
In foreign lands their memory be lost,
Regardless whether good or evil fame.
But God who oft descends to visit men
Unseen, and through their habitations walks
To mark their doings, them beholding soon,   50
Comes down to see their city, ere the tow'r
Obstruct Heav'n tow'rs, and in derision sets
Upon their tongues a various spirit to raze
Quite out their native language, and instead
To sow a jangling noise of words unknown:
Forthwith a hideous gabble rises loud
Among the builders; each to other calls
Not understood, till hoarse, and all in rage,
As mocked they storm; great laughter was in Heav'n
And looking down, to see the hubbub strange   60
And hear the din; thus was the building left
Ridiculous, and the work Confusion named."
      Whereto thus Adam fatherly displeased.
"O execrable son so to aspire
Above his brethren, to himself assuming
Authority usurped, from God not giv'n:
He gave us only over beast, fish, fowl
Dominion absolute; that right we hold
By his donation; but man over men

---

44. The *city* is Babylon, the *tower* Babel.
62. Actually the name "Babel" appears to mean not "confusion,"
as the marginal note in the King James Bible has it (Genesis 11:9),
but rather "the gate of God."

He made not lord; such title to himself   70
Reserving, human left from human free.
But this usurper his encroachment proud
Stays not on man; to God his tow'r intends
Siege and defiance: wretched man! what food
Will he convey up thither to sustain
Himself and his rash army, where thin air
Above the clouds will pine his entrails gross,
And famish him of breath, if not of bread?"

Nimrod (Tower of Babel)

  To whom thus Michael. "Justly thou abhorr'st
That son, who on the quiet state of men   80
Such trouble brought, affecting to subdue
Rational liberty; yet know withall,
Since thy original lapse, true liberty
Is lost, which always with right reason dwells
Twinned, and from her hath no dividual being:
Reason in man obscured, or not obeyed,
Immediately inordinate desires
And upstart passions catch the government
From reason, and to servitude reduce
Man till then free. Therefore since he permits   90
Within himself unworthy powers to reign
Over free reason, God in judgment just
Subjects him from without to violent lords;
Who oft as undeservedly enthrall
His outward freedom: tyranny must be,
Though to the tyrant thereby no excuse.
Yet sometimes nations will decline so low
From virtue, which is reason, that no wrong,
But justice, and some fatal curse annexed
Deprives them of their outward liberty,   100
Their inward lost: witness th' irreverent son
Of him who built the ark, who for the shame
Done to his father, heard this heavy curse,
'Servant of servants,' on his vicious race.
Thus will this latter, as the former world,

Reason

---

101. The *irreverent son* is Ham, "the father of Canaan," who "saw the nakedness of his father" (Genesis 9:22–25).

Still tend from bad to worse, till God at last
Wearied with their iniquities, withdraw
His presence from among them, and avert
His holy eyes; resolving from thenceforth
To leave them to their own polluted ways;   110
And one peculiar nation to select
From all the rest, of whom to be invoked,
A nation from one faithful man to spring:
Him on this side Euphrates yet residing,
Bred up in idol-worship. O that men
(Canst thou believe?) should be so stupid grown,
While yet the patriarch lived, who scaped the Flood,
As to forsake the living God, and fall
To worship their own work in wood and stone
For gods! Yet him God the Most High vouchsafes   120
To call by vision from his father's house,
His kindred and false gods, into a land
Which he will show him, and from him will raise
A mighty nation, and upon him show'r
His benediction so, that in his seed
All nations shall be blest; he straight obeys,
Not knowing to what land, yet firm believes:
I see him, but thou canst not, with what faith
He leaves his gods, his friends, and native soil
Ur of Chaldea, passing now the ford   130
To Haran, after him a cumbrous train
Of herds and flocks, and numerous servitude;
Not wandering poor, but trusting all his wealth
With God, who called him, in a land unknown.
Canaan he now attains, I see his tents

---

113. The *one faithful man* is Abraham.

114. *this side:* i.e., the eastern side.

127. Cf. Hebrews 11:8, "By faith Abraham, when he was called to go out into a place which he should after receive for an inheritance, obeyed; and he went out, not knowing whither he went."

129–146. Michael's account of Abraham's migrations is highly selective, being limited to his journey from Ur to Canaan, whose geographical limits are described in lines 139–146.

132. *servitude:* servants.

Pitched about Sechem, and the neighboring plain
Of Moreh; there by promise he receives
Gift to his progeny of all that land;
From Hamath northward to the desert south
(Things by their names I call, though yet unnamed)   140
From Hermon east to the great western sea,
Mount Hermon, yonder sea, each place behold
In prospect, as I point them; on the shore
Mount Carmel; here the double-founted stream
Jordan, true limit eastward; but his sons
Shall dwell to Senir, that long ridge of hills.
This ponder, that all nations of the earth
Shall in his seed be blessèd; by that seed
Is meant thy great deliverer, who shall bruise
The serpent's head; whereof to thee anon   150
Plainlier shall be revealed. This patriarch blest,
Whom faithful Abraham due time shall call,
A son, and of his son a grandchild leaves,
Like him in faith, in wisdom, and renown;
The grandchild with twelve sons increased, departs
From Canaan, to a land hereafter called
Egypt, divided by the river Nile;
See where it flows, disgorging at seven mouths
Into the sea: to sojourn in that land
He comes invited by a younger son   160
In time of dearth, a son whose worthy deeds
Raise him to be the second in that realm
Of Pharaoh: there he dies, and leaves his race
Growing into a nation, and now grown
Suspected to a sequent king, who seeks
To stop their overgrowth, as inmate guests
Too numerous, whence of guests he makes them slaves
Inhospitably, and kills their infant males:
Till by two brethren (those two brethren call

---

152. Perhaps it is because *Abraham* is the progenitor of the Chosen People that he is the only person so far specifically identified by name.

153. The *son* and *grandchild* are Isaac and Jacob.

160. The *younger son* is Joseph.

Moses and Aaron) sent from God to claim   1:
His people from enthralment, they return
With glory and spoil back to their promised land.
But first the lawless tyrant, who denies
To know their God, or message to regard,
Must be compelled by signs and judgments dire;
To blood unshed the rivers must be turned,
Frogs, lice and flies must all his palace fill
With loathed intrusion, and fill all the land;
His cattle must of rot and murrain die,
Botches and blains must all his flesh emboss,   1ɛ
And all his people; thunder mixed with hail,
Hail mixed with fire must rend th' Egyptian sky
And wheel on th' earth, devouring where it rolls;
What it devours not, herb, or fruit, or grain,
A darksome cloud of locusts swarming down
Must eat, and on the ground leave nothing green:
Darkness must overshadow all his bounds,
Palpable darkness, and blot out three days;
Last with one midnight stroke all the first-born
Of Egypt must lie dead. Thus with ten wounds   1ɛ
The river-dragon tamed at length submits
To let his sojourners depart, and oft
Humbles his stubborn heart, but still as ice
More hardened after thaw, till in his rage
Pursuing whom he late dismissed, the sea
Swallows him with his host, but them lets pass
As on dry land between two crystal walls,
Awed by the rod of Moses so to stand
Divided, till his rescued gain their shore:
Such wondrous power God to his saint will lend,   20
Though present in His angel, who shall go

---

173. *denies:* refuses.
175. The story of the ten plagues ("ten wounds," line 190) ꞯ
told in Exodus 7-12.
180. *emboss:* cover with swellings.
191. In Ezekiel 29:3 Pharaoh is called "the great dragon tha
lieth in the midst of his rivers."
201-214. Exodus 13:21-22.

Before them in a cloud, and pillar of fire,
By day a cloud, by night a pillar of fire,
To guide them in their journey, and remove
Behind them, while th' obdúrate king pursues:
All night he will pursue, but his approach
Darkness defends between till morning watch;
Then through the fiery pillar and the cloud
God looking forth will trouble all his host
And craze their chariot-wheels: when by command   210
Moses once more his potent rod extends
Over the sea; the sea his rod obeys;
On their embattled ranks the waves return,
And overwhelm their war: the race elect
Safe towards Canaan from the shore advance
Through the wild desert, not the readiest way,
Lest entering on the Canaanite alarmed
War terrify them inexpert, and fear
Return them back to Egypt, choosing rather
Inglorious life with servitude; for life   220
To noble and ignoble is more sweet
Untrained in arms, where rashness leads not on.
This also shall they gain by their delay
In the wide wilderness, there they shall found
Their government, and their great senate choose
Through the twelve tribes, to rule by laws ordained:
God from the mount of Sinai, whose gray top
Shall tremble, he descending, will himself
In thunder lightning and loud trumpet's sound
Ordain them laws; part such as appertain   230
To civil justice, part religious rites

---

210. *craze:* smash, shatter.

216–219. Cf. Exodus 13:17, "God led them not through the way
of the land of the Philistines, although that was near; for God
said, 'Lest peradventure the people repent when they see war, and
they return to Egypt.'"

220–222. *for life . . . on:* "life (even life with servitude) is more
sweet (than death) to men, both noble and ignoble, who are untrained in arms, except where rashness leads them to engage in
battle."

Of sacrifice, informing them, by types
And shadows, of that destined seed to bruise
The serpent, by what means he shall achieve
Mankind's deliverance. But the voice of God
To mortal ear is dreadful; they beseech
That Moses might report to them his will,
And terror cease; he grants what they besought
Instructed that to God is no access
Without Mediator, whose high office now   240
Moses in figure bears, to introduce
One greater, of whose day he shall foretell,
And all the prophets in their age the times
Of great Messiah shall sing. Thus laws and rites
Established, such delight hath God in men
Obedient to his will, that he vouchsafes
Among them to set up his tabernacle,
The Holy One with mortal men to dwell:
By his prescript a sanctuary is framed
Of cedar, overlaid with gold, therein   250
An ark, and in the ark his testimony,
The records of his cov'nant, over these
A mercy-seat of gold between the wings
Of two bright Cherubim, before him burn
Sev'n lamps as in a zodiac representing
The heav'nly fires; over the tent a cloud
Shall rest by day, a fiery gleam by night,
Save when they journey, and at length they come,
Conducted by his angel to the land
Promised to Abraham and his seed: the rest   260
Were long to tell, how many battles fought,

232–233. *types/ And shadows:* synonymous technical terms from
biblical exegesis. A type is a person, thing, or event in the Old
Testament specifically ordained by God to symbolize or foreshadow the Messiah. Thus "Moses in figure bears" the "high office"
of the Mediator (lines 240–241). Cf. lines 300–306 below.

249–256. The *sanctuary, mercy-seat,* and *candlestick* are described in Exodus 25. The suggestion that the seven lamps of the
candlestick represent the planets (*heav'nly fires*) comes from
Josephus, *Antiquities,* III, vi, 7.

How many kings destroyed, and kingdoms won,
Or how the sun shall in mid heav'n stand still
A day entire, and night's due course adjourn,
Man's voice commanding, 'Sun in Gibeon stand,
And thou moon in the vale of Aialon,
Till Israel overcome'; so call the third
From Abraham, son of Isaac, and from him
His whole descent, who thus shall Canaan win."

    Here Adam interposed. "O sent from Heav'n,   270
Enlightener of my darkness, gracious things
Thou hast revealed, those chiefly which concern
Just Abraham and his seed: now first I find
Mine eyes true opening, and my heart much eased,
Erewhile perplexed with thoughts what would become
Of me and all mankind; but now I see
His day, in whom all nations shall be blest,
Favor unmerited by me, who sought
Forbidden knowledge by forbidden means.
This yet I apprehend not, why to those   280
Among whom God will deign to dwell on earth
So many and so various laws are giv'n;
So many laws argue so many sins
Among them; how can God with such reside?"

    To whom thus Michael. "Doubt not but that sin
Will reign among them, as of thee begot;
And therefore was law giv'n them to evince
Their natural pravity, by stirring up
Sin against law to fight; that when they see
Law can discover sin, but not remove,   290
Save by those shadowy expiations weak,
The blood of bulls and goats, they may conclude
Some blood more precious must be paid for man,

263–266. Joshua 10:12–13.

267. *Israel* was the name given to Jacob and hence to his descendants, the "children of Israel" (Genesis 32:28 and 32).

274. *Mine eyes true opening* alludes to the false promise of Satan and also continues the theme of faith versus physical sight.

291. *shadowy:* typical, in the sense defined in line 232*n* above, with the added suggestion "insubstantial."

Just for unjust, that in such righteousness
To them by faith imputed, they may find
Justification towards God, and peace
Of conscience, which the law by ceremonies
Cannot appease, nor man the moral part
Perform, and not performing cannot live.
So law appears imperfect, and but giv'n   300
With purpose to resign them in full time
Up to a better cov'nant, disciplined
From shadowy types to truth, from flesh to spirit,
From imposition of strict laws, to free
Acceptance of large grace, from servile fear
To filial, works of law to works of faith.
And therefore shall not Moses, though of God
Highly beloved, being but the minister
Of law, his people into Canaan lead;
But Joshua whom the gentiles Jesus call,   310
His name and office bearing, who shall quell
The adversary Serpent, and bring back
Through the world's wilderness long wandered man
Safe to eternal Paradise of rest.
Meanwhile they in their earthly Canaan placed
Long time shall dwell and prosper, but when sins
National interrupt their public peace,
Provoking God to raise them enemies:
From whom as oft he saves them penitent
By judges first, then under kings; of whom   320
The second, both for piety renowned
And puissant deeds, a promise shall receive
Irrevocable, that his regal throne
Forever shall endure; the like shall sing
All prophecy, that of the royal stock
Of David (so I name this king) shall rise
A son, the woman's seed to thee foretold,
Foretold to Abraham, as in whom shall trust

307–309. Moses cannot lead the Chosen People into Canaan,
which is a type of Heaven, because Moses represents the Old Law,
which "can discover (i.e. reveal) sin, but not remove."

All nations, and to kings foretold, of kings
The last, for of his reign shall be no end. 330
But first a long succession must ensue,
And his next son for wealth and wisdom famed,
The clouded ark of God till then in tents
Wandering, shall in a glorious temple enshrine.
Such follow him, as shall be registered
Part good, part bad, of bad the longer scroll,
Whose foul idolatries, and other faults
Heaped to the popular sum, will so incense
God, as to leave them, and expose their land,
Their city, his temple, and his holy ark 340
With all his sacred things, a scorn and prey
To that proud city, whose high walls thou saw'st
Left in confusion, Babylon thence called.
There in captivity he lets them dwell
The space of sev'nty years, then brings them back,
Remembering mercy, and his cov'nant sworn
To David, stablished as the days of Heav'n.
Returned from Babylon by leave of kings
Their lords, whom God disposed, the house of God
They first re-edify, and for a while 350
In mean estate live moderate, till grown
In wealth and multitude, factious they grow;
But first among the priests dissension springs,
Men who attend the altar, and should most
Endeavor peace: their strife pollution brings
Upon the temple itself: at last they seize
The scepter, and regard not David's sons,
Then lose it to a stranger, that the true
Anointed King Messiah might be born
Barred of his right; yet at his birth a star 360

332. The *next son* is Solomon.
338. *popular sum:* i.e., the faults of the people.
347. Cf. Psalm 89:29, "His [David's] seed also will I make to endure for ever, and his throne as the days of heaven."
353–358. The struggle for the high priesthood in the second
century B.C. is related in 2 Maccabees and in Josephus, *Antiquities*,
XII, iv–v.

Unseen before in heav'n proclaims him come,
And guides the eastern sages, who inquire
His place, to offer incense, myrrh, and gold;
His place of birth a solemn angel tells
To simple shepherds, keeping watch by night;
They gladly thither haste, and by a choir
Of squadroned angels hear his carol sung.
A virgin is his mother, but his sire
The power of the Most High; he shall ascend
The throne hereditary, and bound his reign   370
With earth's wide bounds, his glory with the heav'ns."
    He ceased, discerning Adam with such joy
Surcharged, as had like grief been dewed in tears,
Without the vent of words, which these he breathed.
    "O prophet of glad tidings, finisher
Of utmost hope! now clear I understand
What oft my steadiest thoughts have searched in vain,
Why our great expectation should be called
The seed of woman: virgin mother, hail,
High in the love of Heav'n, yet from my loins   380
Thou shalt proceed, and from thy womb the Son
Of God Most High; so God with man unites.
Needs must the Serpent now his capital bruise
Expect with mortal pain: say where and when
Their fight, what stroke shall bruise the Victor's heel."
    To whom thus Michael. "Dream not of their fight,
As of a duel, or the local wounds
Of head or heel: not therefore joins the Son
Manhood to Godhead, with more strength to foil
Thy enemy; nor so is overcome   390
Satan, whose fall from Heav'n, a deadlier bruise,
Disabled not to give thee thy death's wound:
Which he, who comes thy Saviour, shall recure,
Not by destroying Satan, but his works
In thee and in thy seed: nor can this be,
But by fulfilling that which thou didst want,

_____

383. *capital:* both "fatal" and "pertaining to the head."
393. *recure:* heal.

Obedience to the law of God, imposed
On penalty of death, and suffering death,
The penalty to thy transgression due,
And due to theirs which out of thine will grow: 400
So only can high justice rest appaid.
The law of God exact he shall fulfill
Both by obedience and by love, though love
Alone fulfill the law; thy punishment
He shall endure by coming in the flesh
To a reproachful life and cursèd death,
Proclaiming life to all who shall believe
In his redemption, and that his obedience
Imputed becomes theirs by faith, his merits
To save them, not their own, though legal works. 410
For this he shall live hated, be blasphemed,
Seized on by force, judged, and to death condemned
A shameful and accurst, nailed to the Cross
By his own nation, slain for bringing life;
But to the Cross he nails thy enemies,
The law that is against thee, and the sins
Of all mankind, with him there crucified,
Never to hurt them more who rightly trust
In this his satisfaction; so he dies,
But soon revives, death over him no power 420
Shall long usurp; ere the third dawning light
Return, the stars of morn shall see him rise
Out of his grave, fresh as the dawning light,
Thy ransom paid, which man from death redeems,
His death for man, as many as offered life
Neglect not, and the benefit embrace

---

401. *appaid:* satisfied.

402–465. The following chapters in the Bible are relevant to this passage: Romans 4, 6, 13; 1 Corinthians 15; Galatians 3; and Colossians 2.

407–410. A rather crabbed passage which may be paraphrased as follows: "proclaiming life to all who believe in his redemption, and who believe that his obedience is imputed to them by faith and also believe that it is his merits that save them, not their own works, even legal works."

By faith not void of works: this godlike act
Annuls thy doom, the death thou shouldst have died,
In sin forever lost from life; this act
Shall bruise the head of Satan, crush his strength   430
Defeating Sin and Death, his two main arms,
And fix far deeper in his head their stings
Than temporal death shall bruise the Victor's heel,
Or theirs whom he redeems, a death like sleep,
A gentle wafting to immortal life.
Nor after resurrection shall he stay
Longer on earth than certain times to appear
To his disciples, men who in his life
Still followed him; to them shall leave in charge
To teach all nations what of him they learned   440
And his salvation, them who shall believe
Baptizing in the profluent stream, the sign
Of washing them from guilt of sin to life
Pure, and in mind prepared, if so befall,
For death, like that which the Redeemer died.
All nations they shall teach; for from that day
Not only to the sons of Abraham's loins
Salvation shall be preached, but to the sons
Of Abraham's faith wherever through the world;
So in his seed all nations shall be blest.   450
Then to the Heav'n of Heav'ns he shall ascend
With victory, triumphing through the air
Over his foes and thine; there shall surprise
The Serpent, prince of air, and drag in chains
Through all his realm, and there confounded leave;
Then enter into glory, and resume
His seat at God's right hand, exalted high
Above all names in Heav'n; and thence shall come,
When this world's dissolution shall be ripe,
With glory and power to judge both quick and dead,   460
To judge th' unfaithful dead, but to reward

---

433. *temporal death:* physical death, as opposed to the eternal
spiritual death of the damned.

442. *profluent stream:* running water.

His faithful, and receive them into bliss,
Whether in Heav'n or earth, for then the earth
Shall all be Paradise, far happier place
Than this of Eden, and far happier days."
　So spake th' Archangel Michael, then paused,
As at the world's great period; and our sire
Replete with joy and wonder thus replied.
　"O goodness infinite, goodness immense!
That all this good of evil shall produce,　　　　　470
And evil turn to good; more wonderful
Than that which by creation first brought forth
Light out of darkness! Full of doubt I stand,
Whether I should repent me now of sin
By me done and occasioned, or rejoice
Much more, that much more good thereof shall spring,
To God more glory, more good will to men
From God, and over wrath grace shall abound.
But say, if our deliverer up to Heav'n
Must reascend, what will betide the few　　　　　480
His faithful, left among th' unfaithful herd,
The enemies of truth; who then shall guide
His people, who defend? Will they not deal
Worse with his followers than with him they dealt?"
　"Be sure they will," said th' angel; "but from Heav'n
He to his own a Comforter will send,
The promise of the Father, who shall dwell
His Spirit within them, and the law of faith
Working through love, upon their hearts shall write,
To guide them in all truth, and also arm　　　　　490
With spiritual armor, able to resist
Satan's assaults, and quench his fiery darts,
What man can do against them, not afraid,
Though to the death, against such cruelties
With inward consolations recompensed,
And oft supported so as shall amaze
Their proudest persecuters: for the Spirit
Poured first on his apostles, whom he sends
To evangelize the nations, then on all
Baptized, shall them with wondrous gifts endue　　　500

corrupt church follows earl. Evangelists. lasts in conflict w/ "Spirit" until 2d coming

340   ⋅ৡ   JOHN MILTON

To speak all tongues, and do all miracles,
As did their Lord before them. Thus they win
Great numbers of each nation to receive
With joy the tidings brought from Heav'n: at length
Their ministry performed, and race well run,
Their doctrine and their story written left,
They die; but in their room, as they forewarn,
Wolves shall succeed for teachers, grievous wolves,
Who all the sacred mysteries of Heav'n
To their own vile advantages shall turn   510
Of lucre and ambition, and the truth
With superstitions and traditions taint,
Left only in those written records pure,
Though not but by the Spirit understood.
Then shall they seek to avail themselves of names,
Places and titles, and with these to join
Secular power, though feigning still to act
By spiritual, to themselves appropriating
The Spirit of God, promised alike and giv'n
To all believers; and from that pretense,   520
Spiritual laws by carnal power shall force
On every conscience; laws which none shall find
Left them enrolled, or what the Spirit within
Shall on the heart engrave. What will they then
But force the Spirit of grace itself, and bind
His consort liberty; what, but unbuild
His living temples, built by faith to stand,
Their own faith not another's: for on earth
Who against faith and conscience can be heard
Infallible? Yet many will presume: 530
Whence heavy persecution shall arise
On all who in the worship persevere
Of spirit and truth; the rest, far greater part,
Will deem in outward rites and specious forms
Religion satisfied; truth shall retire
Bestuck with slanderous darts, and works of faith
Rarely be found: so shall the world go on,

---

523. *enrolled:* written down in Scripture.

To good malignant, to bad men benign,
Under her own weight groaning till the day
Appear of respiration to the just,   540
And vengeance to the wicked, at return
Of him so lately promised to thy aid,
The woman's seed, obscurely then foretold,
Now amplier know thy Saviour and thy Lord,
Last in the clouds from Heav'n to be revealed
In glory of the Father, to dissolve
Satan with his perverted world, then raise
From the conflagrant mass, purged and refined,
New heav'ns, new earth, ages of endless date
Founded in righteousness and peace and love,   550
To bring forth fruits joy and eternal bliss."
    He ended; and thus Adam last replied.
"How soon hath thy prediction, seer blest,
Measured this transient world, the race of time,
Till time stand fixed: beyond is all abyss,
Eternity, whose end no eye can reach.
Greatly instructed I shall hence depart,
Greatly in peace of thought, and have my fill
Of knowledge, what this vessel can contain;
Beyond which was my folly to aspire.   560
Henceforth I learn, that to obey is best,
And love with fear the only God, to walk
As in his presence, ever to observe
His providence, and on him sole depend,
Merciful over all his works, with good
Still overcoming evil, and by small
Accomplishing great things, by things deemed weak
Subverting worldly strong, and worldly wise
By simply meek; that suffering for truth's sake
Is fortitude to highest victory,   570
And to the faithful death the gate of life;
Taught this by his example whom I now
Acknowledge my Redeemer ever blest."
    To whom thus also th' angel last replied.
"This having learnt, thou hast attained the sum
Of wisdom; hope no higher, though all the stars

Thou knew'st by name, and all th' ethereal powers,
All secrets of the deep, all nature's works,
Or works of God in heav'n, air, earth, or sea,
And all the riches of this world enjoyedst,   580
And all the rule, one empire; only add
Deeds to thy knowledge answerable, add faith,
Add virtue, patience, temperance, add love,
By name to come called charity, the soul
Of all the rest: then wilt thou not be loth
To leave this Paradise, but shalt possess
A paradise within thee, happier far.
Let us descend now therefore from this top
Of speculation; for the hour precise
Exacts our parting hence; and see the guards,   590
By me encamped on yonder hill, expect
Their motion, at whose front a flaming sword,
In signal of remove, waves fiercely round;
We may no longer stay: go, waken Eve:
Her also I with gentle dreams have calmed
Portending good, and all her spirits composed
To meek submission: thou at season fit
Let her with thee partake what thou hast heard,
Chiefly what may concern her faith to know,
The great deliverance by her seed to come   600
(For by the woman's seed) on all mankind.
That ye may live, which will be many days,
Both in one faith unanimous though sad,
With cause for evils past, yet much more cheered
With meditation on the happy end."
     He ended, and they both descend the hill;
Descended, Adam to the bow'r where Eve
Lay sleeping ran before, but found her waked;
And thus with words not sad she him received.
     "Whence thou return'st, and whither went'st, I
          know;   610

588–589. *top/ Of speculation:* this hill from which we have
looked out.

For God is also in sleep, and dreams advise,
Which he hath sent propitious, some great good
Presaging, since with sorrow and heart's distress
Wearied I fell asleep: but now lead on;
In me is no delay; with thee to go,
Is to stay here; without thee here to stay,
Is to go hence unwilling; thou to me
Art all things under heav'n, all places thou,
Who for my wilful crime art banished hence.
This further consolation yet secure   620
I carry hence; though all by me is lost,
Such favor I unworthy am vouchsafed,
By me the promised seed shall all restore."
    So spake our mother Eve, and Adam heard
Well pleased, but answered not; for now too nigh
Th' Archangel stood, and from the other hill
To their fixed station, all in bright array
The Cherubim descended; on the ground
Gliding meteorous, as evening mist
Ris'n from a river o'er the marish glides,   630
And gathers ground fast at the laborer's heel
Homeward returning. High in front advanced,
The brandished sword of God before them blazed
Fierce as a comet; which with torrid heat,
And vapor as the Libyan air adust,
Began to parch that temperate clime; whereat
In either hand the hastening angel caught
Our lingering parents, and to th' eastern gate
Led them direct, and down the cliff as fast
To the subjected plain; then disappeared.   640
They looking back, all th' eastern side beheld
Of Paradise, so late their happy seat,
Waved over by that flaming brand, the gate
With dreadful faces thronged and fiery arms:

---

630. *marish:* marsh.
635. *adust:* burnt.
640. *subjected:* lying below.

Some natural tears they dropped, but wiped them soon;
The world was all before them, where to choose
Their place of rest, and Providence their guide:
They hand in hand, with wandering steps and slow,
Through Eden took their solitary way.